AA

D0293614

Theatre Sound

John A. Leonard

A&C Black • London

First published in 2001
by A & C Black (Publishers) Limited
35 Bedford Row
London WC1R 4JH

© 2001 John A. Leonard

ISBN 0–7136–4803–1

A CIP catalogue record for this book is available from the British Library.

All rights reserved. No part of this publication may be reproduced in any form
or by any means – graphic, electronic or mechanical, including photocopying,
recording, taping or information storage and retrieval systems – without the
written permission of A & C Black (Publishers) Limited.

Designed and produced by Sandie Boccacci
Typeset in 10/12pt Sabon

Printed and bound in the United Kingdom by Biddles Ltd.
Guildford and Kings Lynn

CORPORATION OF LONDON LIBRARIES	
CLO859953	
Cypher	3.8.01
792.024 LEO	£12.99
AA	

Contents

Acknowledgements

Thanks are due to the following companies and organisations who supplied photographs and information for this publication:

Akai Professional U.K. Ltd
Avid-DigiDesign
Coles ElectroAcoustics Ltd.
Harman International Industries Ltd.
Klark-Teknik
Level Control Systems
Matt McKenzie
Metric Halo
Meyer Corporation
MIDI Manufacturer's Association
Musician's Union
Outboard Electronics (TiMax)
Richmond Sound Design Ltd.
The Royal National Theatre
The Royal Shakespeare Company
Sennheiser UK Ltd.
Shure Incorporated
SiaSoft
Soundcraft
Stage Research
Yamaha Professional Audio

All trademarks used in this book are the property of their owners and should carry the ™ symbol.

Every effort has been made to trace and acknowledge copyright holders. If any right has been omitted, the publishers offer their apologies and will rectify this in subsequent editions following notification.

Introduction

When I applied for my place at drama college, many years before sound design was considered a theatre art, the interviewing tutor asked me what I thought the purpose of lighting design was. I gave a long, and fairly high-brow reply, mostly concerned with the philosophy of painting the stage with light, artistic expression and mood creation. 'Anything else?' he asked. 'No, I don't think so,' I replied, confident that I had covered all the artistic aspects of lighting design satisfactorily, only to be floored completely by his next question: 'How about making sure that the actors can be seen?'

I have been forcefully reminded of this conversation on a number of occasions during my career, but two in particular stand out. I once worked on a production of 'King Lear', starring a very famous 'old-school' actor, long since dead. During technical rehearsals for the extremely complex storm scene, he became more and more frustrated at the delay whilst we were setting levels for thunder, wind and rain. Finally, he stalked from the stage to the operating position and, in his beautiful, classically trained voice, pronounced 'They've come to see *me* laddy, not to listen to your sound effects!'

More recently, I was interviewing a student who, it was thought, showed great potential as a sound designer. We talked about the project that the student had undertaken, and for which she had designed a multitude of long and complex sound sequences, all beautifully assembled and meticulously plotted. Not having seen the production, but knowing the play well, I was intrigued to know how these long sound montages had fitted in to a show that relied for its impact on a series of short scenes, rich in dialogue, flowing seamlessly into one another. 'Oh, they were all cut,' I was told. 'The director said that they got in the way, and that it wasn't what he wanted at all.' I asked if they had not discussed the form of the play and the director's thoughts at an early stage, and was told that, yes, the conversation had taken place, but it was not what the student had wanted to do, so she had gone away and prepared the work in the way that she felt was right. The student felt aggrieved that her work had been dismissed as impractical, and had been reluctant to make the changes required by the director. 'It was just a few sound effects and the music specified in the script – nothing creative at all.'

It seemed to me that one of the most basic tenets of working in theatre was being ignored here, on both the part of the director and of the student. In most cases, theatre productions are a collaborative process; ideas are explored and rejected or accepted through a process of discussion and rehearsal. It serves no practical purpose for any member of the creative team to go their own way simply because they do not believe that the part assigned to them is interesting enough.

Now that there is a recognised role for the sound designer in the creative team, a very real danger exists that we will try to make our presence felt. In doing so, we can create a situation in which, instead of adding to the production as a whole, we provide a distraction, making the work of the actors, writers and directors far more difficult. True, there are many plays, multi-media productions, musicals and operas where the work of the sound designer is of tremendous importance, and full rein can be given to creative input on these occasions. But there are also many more productions where the place of the sound designer is to support the play, the directors and the actors, and for the rest of the time to keep out of the way. The work that you do on shows like these will be appreciated just as much for the latter quality as it will for the stunning effects sequences or transparent sound reinforcement that will get your name in the reviews.

Like all other branches of theatre, sound has become more and more specialised over the years, from the early days, when mechanical sound effects were the preserve of the property master, through the period when an assistant stage manager would juggle with live and recorded sound effects, and finally escaping from the clutches of the enthusiastic electrician to become a fully fledged creative department in its own right. Over the twenty-five years that I have been involved in this branch of the profession, techniques have changed beyond all recognition, and areas of responsibility have increased to cover video, wireless communications and computer skills. Yet although the type of recording and replay equipment that we have at our disposal and the resulting techniques in effects creation and sound reinforcement have changed radically, the fundamental purpose of theatre sound has changed very little. When I first began making sound for theatre, I worked for a company that ran three theatres and opened a new show in each theatre every four weeks. I worked in a department of one, and had a studio with very little in the way of equipment or resources. Consequently, I learned how to make the most of what was available, and how to cope with the demands of all types of production in a very short period of time.

As my career and technology became more and more advanced, I was still able, when necessary, to fall back on the many basic techniques that I had learned at the beginning of my working life. I therefore make no apology for covering some of these aspects of theatre sound in this book. There will always be occasions on which it is necessary to create the best possible sound with the worst possible equipment, and in such cases the ability to fall back on the lessons learned early in one's career is invaluable.

How To Use This Book

This book is intended as an introduction to theatre sound and is aimed at stage-management and technical theatre students, and those with an interest in technical theatre but little hands-on experience or knowledge. It deals with practical and artistic considerations of theatre sound, but is not intended as a technical reference manual. Important technical points are taken into consideration, however, as are the areas of computers and show control, including the immensely powerful facilities offered by the Musical Instrument Digital Interface (MIDI) standard, and the increasing use of automation systems.

The book may be read in its entirety, but is organised in such a way that specific areas of theatre sound may be accessed easily. There are numerous cross-references where details in one section are expanded in other sections, and these will be identified and the reader guided to the relevant chapters.

In the course of producing this book, I have had to rewrite the equipment sections a number of times as the equipment available to the theatre sound engineer and designer is changing at a rate that could not have been foreseen a few years ago. Indeed, some of the equipment and techniques described here may already be dated by the time of publication. Such is the pace of this change that I cannot forecast accurately what equipment I will be using in a few months time, much less in a few years. In order to try and keep the book current, I shall be maintaining a website on the Internet where the reader will find information on the continuing development of theatre sound design, as well as links to other related sites, mailing lists and articles. I cannot stress too highly how important the Internet has become as a medium for the advancement of ideas in the last few years, as well as a vital tool for developing systems. The availability of software updates from manufacturers on the other side of the world via a few minutes of download time and a local telephone call has transformed the way in which many organisations and companies develop their systems, and the ease with which the end-users can make their ideas and requests known to manufacturers has helped to make the products reflect far more accurately the needs of the market. My website can be found at the following Internet address:

http://www.aurasound.co.uk/theatre-sound

My e-mail address is:

johnaura@btinternet.com

Feel free to write and I'll do my best to respond.

Thanks are due to a number of people for their help with the preparation of this book, listed here in no particular order: Matt Mackenzie for his help with and enthusiasm for all things MIDI, and for showing me the MIDI light in the first place; Charlie Richmond of Richmond Sound Design for persistence in the face of my questions about Show Control systems; Phil Lever and Terry Saunders at Autograph Sound Recording for their unflagging patience in putting me right on any number of technical points; John Owens for expert assistance as a Production Sound Engineer on many of my shows; Howard Davies and Val May at the Bristol Old Vic for encouraging me to explore the world of sound in theatre from the very beginning; Terry Hands, Trevor Nunn, Ron Daniels and many other Royal Shakespeare Company directors for continuing that encouragement during my time at the RSC; Tony Hill of the RSC Education Department for making me push the boundaries of random access sound; John Kilgore at Masque Sound Inc. NYC for making me welcome in my second favourite city and for putting me right about US matters; Andrea Hess, for Zeppelin effects and for being married to me; and Tesni Holland at A&C Black for not murdering me.

It would be invidious not to mention the authors whose work I have consulted and enjoyed in the preparation of this book, and their names can be found in the bibliography.

Chapter 1

History of Theatre Sound

Almost all theatre productions involve sound; in its most basic form, it is the sound of the actor's voice, and even the Ancient Greeks used a form of processing via masks to distort and project the voice of the performer.

In the main, however, sound in classical drama involved the imitation of natural sound by artificial means. Where no device existed to produce a sound, one was either invented by a resourceful craftsman, or the information was written into the text. Information about time of day, the weather, the seasons of the year and the location is given in the text of these plays, and the audience used their imagination to fill in the gaps. Shakespeare's plays are full of location hints: 'This is the Forest Of Arden . . .'; 'What country, friend, is this? It is Illyria, my lady . . .', and statements about the weather, surroundings and time of day: 'This castle hath a pleasant seat . . .'; 'How goes the night, boy?'; 'The night has been unruly. Where we lay/Our Chimneys were blown down . . .'.

Chekov, Ibsen and Shaw all wrote complex sound effects into their plays, and the sound designers of the past hundred years were required to produce these by purely mechanical means. Much ingenuity went into the production of devices such as wind machines, rain boxes, thunder sheets and thunder runs to serve the demands of the play, and it is a sobering thought that it is only in the second half of the twentieth century that the complex system of recording and playing back sound and music that we are so familiar with has been available.

Ibsen demands an avalanche in *When We Dead Awaken*; Shaw requires a plane to crash offstage in *Misalliance*, and a full-scale Zeppelin raid in *Heartbreak House*. Both *Journey's End* by R. C. Sherriff and *The Ghost Train* by Arnold Ridley require extremely complex sound effects plots. The instructions on how to recreate a First World War battle or to make the sound of a phantom steam engine may seem very funny to today's sound designer, but just think of the ingenuity that went into designing those effects and into making them happen night after night. I believe that it must have been more satisfying than going to the effects library and pulling out a stock steamtrain recording.

The point here is that playwrights would use stage directions for effects only when they thought the play required them. We have no way of knowing whether Shakespeare would have included sound effects of Italian crickets for the balcony scene of *Romeo & Juliet*, or a continuous track of Arden Forest birdsong during most of *As You Like It*, but we can be pretty sure that he was more concerned with the text than with the sound effects. When the famous actor-manager Sir Herbert Beerbohm-Tree produced a super-realistic production of *As*

You Like It at the Haymarket Theatre in London, complete with real grass, foliage and rabbits, one critic complained that, 'You couldn't see Arden Forest for the Beerbohm Trees'.

I'm not advocating a purist approach to all classical drama, or that we return to the days of mechanical sound effects – apart from anything else, no theatre company would be able to afford the sheer manpower (eleven people for *The Ghost Train*) required to make those effects happen in the theatre – and of course, final consideration must always be given to the overall vision of the director, who may well feel that the use of sound and music will greatly enhance the written word. What I do suggest is that when you approach a period piece of work, you stop and consider why the effect is there, and how it might have been integrated into the production at the time it was written.

In *Heartbreak House*, for example, the final act includes references to an airship flying overhead and dropping a series of bombs that gradually get louder and louder. Shaw has the actors refer to the sound of the airship as being musical – like Beethoven, a great drumming in the sky. This almost certainly gives us a clue as to how the noise was produced; in all probability a bass drum and maybe a cello or a double bass live in the wings of the theatre produced a constant drone. The musicians could easily vary the level of the effect so as not to mask the dialogue, just as today's sound engineer can reduce the level of the fader on the mixing desk. The more distant explosions would have been produced with drums, whilst the closer explosions would have involved a type of pyrotechnic known as a thunderflash, or theatrical maroon.

Taking this as a starting point, in the late John Dexter's production of the play at the Haymarket Theatre, London, in 1983, I used a stock recording of an airship, but mixed it with a recording of a cellist bowing two strings simultaneously and varying the pitch of one slightly to produce randomly pulsating 'beat frequencies'. I have used the resulting sound, with some modification, for two further major revivals of the show; without the musical element of the cello the effect would not be nearly so powerful.

Some of the mechanical devices used in the early part of the twentieth century are still in daily use in modern theatre: the 'door-slam' device, consisting of an open-backed box with a scaled-down door and various types of lock, chain, knocker and latch can be found in most theatres. Others, such as 'wagon trolleys', small trucks loaded with weights and with uneven wheels, meant to simulate the sound of horse-drawn carts and carriages, have long since disappeared, banished into the mists of time by high-quality portable loudspeakers and digitally recorded library effects. But banished along with them was the physical effect of mechanical vibration that they achieved. Sound designers who have attempted to recreate the train effect in *The Ghost Train* can testify to the difficulty experienced in attempting to reproduce the set-shaking effect of pulling a heavy garden roller over wooden slats nailed to the stage floor.

In the world of musical theatre, there is another lesson to be learned. Before the advent of amplification, composers, arrangers and directors had two major resources to call on: how the song was arranged, and which singer was going to

1a

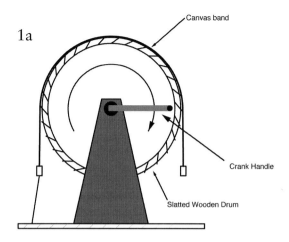

Figure 1a *A Wind Machine: the handle turns a slatted drum against a strip of canvas.*

Canvas band

Crank Handle

Slatted Wooden Drum

Figure 1b *A Rain Box: the box is rotated causing the dried peas to run from one end to the other. The pegs cause the peas to move around in a random fashion.*

1b

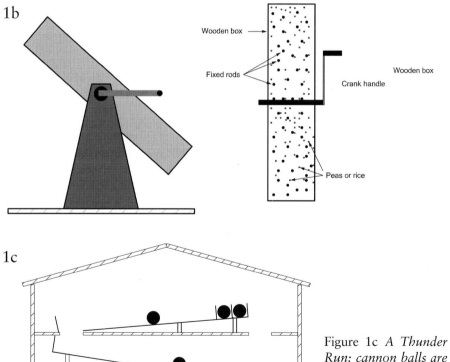

Wooden box

Fixed rods

Wooden box

Crank handle

Peas or rice

1c

Figure 1c *A Thunder Run: cannon balls are dropped into the trough and allowed to roll down to generate thunder sounds.*

deliver it. Singers were cast on their ability to project a song lyric to the rear of a large auditorium without the need for amplification, and musical scores were arranged so that the vocal line fitted into spaces left in the orchestration. Once again, I'm not simply being nostalgic; in a world where advanced sound and music technology is freely available to composers and sound engineers, the craft of the sound designer can all too often simply replace the skill of the artist. It can be argued that, for example, the use of wireless microphones allows more freedom in the choice of actor who can be cast in a musical, and that modern musical staging is far more exciting than it was fifty years ago, and I do not disagree with this. However, it also encourages performers to rely on technology to make up for weaknesses in basic performance techniques. There is no substitute for properly trained vocal projection skills, as many performers who have spent their lives in film and television discover when they make their first foray into live theatre.

This can also apply to straight plays. I have seen a number of film and television stars come to grief when faced with a supporting cast of experienced, classically trained actors and a theatre that has no desire to employ a vocal reinforcement system. Inevitably, the untrained voice cannot compete with the trained voice and the result is almost always a barrage of complaints to the theatre about the inaudibility of the star of the show. It may come as a surprise to North American readers of this book, that very few theatres in the UK use vocal reinforcement systems in straight plays as the practice is widespread in the USA.

As far as music is concerned, the synthesiser, sampler and computer-based music sequencers are now so freely available and inexpensive that they are often used in place of live musicians, both for straight plays and for musicals, where an imagined need to save money leads to whole string or woodwind sections being replaced by a single keyboard player and a bank of sound modules. No amount of technology can make up for the instant reactions and subtlety of shading that a skilled pit or session musician can bring to a performance, and we are in danger of producing a generation of composers, directors, sound designers and audiences who have never heard a live performance by real musicians.

It is tempting to believe that because we are so advanced technically in present day theatre, we should ignore the past and how our predecessors managed things. After all, we have a bewildering range of play-back options, from recordable Compact Discs (CD-R) to Random Access Memory (RAM) based systems; we have computers, samplers, synthesisers, digital signal processing, assignable mixing desks, smart loudspeakers and high power, lightweight amplifiers; and in the field of reinforcement we have the smallest of microphones that can be hidden in an actor's hair and powerful miniature radio transmitters that can be hidden on an actor's body.

The creative technicians who came before us initially had no access to stored sound, and only much later to disc and tape replay. There were no hidden microphones, no miniature transmitters, no artificial echo and reverberation devices,

no compressors, no limiters, no digital delay lines, and far more basic microphones, amplifiers and loudspeakers, so why should we consider how they
achieved their results?

I think that we can draw a parallel with the music recording industry here:
most recording studios today have equipment that would astound the average
studio engineer of thirty or forty years ago. However, that same engineer may
well draw a few unfavourable comparisons with the work that he or she was
doing with far less complex equipment. Listen to the Beatles' recordings of the
mid-1960s and marvel at the immense detail achieved by using a four-track
magnetic tape-based recording machine and the most basic effects devices.

Tempting as it is to fill our studios and theatres with all the latest kit, and our
productions with continuous sound effects and music, very often less is more. To
give a final example, in W. Somerset Maugham's play, *Our Betters*, the stage
directions call for the sound of a pianola (a mechanical piano using punched
paper rolls and a vacuum system operated by the player pedalling a pair of bel-
lows) to be heard off stage. A point is given for the music to begin, and another
for the music to stop, however in a recent production, the director was concerned that the constant background music would distract from some fairly
crucial plot development. The answer was extremely simple: during the scene,
various characters enter and leave the room; when the room door was open, we
heard the pianola, and when the door was closed, we did not. The problem was
solved by reducing the amount of sound in the show rather than increasing it.
Ultimately, it's intelligent and imaginative choices in the use of sound and music
that counts in theatre, rather than how much equipment you've got at your disposal to reproduce it.

Chapter 2

Theatre Types

Over the past fifty years, there has been a change in the fundamental concept of the design of theatre buildings. Prior to the Second World War, most London and provincial theatres followed the same pattern: a proscenium arch divided the stage from a horseshoe-shaped auditorium, which usually consisted of seating at various levels. The stalls were at stage level, with a dress circle above, and then a balcony, often referred to as 'the Gods', where the seats were the most uncomfortable and also cheapest. Many of these theatres were built in the early nineteenth century, whilst some, like the Bristol Old Vic, survive from the mid-eighteenth century; sadly, many were destroyed in the 1940s as a result of bombing raids. Many European theatres are built along similar lines, but usually with the addition of a series of boxes around the side and rear walls of the auditorium.

After the Second World War, most new theatres were built to a number of different patterns, but rarely to the size and scale of their Victorian counterparts.

Figure 2 *The Olivier Auditorium at the Royal National Theatre. Photograph by Mike Smallcombe.*

Two notable exceptions to this rule are the theatre complexes of the Royal National Theatre and the Barbican Centre, until recently the permanent London base of the Royal Shakespeare Company (RSC). The Royal National Theatre has three auditoria: the Cottesloe, a small 'black box' studio theatre; the Lyttleton, a small proscenium arch theatre with a two-level rectangular auditorium; and The Olivier, with a multi-level fan-shaped auditorium.

The Barbican Centre has a large concert hall, as well as a 1,500-seat auditorium, and the Pit Theatre, a tiny studio theatre converted from a rehearsal room by the RSC's in-house technical and design team responsible for shows at the RSC's Stratford Studio Theatre, the Other Place (recently rebuilt).

The different styles of performing space break down into the following general categories: Proscenium Arch, Thrust Stage, Traverse, Theatre in the Round, Adaptable Spaces and Promenade Performances.

It's worth taking a quick look at each type, and some of the problems that they throw up, before we move further into an examination of theatre sound systems.

Finally in this chapter, I will address the problem of control areas for sound in theatre.

Proscenium Arch

The auditorium of this type of theatre is separated from the (usually) raised stage by a large arch, and sometimes a pit in front of the stage which accommodates an orchestra. There is almost always space at the sides of the proscenium arch to allow loudspeakers to be mounted one above the other to cover the auditorium, but the rear of the auditorium is sometimes difficult to reach with a proscenium-mounted loudspeaker, so for amplified musicals it has become customary to mount delay loudspeakers under the circle and balcony overhangs, a technique discussed in Chapter 5.

On stage, the sound designer is normally restricted to placing loudspeakers at the sides and corners of the stage, to allow for the entrances and exits of actors and the movement of scenery on and off stage. Speakers can be hung from flying bars over the stage for thunder or bird-song effects, and the stage, particularly in older theatres, is often well supplied with small trapdoors called dip-traps that allow cables to run under the stage floor for safety and convenience.

The biggest problem with most proscenium arch theatres is their age. Built in an era before amplification was the norm, they provide little in the way of access and space for installing amplifiers, mixing desks and the other paraphernalia of modern theatre sound. On the plus side, older theatres are normally superb acoustically, always assuming that they have not been 'improved' by ill-considered rebuilding, a fate that has sadly befallen a number of once acoustically perfect theatres in the UK.

Figure 3 *A traditional proscenium arch theatre: the Bristol Old Vic Theatre Royal.*

Thrust Stage

In a thrust stage theatre, the stage projects out into the auditorium and the audience surrounds it on three sides. Greek amphitheatres were to all intents and purposes thrust stages, with the audience seated in a hemispherical arrangement.

The Swan Theatre in Stratford-upon-Avon is an excellent example of a small-scale thrust stage, whilst the Chichester Festival Theatre, Sheffield Crucible Theatre and the Festival Theatre at Stratford, Ontario are thrust stages on a much larger scale. In modern theatre productions, stages like these involve the audience

Figure 4 *The Greek amphitheatre:* the Odeion of Herodes Atticus in Athens.

Figure 5 *The Swan Theatre, Royal Shakespeare Company, Stratford-upon-Avon.*

in the action to a greater degree, but can present a problem for the sound designer in managing to provide smooth sound coverage for the entire audience.

Sound effects that need to be located to one side of the stage can also cause problems, and often compromise levels have to be set so that those members of the audience sitting closest to the side on which the effects originate are not exposed to a higher level than is realistic.

Traverse

A traverse theatre involves the audience sitting either side of the stage, usually on raised seating units, whilst the action takes place in the middle. Once again, problems arise with the siting of loudspeakers, and positions above and sometimes behind the audience are employed. In the UK, the Traverse Theatre in Glasgow is the most well known of such venues.

Theatre In The Round

This type of theatre building, where the audience sits all around a central acting area, is less common as a permanent structure and more likely to be part of a repertoire of seating styles available in adaptable spaces. Two of the most famous in the UK are the Royal Exchange Theatre, Manchester, where the audience surrounds the action on three levels, and the Victoria Theatre, Stoke On Trent, where a single raked auditorium surrounds the stage.

For the sound designer, this type of theatre presents a number of problems, particularly with regard to placing sounds in a realistic way. As there can be very little scenery in this type of theatre, the sound designer is denied the luxury of flats and wings to conceal loudspeakers, and the proscenium arch positions for main audience coverage.

More often than not, this leads to loudspeaker clusters suspended over the stage, and small speakers hidden in scenery items on the stage. Loudspeakers can also be placed in the gaps in the auditorium designed to allow actors to enter and exit from the stage. At the Royal Exchange Theatre, each audience level is covered by a ring of loudspeakers that drop down from the front of the balcony above, as the auditorium is too high to allow an overhead loudspeaker cluster to be used as anything more than a source for sound effects.

Adaptable Spaces

In the middle of the 20th century, a large number of studio theatres were built that had no formal seating/acting area relationship. The seats were arranged on moveable units that could be adapted to encompass almost any suitable arrangement depending on the requirements of the production.

University drama departments very often have adaptable theatre spaces, so that students can experiment with different types of theatre. The Guildhall School of Music and Drama in London has an excellent arrangement, with a space that can be converted to a conventional proscenium arch theatre, with or without an orchestra pit; or by lowering the safety curtain, an intimate space can be created for small-scale theatre. If the safety curtain is lifted, it is possible to move seating units on to the stage and create a traverse space.

Promenade Performances

In this type of theatre, the action moves around the theatre space and the audience follows. Typically, promenade performances take place in lots of different locations; for example, *The Dillen*, presented by the RSC in Stratford, started out in the Other Place Theatre, moved to the car park, then to the riverside gardens, then along the side of the river to a disused railway bridge, then along the old railway line to a grandstand-type edifice, then to a tent, then through the streets of Stratford to the war-memorial, then back to the river-side gardens, then back into the theatre; so there is no specific performance space related to promenade performances.

This type of performance presents special problems for the sound designer, and considerable planning must be undertaken to ensure that the action can be followed by the entire audience. This may involve the use of multiple speaker set-ups, wireless microphones, portable mixing desks and duplicate sets of equipment to allow the operator to move quickly from one location to the next.

Working in the Open Air

At some point in your career in theatre sound, you may have to mount a production in the open air. Whilst many of the problems that beset the sound designer in an enclosed space are removed, a whole new set of problems are created that demand special attention. Not least of these is the weather: rain and wind can play havoc with efficient sound reinforcement, and water and electricity do not mix at all.

In an enclosed space, sound behaves in a more-or-less predictable way; temperature can be controlled and reflective surfaces treated to ensure that the acoustics of a performance space are helpful rather than destructive. Outside the confines of a building, things are rather different. The effects of humidity, air temperature, ground temperature and wind all come into play when a theatre production is mounted outdoors, as do unwanted reflections from adjacent buildings. These problems can be overcome in a number of ways, but the most basic solution is to try and minimise the effects by choice of location. Natural amphitheatres, where the audience is arranged above the acting area, are advantageous to outdoor productions, and if a natural amphitheatre cannot be found, raising the audience on bleacher seating is often the next best thing. The Minack Theatre in Cornwall is an excellent example of this type of outdoor location.

Extraneous sounds such as road, rail-traffic and aircraft can raise the ambient noise level to a distracting degree, and care should be taken to site outdoor events away from motorways and aircraft flight-paths wherever possible. I know this all sounds a little elementary, but it is surprising how many organisers of outdoor events fail to take this into account. I once provided a soundtrack for an outdoor show whose organisers had managed to arrange for the main stage of the first venue to be next to a major construction site, and a full-scale fun-fair complete with heavily amplified dance music to be present in the second. Trying to compete with a pile-driver and the screams of roller-coaster riders was more than my system could cope with, and extra speakers and amplifiers needed to be employed, rather to the detriment of my subtle soundtrack.

The weather is something that the sound designer has no control over. The effects of wind and humidity can severely reduce the high-frequency content of sound-waves, and extra speakers are often needed at various points throughout the audience to address this problem. If possible, it is always preferable to arrange an outdoor site in an area that is well protected from strong winds, or at least where the prevailing wind direction is from the stage towards the audience.

Safety is a major concern in outdoor venues and particular attention should be paid to the weatherproofing and earthing of all electrical equipment. Cancelling a performance in wet weather is always a possibility and safety concerns must take precedence over commercial concerns.

Operating Positions

All indoor theatre spaces need an operating position, where the control equipment can be grouped together to ensure efficient operation of the show.

Many theatres spend large sums of money on buying and installing state-of-the-art sound equipment, and then position the operator in a booth where, if the live performance can be heard at all, an accurate perception of the balance of a soundtrack is impossible. This is primarily due to the physical size of the mixing console, but even when new theatres are planned and built, the sound position is too often confined to a glassed-in booth in the rear wall of the house. There seems to be a feeling that it is only necessary for the operator to be able to hear in the case of a musical, however, all but the most simple of shows benefit from having the operating position in the auditorium.

It is essential for a sound operator to be able to judge accurately whether a particular effect is being played at the correct level, and the only way that this can be achieved is for the operator to be in the same acoustic space as the audience. In most of the productions that I am involved in for commercial theatres, whether they are musicals or not, producers realise this fact and arrangements are made accordingly.

In many of the subsidised theatres that I work in, the operator is required to be in a completely unsuitable control room where he or she can have only the smallest idea of how the audience is perceiving the sound. Actors and musicians vary their performances on a nightly basis, dependent on many factors, such as the size or responsiveness of the audience, and it is often necessary for the operator to modify the way in which the sound is integrated into the production accordingly. Theatre managements, architects and theatre consultants who think otherwise should consider the costs involved in building the 'soundproof' booth of which they seem so fond, against the fact that most sound operators and sound designers will spend much of their career looking for ways to avoid using these rooms.

By all means build a control room, but please also allow for an operating position in the body of the house. More importantly, let this be an area that *cannot* be used for audience seating; once the space is lost to a paying customer, it will be very difficult to recover it for its intended use.

Operating a show from within the auditorium does present certain restrictions, however, in that the equipment used must be silent in operation and the operator must be careful that the running of the show is conducted in a way that presents the minimum of disturbance to the audience. It is, of course, essential that the operator should be able to leave the operating position as unobtrusively as possible in case of an emergency or a technical problem, and some thought needs to be given as to how best this can be achieved. Siting the mix position at the rear of the auditorium often presents the best compromise between access and contact with the performance, although the deep balcony overhangs found in some theatres can cause problems of audibility and frequency response anomalies.

Chapter 3

The Theatre Sound System

Basics of Sound Theory

Before we examine the different elements involved in a theatre sound system and their use, we need to look at the basic theory of sound transmission, including the collection, storage, amplification and retransmission of sound by mechanical and electrical means.

When we talk about sound, we usually have one of two meanings in mind: what we perceive as the physical sensation of hearing, for example, 'The sound of the sea is very restful', or the actual transmission of a complex set of vibrations through a conducting medium that leads to the former sensation, for example, 'The speed of sound through air is 340 metres per second at room temperature'. A knowledge of the link between these two meanings is essential to our further understanding of the subject of sound and sound control in theatre.

In order for sound-waves to be created, an object has to vibrate, and that object must be in contact with a medium through which the vibrations can be transmitted. Sound-waves can travel through liquids and solids, but at greatly differing speeds, and for our purposes it is simplest to assume that we are dealing with sound-waves that are travelling through the air around us. The vibrating object, be it a guitar string, a drum skin, a set of vocal chords or a loudspeaker diaphragm, causes minute variations above and below the normal atmospheric pressure and sets up waves of compression and rarefaction that travel through the air; the further these waves travel from the source of the vibration, the less intense the changes in air pressure become until they are so small as to be insignificant. The law governing this change is known as the inverse square law (see Appendix A). If these waves are intercepted by the human ear, they are transmitted via the ear-drum and the extraordinarily complex chain of bones and cavities that form the inner ear, to the auditory nerves that produce the perception of sound in the brain.

The process of an initial increase in atmospheric pressure from a steady state, followed by a corresponding drop below the steady state, and then a return to a steady state, is known as one complete sound-wave cycle. The faster the object vibrates, the greater the number of sound-wave cycles produced over time, and we express the number of waves produced in a second as the frequency of a sound-wave. The frequency of a single sound-wave is related to what we know as pitch, or the relative position of a sound in the musical scale. Slow vibrations produce sound-waves at a low frequency, and we perceive these as being low in pitch, or towards the bottom end of the musical scale. Fast vibrations produce sound-waves at a high frequency that we perceive as being high in pitch, or towards the top end of the musical scale. The frequency of a sound used to be measured in units called cycles per second, or cps, now we use the term Hertz, abbreviated to Hz, after the scientist Heinrich Hertz. It must be realised that there is not actually a direct correlation between the frequency of a note and its perceived pitch. Pitch is purely a subjective sensation, and a very small change in the frequency of a sound-wave does not necessarily produce a sensation of change of pitch in the listener.

Frequencies over 1000 Hz are usually quantified using the suffix kHz, or kiloHertz; thus a frequency of 12,560 cycles per second would be expressed as 12.56 kHz. The lowest frequency that the human ear can perceive as sound is around 15 Hz. The highest frequency depends very much on both the sex and age of the person concerned. Young women tend to be able to hear much higher frequencies than men of the same age, often as high as 20 kHz. An upper limit of between 15 kHz and 18 kHz is more common for the average listener. The ability to hear high frequency sounds decreases with age, or with constant exposure to a high level of sound; the loss of high frequency perception can be an early sign of deafness.

Complex Sounds

A sound produced by blowing over the top of a closed tube, for example, will have a simple sinusoidal wave-form and can be referred to as a pure tone. In practice, very few of the sounds that we hear consist of pure tones; they are complex combinations of frequencies at different levels. The sound-wave-form produced by playing middle C on a piano looks like this:

Figure 6

The more component parts there are to a wave-form, the more complex it becomes and we begin to have difficulty determining what the sound is. Complex wave-forms of this type are simply identified as noise.

At this point, it must be understood that all sound is subjective; no two people will hear a sound in exactly the same way. This is part of the process that marks us out as individuals, but it can also lead to confusion when trying to discuss aspects of sound reproduction systems.

Speed of Sound, Frequency and Wavelength

At room temperature, sound travels at 340 metres per second, which is 1238.4 kilometres per hour, or 769.7 miles per hour, or 1,115 feet per second. We can use this measurement to help us explore the relationship between the speed of sound, frequency and a third aspect of sound – waves: the wavelength.

Figure 7 shows a graph of a sound-wave plotted as compression or rarefaction of sound pressure against a time axis. The distance between equal points on each wave is known as the wavelength, and there is a simple formula that shows the important correlation between the wavelength and frequency of a sound-wave.

We know that sound-waves travel at a fixed speed, and that we can determine the number of cycles that a sound source vibrating at a fixed frequency produces per second, so it is extremely simple to determine the wavelength of a sound-wave by dividing the speed of a sound-wave by its frequency. A sound-wave that has a frequency of 100 Hz (cycles per second) will have a wavelength equal to the speed of sound divided by the frequency: in this case, 340 metres per second divided by 100 cycles per second. The result is a wavelength of 3.4 metres.

By mathematical substitution, we can therefore determine the frequency of a wave by knowing its wavelength. For example, a sound-wave with a wavelength of 50 centimetres has a frequency of 340 divided by .5. The result is 680 Hz.

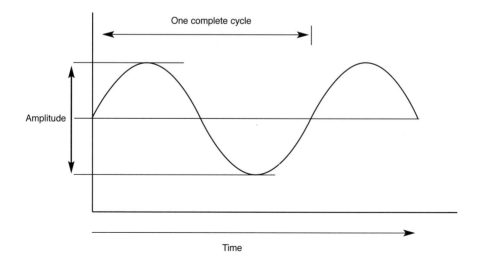

Figure 7 *A pure tone waveform plotted as a graph of amplitude against time.*

Amplitude, Harmonics and Timbre

The maximum change in air pressure in a sound-wave (i.e. the height of the waveform in Figure 7) is called the amplitude of the sound-wave, and determines the strength of the wave and thus its perceived loudness by the ear. Owing to certain anomalies in the sensitivity of the ear, different frequencies at the same amplitude may seem to have different degrees of loudness. A low-frequency sound, for example, will not appear to be as loud as a mid-frequency sound of the same amplitude.

Figure 8 shows the relative sensitivity of the ear at various frequencies and intensities.

The quality, or timbre, of a complex sound is largely determined by the presence and relative levels of harmonics. These are additional wave-forms with frequencies that are always exact multiples of the fundamental frequency of the sound. For example, a musical instrument may produce a sound that has a fundamental frequency of 440 Hz, but it may also contain frequencies of 880 Hz, 1,760 Hz, 3,520 Hz, and so on. As the multiples in the frequency range get higher, they become less powerful.

The presence and varying strengths of these harmonics is the aural clue that helps us differentiate between two musical instruments producing the same note. However, do bear in mind that many other factors determine the timbre of a sound, including the relationship of the listener to the source and the listeners' and players' surroundings.

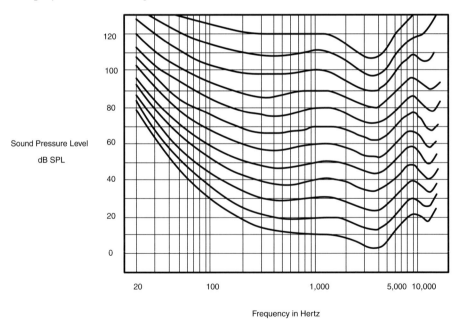

Figure 8 *The Robinson-Dadson curves showing the ear's perception of equal loudness at various different frequencies and intensities.*

Resonance

The vibration of air particles that I have described as sound-waves can cause vibrations in anything that stands in their path. All objects with mass and stiffness will vibrate more at one particular frequency than at any other, and this is said to be the resonant frequency of an object. Sound-wave reflections in a room, determined by the size and shape of the room, will also have a resonant frequency, or many resonant frequencies, and these can become troublesome if the room is to be used for sound reproduction or recording. An expert in acoustics is usually consulted to avoid the creation of troublesome room resonances.

Reflection of Sound-Waves

It is well known that if you shine a light on to a mirror, you will get a reflection of the light-waves back from the mirror's surface. Sound-waves behave in much the same way, the difference being that light-waves are very small (visible light-waves vary between 0.76–0.39µm) and will reflect from even the smallest object. Sound-waves, especially low-frequency sound-waves, are very much bigger and will therefore only reflect from certain sized objects.

Applying our formula to find the wavelength of a low-frequency sound-wave, say 50 Hz, we find that the wavelength is: 340 (metres/second – the speed of sound) divided by 50 (cycles/second), which equals 6.8 metres (22.3 feet). A high-frequency sound-wave, say 15 kHz, has a wavelength of 340 divided by 15,000, which equals 2.266666667 centimetres (0.9 inches).

If a solid object such as piece of scenery is placed in the path of a sound source such as a loudspeaker, the size of the object will determine which frequencies are reflected from the object, and which will flow around the object. When sound-waves are reflected from an object, a sound 'shadow' is created in front of that object, causing a drop in our perception of the reflected frequencies. It's easy to see that the frequencies most likely to be reflected by a large, solid piece of scenery are the high frequencies, whilst the low-frequency sound-waves will be bent, or diffracted, around it.

Objects placed in the path of sound-waves also absorb some of the energy of the wave, and some materials are better at absorbing sound than others. Soundproofing materials are especially designed to absorb as much sound as possible, whilst other materials are designed to absorb sound-waves of certain frequencies and can be used to change the acoustic properties of a space. Thick cloth, of the type used for theatrical drapes, is very good at absorbing high-frequency sound-waves and presents a further problem for the sound designer. It is important that these facts are taken into consideration when deciding where to place loudspeakers and microphones on a theatre set.

The way in which sound behaves is always governed by surroundings. Outdoors, in a space free from any reflecting or absorbing objects, sound behaves in accordance with the inverse square law, a condition known as free-field, but such conditions are rarely, if ever, encountered in our everyday work. We work in places with floors, walls, ceilings, scenery and people, all of which affect the way that sound-waves travel.

Sound-waves from a source within an enclosed space bounce off the walls, floors and ceilings, and these reflections combine with the original wave to a greater or lesser degree depending on where the listener is in the room. The closer to the source, the less apparent the reflected waves will be, the further away, the more apparent, until the combined effect of all the reflected sound-waves obscures the original. The point at which the energy direct from the source equals the energy from the reflections is known as the critical distance, and this distance will vary according to the acoustic characteristics of the room. At a point outside the critical distance, the reflected sounds form a diffuse energy source known as a reverberant field, and when we want to describe a room with many reflective surfaces we describe it as having a long reverberation time. Some reverberation is useful for adding character to speech and music, and composers who write music for churches often use the reverberant characteristics to complement the overall sound. The long reverberation times of a church are not suited to speech, however, and the overall effect is often a loss of clarity. A room which has no reverberation at all, however, is a pretty unpleasant place to be, unless you are testing loudspeakers and microphones, and artificial reverberation is sometimes needed to enhance sound in spaces which are too absorbent.

In some spaces, sound-waves bouncing from highly reflective surfaces arrive at the listener so late (more than 50 milliseconds after the original), that they are perceived as echoes, and can be highly disturbing to the listener. A room which produces echoes and has a high reverberation time is of little use in theatre unless complex measures are taken to treat the offending surfaces with absorbent material (See Appendix A).

Sound as an Electrical Signal

In order to manipulate sound-waves we need a number of tools that are capable of capturing these waves and converting them into a form that allows us to amplify, record, store, alter and then release them as sound-waves again. Before scientists had succeeded in harnessing the power of electricity, the only way to do this was to change the acoustic energy of a sound-wave into mechanical energy. Edison discovered that by connecting a needle to a membrane stretched tightly across the narrow end of a hollow, horn-shaped funnel, he could make the membrane and needle vibrate when he spoke into the wide end of the horn. Using a rotating cylinder covered in metal foil, he could then make indentations in the foil that corresponded to, or were an analogue of, the vibrations of the needle. By capturing these indentations in a continuous spiral track around the circumference of the cylinder, he was able to make recordings of short pieces of speech or music. Once the recording process was complete, the needle was returned to the beginning of the spiral track and the cylinder was rotated. The needle followed the track, and the variations in the depth of the indentations made the needle and the membrane vibrate. The resulting vibrations caused changes in the air pressure that were a copy of those that caused the membrane to vibrate during the recording process and the result, amplified by the shape of the horn, was the reproduction of the recorded sound.

The beginning and the end of the process is much the same today, but with the advent of electricity came much more sophisticated methods of harnessing and treating our sound-waves. To capture the minute and complex changes in air pressure faithfully, we need a microphone, a device that, when placed in the path of a sound-wave, converts these changes into an electrical copy, or analogue, of the sound that can be transmitted along an electrical conductor. To release the sounds as changes in atmospheric pressure, we use a loudspeaker, a device that changes electrical energy into vibrations that cause changes in air pressure. The amplitude of the original wave-form directly corresponds to the voltage produced at the terminals of a microphone, just as the voltage applied to the terminals of a loudspeaker directly correspond to the amplitude of the wave-form produced. Similarly, just as the changes in air pressure consist of compression and rarefaction about a steady state, so the current flowing at the terminals of a microphone and in the rest of a sound system changes from positive to negative: what we know as alternating current (AC).

In between microphone and loudspeaker, there are now a huge number of ways to store, treat and amplify these sound-waves, as well as methods of generating sounds artificially, and we need to know how to use the different types of equipment that are available. Before we do this, we should examine the different transmission and storage methods available in an audio system, and the electrical connections between the different parts.

Equipment Overview

Traditionally, theatres have always been the poor relation of the audio industry, with much smaller budgets for equipment than their counterparts in the music, film and broadcast industries.

Regrettably, this has led to the wholesale adoption of so-called semi-professional equipment in many theatre sound systems. This in turn has meant that those in control of capital expenditure budgets do not expect to pay the higher prices required for professional audio equipment, and the theatre sound department that has equipped itself with low-end equipment often finds it very difficult to persuade the accountants to part with the extra sums involved in the purchase of replacement high-end equipment. Thus it is quite usual to find theatre sound departments using equipment intended for domestic use, or for use in 'home recording studios' where they are extremely unlikely to be subjected to the intensive use required in theatre. The knock-on effects are also tremendous. Domestic equipment comes fitted with connectors that are intended to interface with home hi-fi systems, and small controls that are made to be used in a brightly-lit environment. Home studio equipment is often produced using

When digital audio equipment first became available, the high cost prevented most theatre companies from taking advantage of it, but as the cost of producing such equipment has fallen dramatically over the past few years, there are now few theatre companies that do not make use of digital audio technology in one form or another. This has lead to a dramatic change in the way in which theatre sound systems are put together, and will continue to have far-reaching effects as the quality of the equipment increases and the cost decreases.

Regardless of whether the component parts of a sound system are analogue or digital, the link between them is still established electrically, and there are standards that govern the size of the electrical signal and how it is carried from one piece of equipment to another.

Audio Signal Levels

Now that we have established that sound can be distributed electrically, we need to look at the various signal voltages associated with different types of equipment. Broadly speaking, these can be divided into three distinct parts.

(1) Microphone Level

The voltage present at the output terminals of a microphone is very small and is measured in thousandths of a volt. Great care must be taken in ensuring that the electrical circuit that carries these signals, including any connectors, is of the highest quality and not subject to dirt or corrosion, which may lead to distortion or partial transmission of the signal. This is particularly true of patch-fields (see page 40). Microphone signals are increased in level at the input stage of a mixing desk, by a part of the desk known as the microphone amplifier, which allows microphones with differing output levels to be brought up to a standard level for routing and processing within the mixing desk.

(2) Line Level

Equipment such as CD players, tape recorders, samplers, mixing desks and processing equipment transmit, and in some cases receive their audio signals at a much higher level than microphones, but still at a relatively low level. There is a standard nominal level at which professional audio equipment operates, which is generally known as line level, and it is set at 0.775 volts, usually referred to as 0dBu (see Appendix A – 'The deciBel'). Digital signals transmitted electrically are sent at a slightly higher level, but can usefully be grouped with line level signals.

(3) Loudspeaker Level

Audio signals at line level are insufficient to make a loudspeaker produce sound at a useful level, and so need to be increased by means of a power amplifier. The more powerful an amplifier, the greater the voltage delivered at its output, and depending on how well the loudspeaker converts the electrical energy into sound-waves, the louder the resultant sound. Most power amplifier manufacturers will quote an output level with reference to the size of the signal coming into the amplifier, which may produce anything up to 50 volts.

Balanced and Unbalanced Interconnection

When an audio signal is being carried in an electrical circuit, it can be subject to interference from a number of outside sources: electromagnetic radiation from power cables and transformers, or electrical noise from lighting control dimmer switches, for example. In order to minimise this interference, many manufacturers of professional audio equipment use an interconnection system called a balanced line.

In contrast, most domestic and semi-professional audio equipment connects to the next piece of equipment using an unbalanced line (see Figure 9a). This consists of a simple two-wire circuit, with the 'send' part of the signal carried on a single cable that is surrounded by a braided or lapped screen, or shield, which also acts as the 'return' part of the circuit. The screen is either made of a closely woven braid of fine wire, or of an overlapping strip of metalised plastic foil which is in physical and electrical contact with a 'drain' wire for ease of termination. The screen acts as a barrier to external electrical interference, but is not 100 per cent effective, particularly over long cable runs. In the case of the very low levels encountered in microphone circuits, the level of interference induced in an unbalanced circuit can often be much higher than the signal produced by the microphone, thus rendering the signal unusable.

A much better solution, but one that is more expensive to implement, is the balanced line (see Figure 9b). A transformer, or electronic balancing circuit, is

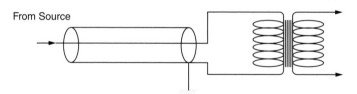

Figure 9a *Unbalanced line – any interference is passed through to the following equipment.*

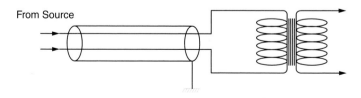

Figure 9b *Balanced line – any interference is cancelled out in the balancing transformer.*

inserted at the input and output of each piece of equipment and the signal travels, as a positive and negative, through two conductors which run inside a screen or shield as described above. The screen simply provides protection against interference and is not used as part of the audio circuit. Any interference that does affect the signal wires is induced equally and in phase in both conductors. When the two identical interference signals are combined at the input section of the next piece of equipment, they cancel each other out, whilst the positive and negative sides of the audio signal recombine.

In the electrically hostile world of theatre sound, the balanced line system is the only sensible approach to take. Equipment with unbalanced inputs or outputs should only be used if no other alternative is available, and even then, the use of stand-alone balancing amplifiers is highly recommended.

There are also two types of digital audio interconnection – the AES/EBU standard, which uses a balanced connection, and the Sony/Philips Digital Interface (S/PDIF) standard, which uses an unbalanced connection.

Cables and Connectors

A note about numbers: as usual, the conservative nature of the sound engineer brings some contradiction in the use of measurements. A deep reluctance to part with the imperial standard of measurement means that many physical measurements are still expressed in inches. This applies to the standard measurement of panel size in rack-mounting equipment, where panel width is standardised at 19 inches and panel height at multiples of $1\frac{3}{4}$ inches. This carries through to some connectors, the $\frac{1}{4}$-inch jack plug being one example. Oddly, the miniature version of this connector is more widely known by its metric measurement – 3.5 millimetres.

Connectors: a Lesson in Confusion

In an ideal world, the connection of the various parts of the audio chain would be a very simple one, and for very many years in professional recording and broadcast studios there were really only two types of connector to consider: the ITT Cannon XLR three-pin connector in its male and female versions, and the Post Office Tip-Ring-Sleeve (TRS) jack-plug. The XLR was used for both microphone and line connections to and from the mixing desk and associated equipment, and the Post Office jack was used for patch-bays. As both connectors were three-circuit, they could be used with balanced lines, and were small and compact enough not to take up too much room on connection panels. Connectors for loudspeakers were pretty much unheard of, and various manufacturers used either banana plugs or binding posts to connect amplifier and loudspeaker.

In the world of theatre sound, these conventions were once followed fairly closely, but a connector was desirable for loudspeakers, and in the UK at least, the Cannon four-pin connector was the standard for a while. This connector had a number of problems, not least of which was that it was too small, both in terms of its current handling specifications and the size of cable that could be fitted into the connector cover. Further confusion arose when an attempt was made to reach a wiring standard for the connector, which specified two pins for low-voltage applications, i.e. connection to a standard 4-16Ω loudspeaker, and the other two pins for high-voltage applications, i.e. 100 volt line systems. The specification was never resolved to anyone's satisfaction and a number of new theatres were wired to different standards. The XLR four-pin connector also appeared on some equipment used in film and television as a low-voltage DC power connector, so it was something of a relief when the Swiss company Neutrik produced the NL4 speakon connector which now seems to have become the standard for most loudspeaker manufacturers.

As discussed, the lack of funds allocated in theatres for sound equipment meant that many adopted semi-professional or domestic equipment with un-balanced input and output connectors, where previously costs had been kept down by using the RCA Phono connector, sometimes known as the RCA Cinch connector. Additionally, some equipment intended for the rock music market was also adopted for theatre use, and came with unbalanced (two-circuit) $^{1}/_{4}$in jack sockets fitted as standard. To make matters even more confusing, some manufacturers started to use the three-circuit version of this connector, pre-viously used as a connector for stereo headphones, as either a balanced input and output connector, or as an insertion connector, with the send and return using two of the poles and a common ground signal on the third. There is no standard way of wiring up the connector in this circuit, and various manu-facturers adopted different methods, with at least one producing different versions of its desks with the inserts configured in opposite ways.

The advent of computers, MIDI equipment and digital audio in theatres has added yet more connectors to the many that the theatre sound engineer has to cope with. Many computers have their audio output appearing on the 3.5mm mini-jack, also associated with the headphone output of personal stereo systems, whilst the MIDI standard is a five-pin DIN connector, of which only three pins are connected. There is a proviso in the MIDI standard for the XLR 3 to be used in professional applications, and many sound engineers make their own adapters to allow them to use existing cables for running MIDI.

Digital audio equipment also offers a range of connection possibilities, with the professional standard AES/EBU signal appearing on XLR 3 connectors, the domestic S/PDIF signal using the RCA Phono connector, and optical digital sig-nals usually appearing on the TOSLink connector, although Sony have their own version of an optical connector that allows the same socket to be used for both digital and analogue signals. Some Akai samplers offer the user either TOSLink or an AES/EBU connector based on the three-pole $^{1}/_{4}$in jack, whilst others offer AES/EBU on XLR three-pin and S/PDIF on RCA Phono.

Add to this the fact that most theatre sound engineers will also be dealing with video and RF equipment, and that video equipment manufacturers also can't make up their minds as to which connector to standardise on, offering at least three for composite video signals, including the ubiquitous RCA Phono con-nector; and that the manufacturers of wireless microphones offer a similarly eclectic range of connectors both for signal and RF connections at transmitter and receiver ends, and the user is faced with a huge and confusing range of connectors to choose from.

There is very little that can be done about this profligate proliferation of plugs and sockets, except to make sure that in your own system, the number of different types is kept to the absolute minimum. In order to try and make sense of the confusion, the following section gives the most common usage and pin configurations of the connectors you are likely to encounter. The author's personal prejudices will also be mentioned.

Balanced Line Level Analogue Connectors
(1) The XLR/AXR three-pin connector
Developed by Cannon, with variations now manufactured by Switchcraft, Neutrik and others, this is a robust latching connector available in male and female cable and panel-mount versions, suitable for interconnection of a wide range of audio equipment. Early versions used small screws (which were easily misplaced) for fixing the plug insert to the shell and for cable strain relief, but modern versions are constructed in a much more user-friendly way and do not need any tools for assembly. This is an excellent and versatile connector that has stood the test of time and is the preferred connector for all professional equipment.

The pins are numbered on the body of the plug or socket, and the accepted standard wiring configuration is as follows:

Pin 1 – Screen/Shield
Pin 2 – Line or positive phase of a balanced signal
Pin 3 – Return or negative phase of a balanced signal

This is very easy to remember – the letters XLR relate to pins 1, 2 and 3, and Screen, Line and Return respectively. Until recently, the North American standard had pins 2 and 3 reversed, which caused problems in certain applications, but this has now been altered and the XLR 3 standard is the same world-wide. Some older pieces of equipment may still be wired to the old US standard, however, and it is worth checking this with the manufacturer before connection.

As a general rule, the male half of the connector carries the output signal, and the female half accepts the input signal. The mnemonic for this, apart from the obvious sexual connotations, is that the pins on the connector always point in the direction of signal travel. Thus audio signal outputs will always appear on male connectors and inputs on female connectors.

Note that a miniature version of this connector is used by some microphone manufacturers, but it is difficult to wire and not nearly as strong as its full-sized counterpart. There is also a large version, known as the EP connector, that comes in different pin configurations and is used by some manufacturers, notably Meyer, as a loudspeaker connector. Unfortunately, in the USA, the four-pin version is used, and in the UK, where the four-pin Cannon EP has traditionally been used as a 250-volt AC connector in film and television, the five-pin version is used, even though the four-pin EP no longer complies with any safety regulations and is rarely encountered as a mains voltage connector.

At one time, some amplifier manufacturers offered the XLR 3 as a loud-speaker connector, but it does not meet safety recommendations when used in the orientation described above, and some rental companies reversed the connector orientation on their amplifier racks, with the female socket carrying the signal, connected across pins 1 and 3.

(2) The Post Office Tip/Ring/Sleeve Jack-Plug/Socket

This is the connector that you see being used in telephone exchanges in old movies. It suffers from terminology overload because different generations call it different things: I used to call it a GPO jack, after the old British General Post Office, but its correct name is the Type 316 jack, which is the model number of the company that originally manufactured the plug. You may also find it referred to as a B-gauge jack, or simply as a balanced telephone jack. The nominal diameter of the shaft of the plug is $\frac{1}{4}$in.

The plug is usually constructed from brass, and in its patch-bay plug incarnation has a thin plastic insulating sleeve to allow a large number of connectors to fit in a small space. There is a special type of cable associated with these connectors when used in patch-bays, which is extremely flexible, but difficult to terminate without special equipment. A standard version is also available with a metal outer sleeve and a screw-down cable strain-relief bush, but these do not allow for the same panel density to be achieved and are usually used with balanced cables for connection to stand-alone pieces of equipment.

The socket is most often available as part of a patch-bay, in which there may be as many as twenty-six sockets in a row on a standard 19in rack panel, with manufacturers offering two, four or eight rows mounted on panels. Twenty-four sockets per row is a more usable layout and tends to be less confusing in terms of labelling, particularly where low light levels are concerned. A single panel-mount socket is also available, as is an in-line cable socket, although extra hardware is needed in the form of a screw-locking collar for both plug and socket to prevent the connection becoming accidentally unplugged.

The wiring configuration is as follows:

> Tip – Line or positive phase of a balanced signal
> Ring – Return or negative phase of a balanced signal
> Sleeve – Shield/Screen

Be warned that in a version offered by at least one manufacturer, the layout of the solder lugs does not, at first sight, correspond to the obvious tip and ring connectors. Always use a circuit-tester to check this out.

This connector is sometimes used as an unbalanced, combined send/return connector on mixing desk inserts, but there is no recognised standard for which contact carries the send or return signal; check with your supplier.

There is a miniature version of this connector, known as the Tiny Telephone,

Figure 10 *Left – the jack-plug family. Below – B-pin XLR MIDI and phono connector.*

or TT jack, sometimes found in on-board patch-bays on recording studio mixing desks. These allow for a much higher density of connector in a small space, but are expensive and extremely difficult to terminate.

(3) The Stereo ¹⁄₄in Jack Plug/Socket (or A-Gauge Balanced Jack)

Adopted as a cheaper alternative to the Type 316 jack, and similar in construction, this connector is not generally suitable for high-density panel applications as few slim-line versions exist. Although it is similar in appearance to the 316 connector, the two are not interchangeable. The tip and ring contacts on a Type 316 plug are considerably smaller than those on the stereo jack, and attempts to force a stereo jack into a 316 socket may well result in the socket contacts becoming deformed and failing. Similarly, plugging a Type 316 plug into a stereo jack socket will almost always result in a failed connection as the contacts on the socket will not touch the smaller tip and ring of the Type 316 plug.

The widespread use of this connector in lower cost professional equipment means that you are now more likely to come across it than the Type 316 as a balanced connector in mixing desks and replay equipment. Like the 316, it is also used as an unbalanced send/return insert connector.

The wiring configuration is as follows:

Tip – Line or positive phase of a balanced signal
Ring – Return or negative phase of a balanced signal
Sleeve – Shield/Screen

When this connector is used as a stereo headphone plug, the wiring configuration is as follows:

Tip – Right-hand channel
Ring – Left-hand channel
Sleeve – Common return

Note: although the 3.5mm stereo jack is widely used in miniature portable equipment, it is rare to find it used as a balanced connector; more often it is used to carry two unbalanced signals, with the sleeve acting as the common return. In this case, the wiring convention is as for stereo headphones.

Unbalanced Line Level Analogue Connectors
(1) Two pole $^{1}/_{4}$in Jack Plug/Socket
Sometimes called a 'guitar' jack, 'rock and roll' jack or $^{1}/_{4}$in mono jack, this connector is the same physical size and construction as its stereo counterpart. It is most commonly found on electrical musical instruments, such as electric guitars, synthesisers and keyboards, and on the processing equipment associated with them. As the connector is unbalanced, short cable runs are best, particularly when noisy electrical equipment such as stage lighting dimmers is in the same area.

These connectors come in a wide range of styles, including locking versions for both panel and cable mounting, but the high-quality professional type such as those manufactured by Rendar, Switchcraft and Neutrik are preferred for heavy-duty theatre work.

The wiring configuration is as follows:

Tip – Signal
Sleeve – Screen/Return

(2) RCA Phono/Cinch Connector
Originally conceived as a low-cost connector for domestic audio equipment, this connector has found its way into many types of equipment, including video and digital audio devices. The plug and socket come in many forms and can be difficult to solder in certain cases, giving rise to short and open circuits. The connector can also come loose easily if the quality of manufacturing is poor. As this connector is unbalanced, it can only be recommended for short cable runs.

The wiring configuration is as follows:

Tip – Signal
Sleeve – Screen/Return

Loudspeaker Connectors
(1) Neutrik NL4 Connector
After many years, the industry seems to have settled on the NL4 as a standard for loudspeaker connectors. The connector has only two forms – a cable connector and a panel-mount connector. Users needing to link two cables together to achieve long runs should use an in-line adapter. The connector uses a twist-

and-latch arrangement to prevent accidental disconnection, and the present arrangement is far superior to the original system whereby it was possible to believe that the connector was latched, when in fact it was not. The new latching arrangement also allows for higher density on a rack-mounting panel. Construction is of high-impact resistance plastic, ensuring that the connector is virtually indestructible.

The connector has four contacts, allowing it to be used for bi-amplified systems, and there is a larger model, the NL8, with eight contacts for more complex or multi-speaker systems.

The contact numbering is arranged for bi-amplified systems and consists of two pairs of contacts labelled 1+ & 1- and 2+ & 2-.

Wiring configurations are as follows:

Single loudspeaker: 1+ – Positive amplifier/speaker terminal
                      1- – Negative amplifier/speaker terminal

Bi-amplified system: 1+ – LF Positive amplifier/speaker terminal
                      1- – LF negative amplifier/speaker terminal

                      2+ – HF Positive amplifier/speaker terminal
                      2- – HF Positive amplifier/speaker terminal

(2) ITT Cannon PDN Connector

The PDN, Positive Drain Negative, was an attempt to produce a loudspeaker connector similar in construction to the XLR/AXR series of connectors, but with higher current handling capacity and a different pin/key-slot configuration. Its early version suffered from a number of problems, and later versions were not backwardly compatible, unlike the Neutrik NL4. As the connector has only three circuits, the third intended as a safety earth, it could not be used for bi-amplification purposes. Additionally, the cable-entry gland on the cable-mount version is too small to accept the large cross-section speaker cables used in today's high performance loudspeaker systems.

Although the connector enjoyed some small success, with the Association of British Theatre Technicians (ABTT) recommending it for a time, the design problems mentioned above made it unsuitable for most manufacturers.

The wiring configuration for this connector is self-explanatory: the letters P, D and N appear on the body of the connector, and connection is to the positive and negative terminals of the amplifier/loudspeaker. The third contact, Drain, is seldom used and should be considered non-connected (N/C).

(3) ITT Cannon XLR/AXR three-pin Connector

As described, this connector is sometimes used for loudspeaker applications. The sex of the connectors varies with manufacturer, as does wiring configuration, but the most common is as follows:

Amplifier output – Panel-mount male
Loudspeaker input – Panel-mount female
Pin 1 – Negative terminal amplifier/loudspeaker
Pin 3 – Positive terminal amplifier/loudspeaker

(A notable exception to this is Bose Loudspeakers, who use reverse sex connectors to those described above, on some of their products.)

(4) Two pole $^1\!/_4$in Jack Plug/Socket

Few loudspeaker manufacturers still use this connector for loudspeakers, although once again, Bose and some early ElectroVoice speakers are an exception.
   Wiring configuration is as follows:

Tip – Positive terminal amplifier/loudspeaker terminal
Sleeve – Negative terminal amplifier/loudspeaker terminal

(5) RCA Phono/Cinch Plug/Socket

Any loudspeaker or amplifier with RCA connectors for loudspeakers is certainly a domestic product and has no place in professional theatre. Avoid like the plague.

(6) Cannon EP4/5

Some loudspeaker manufacturers, notably Meyer, use the EP4 or EP5 connector to deliver a bi-amplified signal to their loudspeakers. The standard in the USA is the EP4, and in Europe the EP5, for reasons outlined above.
   The wiring configuration is as follows:

Pin 1 – Low frequency +
Pin 2 – Low frequency -
Pin 3 – High frequency -
Pin 4 – High frequency +

Where a five-pin connector is used, Pin 5 is not connected.

Balanced Digital Audio Connectors (AES/EBU format)

(1) ITT Cannon XLR/AXR three-pin Connector

Industry standard. See remarks for analogue balanced line, page 27 and Figure 9a page 27.
   The wiring configuration is as follows:

Pin 1 – Screen/Shield
Pin 2 – Positive phase
Pin 3 – Negative phase

Unbalanced Digital Audio Connector – Electrical (S/PDIF format)
(1) RCA Phono/Cinch Plug/Socket

Industry standard. See remarks for analogue unbalanced line, page 27 and Figure 9b page 27.

The wiring configuration is as follows:

    Tip – Positive phase
    Sleeve – Negative phase/screen

Unbalanced Digital Audio Connector – Optical (S/PDIF format)
(1) TOSLink Connector

Industry standard optical coupler using fibre-optic cable. Although the panel-mount socket and cable-mount plug are both identical for input and output, it is very easy to tell one from the other as an optical digital output will glow red when the equipment is powered on. If you can see a red light at either the socket or the end of the cable, you are looking at a digital output; no light and it's an input. That's the kind of connector I approve of!

The TOSLink system has also been adopted by Alesis as a multi-channel connector for its A-DAT digital multi-track systems, and a number of other manufacturers produce so-called A-DAT bridges which allow the single TOSLink cable to break out to eight electrical digital connections.

MIDI Connectors

At the time of writing, there is only one commonly used MIDI connector, and that is the 5 Pin DIN (Deutsche Industrie Norm) connector. Unfortunately, this connector was also used as a combined stereo input/output unbalanced line connector in domestic audio systems, with a significant number of wiring variations, and users should be absolutely certain that any ready-made cables that they buy are MIDI cables and not audio cables.

A five-pin connector was specified to allow for future, so far unrealised, expansion, and only two pins are used, with a third being used as a screen only, having no electrical connection to a MIDI circuit.

Most low-cost MIDI cables use a connector that is flimsy and can be easily broken or distorted if subjected to rigorous use. My recommendation would be to use only the substantial, metal-shelled version of the connector, either when making up cables or when buying ready-made units.

The connection standard is that all MIDI equipment contains the female or socket version of the connector, and all cables have the male or plug version of the connector at either end. Once again, therefore, any extensions will need to be made using an in-line female to female adapter.

The wiring configuration is as follows:

    Pin 2 – N/C (Shield/Screen only)
    Pin 5 – Data
    Pin 4 – Data

Note: cable connection is like-pin to like-pin, i.e. connect pin 5 to pin 5, and pin 4 to pin 4. See also the MMA Data sheet in Appendix C regarding the use of MIDI connectors on Personal Computer Sound Cards, and the avoidance of hum-loops in audio/MIDI systems.

It is not uncommon for sound engineers sending MIDI data over long distances to build converters from the 5 Pin DIN to the XLR 3 connector, with DIN contact 4 connecting to XLR pin 2, and DIN pin 5 connecting to XLR pin 3.

Cables

It is just as important to make sure that the correct cable is used for connecting equipment as it is to use the right connector. Once again, the choice is bewildering, with varying types of cables appearing to do the same job, but with vastly different specifications and prices. The situation has been further complicated by the manufacturers of cables for high-end hi-fi equipment making often extravagant claims for various exotic formulations of metals used in the construction of their invariably expensive accessories. Leaving most of these aside, it does seem that the use of oxygen-free copper in the manufacturing of line level audio cables is an effective way of reducing distortion over long distances.

Audio cables receive very rough treatment in most theatres, and it is therefore sensible to ensure that you use a cable type that will withstand such abuse without sustaining damage. Microphone, line level and loudspeaker cables that are to be used to connect equipment on a temporary basis should be flexible enough to coil easily and to lie flat on a stage surface to avoid the danger of tripping. Any cables that run across access ways, entrances to the set or in public areas, should either be taped securely, run overhead, laid under temporary carpeting or contained in one of the proprietary cable containment systems produced for this purpose. These are usually made of rubber or a similarly flexible compound and allow cables to be safely contained within them.

Microphone and Line Level Cables

Cables for connecting microphones and line level audio signals should always be of the balanced line type, consisting of a central pair of conductors, surrounded by a tightly braided or lapped metal screen, and protected by a flexible insulating

Figure 11 *Cross-section through a cable cover.*

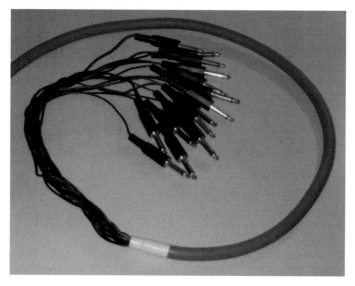

Figure 12 *A multi-core cable termination.*

jacket. When there is a need to run many signal paths together, to connect a mixing desk with a large number of microphones, for example, a multi-pair cable, or 'snake', is commonly used. This consists of a number of pairs of conductors, each with its own individual screen, protected by an overall insulating jacket. Usually, these cables are fitted with multi-pin connectors that allow for connection either to 'break-out' boxes fitted with multiple microphone or line connectors, or 'tails', which have separate cables terminating in individual connectors.

Loudspeaker Cables
Loudspeaker cables have to carry a much higher electrical power than microphone cables, and the conductors must therefore have a greater cross-section. A minimum cross-section of 2.5sq mm is recommended, with high-power systems requiring heavier duty cables. Loudspeaker cables for high-performance systems can be very large and heavy and care should be taken in planning suitable routes from the amplifier racks to the loudspeakers.

Ideally, the distance between the amplifier and the loudspeaker should be as short as possible to avoid any degradation of the signal, and it is not uncommon to have amplifier racks situated at various locations throughout a large theatre. To overcome the problem of long speaker runs, a number of manufacturers have produced loudspeakers in which the controllers and amplifiers are built-in to the loudspeaker cabinet. All that is needed is a local source of mains power and a balanced line level signal from the mixing desk. Such systems have much to recommend them and are increasingly finding favour with sound designers all over the world.

How the System Goes Together

Let's look at a theatre sound replay/reinforcement system overall, before examining each section individually. Almost all theatre sound systems have the following components in one form or another.

1. Sound sources – equipment that generates sound as an analogue, electrical or digital signal. For example, a microphone, a CD player, an electronic keyboard or sampler.
2. A mixing desk in which to collect, treat and balance the various sound sources. This may have a selection of inputs to allow most types of sound sources, including digital, to be connected and then distributed to the next part of the chain.
3. Processors – these allow the sound sources to be treated in a number of ways so that the sound quality is changed. Processing equipment may include echo and reverberation devices, compressors, limiters, equalisers, and time delay devices.
4. Amplifiers – these increase the mixed and treated electrical signals to a high level for transmission to the loudspeakers.
5. Loudspeakers – to convert the electrical signal into sound-waves and direct the resultant sound to the desired part of the auditorium.

A most important part of the system is a cable infra-structure to allow easy and accurate connection of all the items in the system. This needs to embrace each of the above items as well as cue-lights and communications for the entire theatre. A well-designed and laid out cabling system can save many hours in setting up and trouble-shooting a complex sound system, allowing the sound engineer to access all connections in the system with ease.

Central to the cabling system will be a patch-bay, sometimes called a patch-field, where all of the inputs and outputs are gathered together in one place. Each piece of equipment, or potential signal source, such as microphone points around a theatre, has its inputs and outputs connected to sockets on the patch-bay, and special cables are used to connect these together as required. There may be a number of these in a complex system, one which has all the inputs, outputs and insert points for the theatre's sound control desk, one dealing with digital signals, one with microphone and line level outlets, and one with loudspeaker signals. Additionally, there may be patch-fields dealing with communications and cue-light circuits. A typical line level audio jack-field using Type 316/B-gauge balanced jack connectors is shown on page 40.

The layout of a patch-bay can help or hinder the sound engineer, depending on how much thought has gone into its design. Much use is made of a system known as normalling.

Let's assume that the main left and right outputs of a CD player are normally connected to the first two inputs on the theatre's twelve-input mixing desk, the MiniDisc player is normally connected to the next pair of inputs, and a sampler is connected to the remaining eight inputs. A patch-bay associated with this

Figure 13 *Type 316 patch-field.*

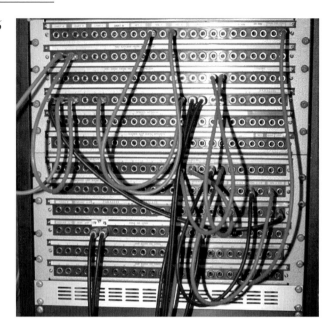

system would have a row of twelve sockets that were directly connected to the equipment outputs, and a further row of twelve sockets that were directly connected to the mixing desk inputs. Without a normalling system, twelve patch-leads would be needed to connect the equipment outputs to the mixing desk inputs. With a normalled system, however, each output is connected to the relevant desk input by connecting a special set of contacts on the rear of the patch-bay sockets.

If there is no plug in either socket, a direct connection from equipment output to desk input exists. As soon as a plug is inserted in either an equipment output socket or a mixing desk input socket, however, the direct connection is broken and the engineer can then choose to redirect the signal to another desk input, by plugging in the other end of the patch-lead to a different mixing desk input. In the process, the connection that normally exists for that input is broken, and remains so until the plug is removed from the socket.

Further variations of normalling, known as half-normalling and double normalling, as well as the provision of parallel sets of connectors for equipment outputs (sometimes known as 'listen' or 'sniff' jacks), make the patch-bay an essential item in any sound system.

Microphones

Microphones are at the beginning of the audio chain, and along with replay devices and electric musical instruments provide a sound source for the engineer to work with. A microphone picks up sound-waves, and translates the changes in air pressure into an electrical signal that can then be sent to a mixing desk, or a recording device for processing.

Not all microphones produce their electrical signal in the same way, nor do they respond to sound-waves in the same way. Broadly speaking, there are three operational types of microphone – moving coil, ribbon and capacitor – and four ways to describe the directional characteristics of a microphone – omni-directional, figure-of-eight, cardioid and hypercardioid.

Let's look at the operational types first.

Moving Coil Microphones

An alternating current applied to a coil in a magnetic field will cause the coil to move in direct relationship to the strength of the current. This fact gives us the basic mechanics of a moving coil *loudspeaker*.

By using the same theory, but changing the motive force, we can observe another effect. If a coil moves within a magnetic field, then a voltage will be induced in the coil, related to the direction and strength of the coil movements. If the movement of the coil can be related to sound-waves (variations in air pressure), then the voltage produced will also be related to the sound-waves. This fact gives us the basic mechanics of a moving coil microphone (see Figure 14).

The component parts of a moving coil microphone are the same as those of a moving coil loudspeaker – magnet, voice coil and diaphragm – but they are of a much more delicate nature than those in loudspeakers, and the voltage produced is measured in millivolts.

Moving coil microphones, often known as dynamic microphones, are generally sturdy and will take a great deal of rough treatment before failing. They are thus ideal for general stage work, especially where untrained users are involved.

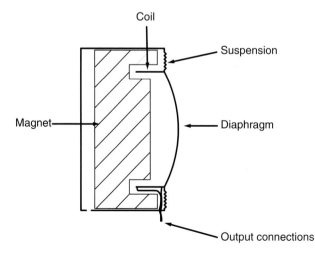

Figure 14 Cross-section through a moving coil micro-phone.

Ribbon Microphones

In a ribbon microphone, a thin metal strip, or ribbon, is suspended in a magnetic field; movement of the ribbon in the magnetic field produces a voltage at either end of the ribbon (see Figure 15). The ribbon is corrugated for strength, and is very susceptible to sudden blasts of wind. Microphones employing ribbon elements are very delicate and are generally unsuitable for heavy duty work, being used more in recording and broadcast studios.

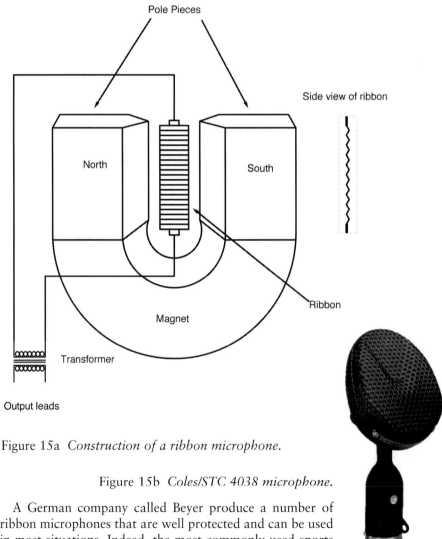

Figure 15a *Construction of a ribbon microphone.*

Figure 15b *Coles/STC 4038 microphone.*

A German company called Beyer produce a number of ribbon microphones that are well protected and can be used in most situations. Indeed, the most commonly used sports commentary microphone, the Coles 4104B, is a ribbon microphone. The same company also produces a classic ribbon microphone, the 4038, with a figure of eight polar pattern. This microphone was designed over forty years ago and is still considered to be one of the best for speech in broadcast studios.

Capacitor or Condenser Microphones

The construction of a capacitor microphone is shown in Figure 16. The diaphragm behaves as one plate of a capacitor, whilst a fixed backplate forms the other. These plates have a polarising voltage or charge applied to them, and form part of an electrical circuit.

As sound-waves cause the diaphragm to move in relation to the backplate, so the capacitance changes, and an electrical signal, analogous to the changes in air pressure, is generated in the circuit. This signal is very small, and needs to be amplified before it is suitable for transmission down a cable, so most capacitor microphones incorporate a pre-amplifier in the body of the microphone. To provide the necessary power for this pre-amplifier, and also to provide the polarising voltage for the capacitor 'plates', an external DC source is needed. This can either come from batteries held within the body of the microphone or in an external battery pack, or from the mixing desk or recorder to which the microphone is connected. Such a source is known almost universally as 'phantom power', although this is the trademark of a German company, Georg Neuman.

Phantom power is so-called because it is a DC voltage, ideally 48v, but often anything between 12 and 50v, that is superimposed upon the audio (AC) signal in a microphone cable without affecting that signal. A simple combination of resistors and capacitors at both the mixing desk and the microphone ensure that

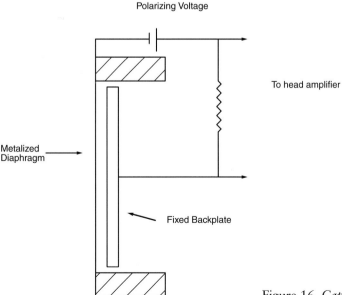

Figure 16 *Capacitor microphone.*

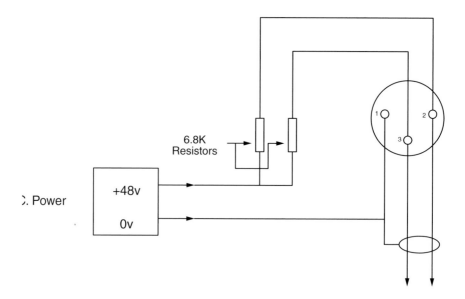

Figure 17 *Phantom Power Supply circuit.*

the DC voltage is available to the microphone as a power supply, but does not interfere with the generation and reception of the audio signal (see Figure 17). Moving coil and ribbon microphones, which do not need this DC voltage, are unaffected by its presence, unless they are connected to the mixer via unbalanced (single core and screen) cable instead of balanced (twin core and screen) cable.

Most professional mixing desks have a switch with which to turn the phantom power on and off as required, and it is good practice to switch the supply off when capacitor mikes are not being used.

A variation in capacitor microphone design is the Electret capacitor, in which the diaphragm and backplate have a polarising voltage imposed on them at the manufacturing stage, and do not need a separate supply for this purpose. They do need a separate voltage for the pre-amplifier, however, and this can either be supplied via a battery or by phantom power.

Capacitor microphones are capable of very high fidelity, and are found in broadcasting and recording studios. In certain designs it is possible to separate the capacitor capsule or head from the pre-amplifier or body, connecting the two with fine cable or a thin supporting tube that carries such a cable. The tiny microphones used in most theatre musicals are capacitor microphone capsules connected to a pre-amp/power supply and radio transmitter, so that the performer is free to move on stage.

It is also possible to construct condenser microphones so that they are capable of exhibiting different polar patterns, thus increasing their usefulness in studios and theatres.

Polar Patterns

A microphone can be designed so that it is sensitive to sounds arriving from particular directions. The graphic plot of this sensitivity is called the polar pattern, or polar response of the microphone, and four main polar patterns are commonly used in sound recording and reproduction. These are illustrated below.

It is important to know the polar pattern of a microphone, as it can determine whether a particular model of microphone is capable of performing the task allotted to it.

a) Omni-directional microphones are sensitive to sound-waves from all around, and are less susceptible to wind, breath and handling noise than their directional counterparts. They are used extensively in classical music recordings and by radio interviewers when acoustic conditions are favourable. They are not so useful where there is excessive background noise, or in close proximity to loudspeakers in sound reinforcement systems.

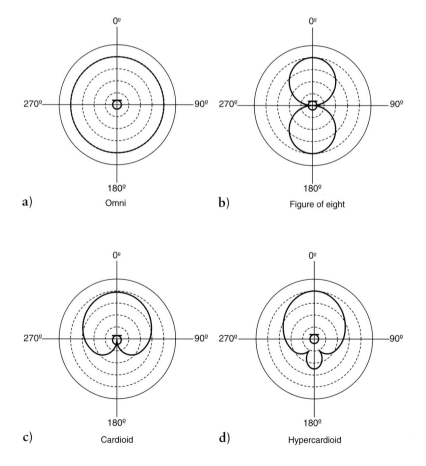

Figure 18 *Microphone polar patterns.*

A boundary microphone, or PZM (Pressure Zone Microphone, a trade name of the American company, Amcron, which developed this type of microphone) contains an omni-directional microphone capsule mounted in a support and facing directly down on to a boundary plate. A very narrow gap is left between the capsule and the plate, ensuring that all sound-waves arrive at the diaphragm at the same time, thus minimising any phase cancellation effects. It is meant to be used mounted on a surface such as a floor, a wall or a desk-top. The omni-direction characteristic of the capsule is limited by this surface mounting, and the actual polar diagram is more correctly described as hemispherical.

b) **Figure of Eight** or **Bi-directional** microphones are sensitive to sound from front and back, but reject sound from the sides. This makes them especially useful in radio drama, where two characters may face one another across a single mic, without worrying about intrusive sounds from the side. The BBC owns patents on a number of excellent bi-directional ribbon microphones, and they are also used extensively in a particular form of purist classical music recording pioneered by Alan Dower Blumlein, the father of 'stereo' recording. Ribbon microphones lend themselves to the figure of eight response by virtue of their mechanical construction, and ribbon mics are often constructed as bi-directional units.

c) **Cardioid** microphones are more sensitive to sounds coming from the front. The term 'cardioid' relates to the 'heart' shape of the polar pattern. These microphones are perhaps the most widely used in sound recording and reinforcement, as they offer a degree of control and off-axis discrimination to the user. Sounds that are not required can be minimised by positioning the microphone so that the unwanted sounds are outside the polar pattern, or 'off mic', and the balance between unwanted and wanted sounds is determined by the engineer rather than by external acoustic considerations.

Cardioid microphones are sometimes known as **uni-directional** microphones, but as this can cover a number of possible polar patterns, the term cardioid is preferred. The same company that produces the PZM hemispherical microphone also makes a version with a specially shaped housing, again made for floor or desk mounting. This microphone is known by its trade name, Phase-Coherent Cardioid (PCC), with various models available.

d) **Hyper-cardioid** microphones are sensitive to sound from the front, but as the name suggests, they have a narrower acceptance angle than cardioids. They are used mainly where ambient noise is a problem, or when the effect of room acoustics needs to be minimised.

Super-cardioid microphones have an even narrower acceptance angle and are sensitive to sounds immediately to the rear of the microphone. They are most often used in film and television recording when off-axis sound is not required and the microphone needs to remain out of shot. These microphones are sometimes referred to as **Shotgun** or **Rifle** microphones.

They are used in theatre when there is a need for remote pickup of sound, however they do frequency response anomalies: they are only directional at middle and high frequencies, and their use is often restricted to supplementary applications, such as general stage pickup or show relay. These microphones are

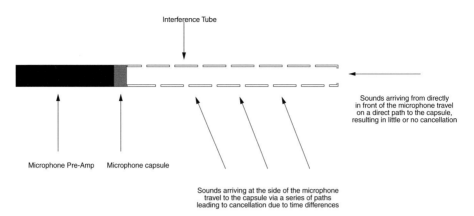

Figure 19 *Cross-section of a rifle microphone.*

physically very large, their construction being based on a principle known as an interference tube (see Figure 19), and they can be difficult to hide on theatre sets.

The Proximity Effect

A directional microphone will produce a signal with an artificially boosted low-frequency content when used close to the sound source. Sometimes known as bass tip-up, the correct name for this is the proximity effect. The effect is exploited by both politicians and performers, who move closer to the microphone when they wish to sound sincere, the extra bass adding warmth to their voices. However, such close-up use of a microphone for vocal purposes can also have a detrimental effect, causing low-frequency overload of the microphone on speech plosives, for example, words beginning with the letter 'p' or 'b', an effect more commonly known as popping the microphone.

To counter the proximity effect, many directional microphones are fitted with a bass cut or bass roll-off switch, which will filter the low frequencies out of the signal. This switch also serves to reduce handling and wind noise. To prevent popping, a high-quality foam wind-shield is needed, or in situations where looks are not important, a fine mesh screen can be positioned in front of the microphone. Some success can be had with a wire coat-hanger and a pair of women's tights.

The proximity effect can also be detrimental in certain aspects of the recording and amplification of musical instruments that have an extended low-frequency content, and care should be taken to avoid overloading recording equipment and/or loudspeakers.

Microphone Sensitivity

All microphones produce a voltage at their output terminals that varies in direct proportion to the changes in sound pressure level at the microphone diaphragm. How much voltage is produced depends on a number of factors: the design of the microphone circuitry, the type of microphone and the specification of the equipment to which it is connected. Very often, a manufacturer will quote figures for the output of a microphone with reference to a known set of conditions, for example, an output voltage will be specified for a known sound pressure level at a fixed distance.

Comparing levels for different microphone types and manufacturers will show a marked difference in output. The sound engineer needs to be aware of this to avoid generating too much unwanted noise in the system, or, at the other extreme, overloading the system.

In general, dynamic microphones (i.e. moving coil and ribbon microphones) produce a lower signal level than capacitor microphones. Some capacitor microphones can produce such a high output that it is necessary to reduce the level at the microphone using a switched attenuator, known as a pad, on the body of the microphone. If such a switch is not provided, then it is usually possible to use a similar attenuator built in to the input channels of most mixing desks.

Choosing and Using Microphones

There are a bewildering number of microphones available for use in theatres, recording studios, film, TV and radio studios. They vary in price from around £25 to over £2,000, and great care needs to be exercised when choosing which microphone to use. If you are lucky, the theatre or studio that you work in will have a stock of the highest quality variable polar pattern and specialist capacitor microphones; more likely, there will be one or two of these, and a larger number of general purpose microphones that are used for everyday work.

There are many microphone manufacturers: the UK companies Calrec and Soundfield Research Ltd, the North American companies ElectroVoice and Shure Brothers, the Austrian company AKG, the German companies Sennheiser, Beyer and Neuman, and the Japanese ATC and Sony. An increasing number of microphones are now available from Eastern European countries, although the build quality of some models leaves rather a lot to be desired.

Theatre companies tend to buy and use moving coil microphones because they are robust, fairly low priced, and more or less suitable for most routine work. Unfortunately, some theatres never get beyond using the very simplest microphones, with the result that they are pressed into service for jobs for which they are not ideally suited.

It is important to understand that there is no such thing as the all-purpose microphone, and you will need to make a series of decisions before you decide which type of microphone to use for a particular job. First, you need to know under what circumstances the microphone will be used. We can break the various situations down into a number of basic groups: recording in a studio; recording on location; amplification of material located remote from loudspeakers; amplification of material located close to loudspeakers.

Each of these groups can be broken down into smaller sections as your requirements become more and more specialised.

Recording in a Studio

There is a tendency to regard any recording studio as a place with controlled acoustics, where noise from outside is not a problem, and instruments and voices can be separated from one another with special screens if required. Unfortunately, this is not always the case, and recording studios have to cope with many different styles of music or speech recording. To this end, many of the larger studio complexes have separate studios for different types of music; large spaces with a 'live' feel for orchestral work, smaller spaces with a more 'dead' feel for rock and pop work and isolation booths for drums, and even smaller rooms, sometimes within a larger studio for voice work, known as 'vocal booths'.

A well-designed studio should not alter or 'colour' the sound produced in it, and the choice of microphone can be much wider than if a recording was being made outside a studio.

Microphones are naturally omni-directional (with the exception of ribbon microphones), and in tailoring the polar response of a microphone it is also likely that the frequency response will be adversely affected. Having said that, microphones designed for use in recording studios will almost inevitably be expensive capacitor mics, usually with variable polar patterns so that the same mic can be used in a number of circumstances. Examples of variable polar pattern microphones made by AKG, Neuman, Sennheiser and Soundfield Research are listed on the next page.

How the microphones are positioned in the studio depends very much on the type of work being recorded. In a studio devoted solely to the spoken word, the microphone will tend to be a cardioid type, mounted on a boom stand overhanging the table on which the actor or presenter places the script. The script surface will often be acoustically treated to prevent stray reflections from causing phase cancellation problems.

Recording on Location

If you wish to record away from a studio, you will need to choose your microphone with slightly more care. If you are actually recording out of doors, then you will have to be prepared for wind noise. The standard foam plastic windshields supplied with most microphones are OK for preventing pops and blasts from a close-up performance, but are no use at all for dealing with even a slight breeze. Omni-directional microphones are better at coping with wind blasts than cardioid types, but best results are obtained with a purpose-made wind-shield.

Two of the most common types of microphone used by TV and radio crews are dynamic omni-directional mics for interviews and vox-pop type shows, and capacitor directional mics for dialogue and effects work in news and drama productions. Sennheiser 816 and 416 rifle mics are a favourite choice, coupled with Rycote wind-shields.

It should be remembered that all microphones, but especially capacitor types, are affected by damp and condensation and may need special handling or protection in wet or humid conditions.

Amplification of Sounds Remote from Loudspeakers

Your choice of microphone can be much the same as for a recording studio situation, with regard for the overall quality of the microphone rather than its susceptibility to feedback or handling abuse. Caveats applied to location recording should also be taken into consideration if your location is exposed to the elements!

Amplification of Sounds Close to Loudspeakers

This situation is the most problematic. Colouration of the sound through loudspeakers being picked up by microphones, and in extreme cases acoustic feedback or howl-round, can cause severe distortion in sound reinforcement systems where the microphone is in close proximity to the loudspeakers.

The use of directional microphones is almost essential to maximise system gain before feedback, although the miniature microphone systems used in most musicals are omni-directional. Recently, there has been a trend in musicals to use microphones mounted on headbands that position the microphone capsule close to the mouth of the performer. These can make a great deal of difference to the level of the signal achieved, but are not really suitable for productions set in the past.

Significant improvements can be gained by making sure that the loudspeaker system is as directional as possible, and the development of directional compact loudspeakers has had a marked effect on the quality of theatre sound systems. This aspect of theatre sound is discussed on page 92.

Sound engineers identify microphones by manufacturer name and microphone type number. Here are a few examples:

Shure SM58	Dynamic	Cardioid
AKG C480B/CK6	Capacitor	Cardioid
AKG D112	Dynamic	Cardioid
AKG C414TL	Capacitor	Multiple
Beyer M201	Dynamic	Cardioid
Beyer M101	Dynamic	Omni
Beyer M88	Dynamic	HyperC
Beyer M740	Capacitor	Multi
Neumann KM184	Capacitor	Cardioid
Neumann U89	Capacitor	Multi
Sennheiser MKH60/70	Capacitor	Rifle
Sennheiser K6 series	Electret	Various
Sennheiser 816/416	Capacitor	SuperC
Amcron PCC160	Electret	Cardioid
Amcron PZM series	Electret	Hemi

General Notes

Many performing artists have their favourite mics and they will not be happy unless these are available. Some cabaret artists travel with their own mics, and will only work with these. Very often this reliance on a particular microphone has little to do with the way it performs, and far more to do with the look and feel. An expensive German capacitor microphone may well perform far better than the cheap American dynamic, but it is hopeless as a stage prop, or as a totem that can be twirled, caressed, licked and generally interfered with.

You will only learn about microphones by trial and error. Most of those that you will come across will be fairly rugged and will cope with the odd mistake, but use your common sense to determine what type of mic you might need, and above all use your ears to hear if you have made the right choice.

Direct Injection Boxes

When it is necessary to connect an electrical musical instrument with an un-balanced output such as a synthesizer or electric guitar, to a mixing desk, problems often occur owing to impedance mismatches and the susceptibility of unbalanced cables to interference. The most common way to approach this problem is to use a device called a Direct Injection box, or DI box.

These devices usually contain either a balancing transformer and a resistor network, or an active balancing unit, powered either by batteries or by phantom power from the mixing desk. The instrument is plugged into the box via a standard quarter-inch jack, and, if required, the signal is then passed through the box to the musician's own amplifier: an XLR connector on the DI box also carries the output of the instrument, but as balanced signal at microphone level. The output of the DI box can then be connected to a standard microphone input channel on the mixing desk.

It should be noted that many guitarists rely on a combination of electric guitar and amplifier to achieve their distinctive sound and may insist that the sound designer uses a microphone in front of the instrument amplifier's loudspeaker. In this case, it may be advantageous to allow two channels of desk input, one for a direct injection box, and another for the microphone. In the case of bass guitars, using a direct injection box is an excellent way of capturing the sound of the instruments. Some instrument amplifier manufacturers provide a balanced direct output that follows any processing that may be contained within the amplifier, but is situated before the amplifier's main level control. This offers the best of both worlds as the musician is able to set a local level that suits him or her, and the sound designer gets a clean feed from the instrument without having to worry about the problems of miking the loudspeaker cabinet. The choice of whether to use a DI box should only be made after discussion with the musician involved and the musical director.

Phase Cancellation

A sound-wave travelling from source to microphone does not simply follow a direct path; in most cases, the sound will radiate in all directions and bounce from any hard surfaces it might encounter. The reflected sound will then arrive at the microphone slightly later than the direct sound, causing a phenomenon

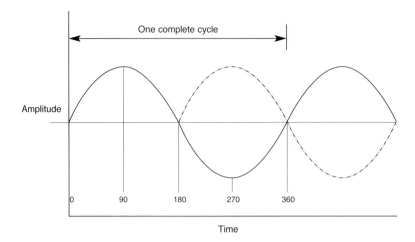

Figure 20 *Phase cancellation: the dotted waveform has its compression period at exactly the same time as the solid waveform has its rarefaction period. Combining the two waveforms will result in total cancellation.*

known as phase cancellation. Similarly, if two or more microphones are in close proximity to the same sound source, the sound will arrive at each microphone at slightly different times. Combining the output of these microphones can also give rise to phase cancellation and produce a sound which is indistinct and unpleasant.

Many mixing desks have a phase reversal switch which allows the polarity of the microphone channel to be switched through 180 degrees, if required. The Yamaha 02R also has the facility to time-delay the incoming signals by minute amounts to allow the phase alignment of multiple microphone set-ups.

A classic example of phase cancellation occurs in musicals when two characters, both wearing wireless microphones, have to sing very close to each other, usually face to face. In this case, each performer's microphone will pick up both the voice of the performer and that of his or her partner, resulting in severe phase cancellation of certain frequencies. One solution to this problem is to drastically reduce the level of one performer's microphone at the mixing desk and allow both performers to be amplified using the remaining channel. It makes sense to leave the microphone of the singer with the weaker voice as the open channel, and considerable dexterity is often required on the part of the balance engineer to maintain a constant level as the performers move towards and away from each other. A second solution is to use dual vocal reinforcement systems with each performer's voice coming through separate loudspeaker systems, sometimes called A/B systems, although this requires complex planning and is considerably more expensive than the first option.

Recording and Playback
Analogue Tape Recorders

Although analogue reel-to-reel and cartridge-based tape recorders and players are still being used in some theatres, the ready availability of more sophisticated digital equipment has meant that increasing numbers of theatres have turned to digital storage and playback devices as a matter of course.

In this section I will examine analogue tape-based systems briefly, before passing on to the digital alternatives most frequently used today.

Analogue tape recorders work in the following way. An audio signal in electrical form is converted to a varying magnetic field by the recording head of the tape machine. A strip of plastic tape on feed spool, on to which a metal oxide has been coated, is pulled past the recording head at a constant speed by a mechanical arrangement of a rotating capstan against which the tape is pressed by a rubber or composition pinch-wheel. The changes in the strength of the magnetic field at the head are recorded on to the moving tape as a constantly varying magnetic pattern. The tape is then fed to a take-up spool, where it is stored.

When the recording is finished, the magnetised tape is rewound and pulled past a replay head, which converts the changing magnetic pattern into a varying electrical voltage, analogous to the voltage applied to the record head. The resulting signal is then fed to an amplifier and on to the rest of the reproduction chain. The faster the tape is pulled past the recording head, the more space there is for the magnetic information to be recorded, and the higher the quality of the resulting recording. Tape recording speeds are usually referred to in inches per second (ips) rather than their metric equivalent, and the two speeds most commonly used in theatre are $7\frac{1}{2}$ ips, and 15 ips (19 centimetres/second and 38 centimetres/second respectively).

Professional tape machines have three heads: the erase head, which wipes any previous recordings, the record head, which presents the varying magnetic field and cut to the tape, and finally the replay head, which reconverts the magnetic pattern into an electrical signal. In domestic machines, the record and replay heads are sometimes combined into one unit, with a resulting compromise in performance.

Because the transfer process is not perfectly linear, extra processing in the form of equalisation of the signal, and the addition of a very high-frequency bias signal are necessary to achieve accurate recording and playback. North American and European recording systems use different types of equalisation, and most tape recorders give the user the option of switching between the two. The North American system is known as NAB, and the European system as IEC/CCIR. The setting up of the equalisation and bias frequencies of a professional tape machine will vary depending on the manufacture of the tape used, and the speed of recording and playback, and the user's manual will almost always contain information on how to achieve optimum settings.

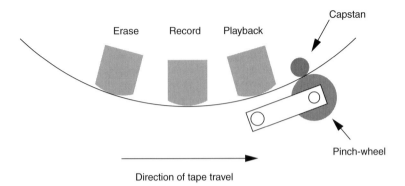

Figure 21 *Analogue tape recorder tape path.*

The process of recording audio information on to magnetic tape in this fashion is the same for all types of analogue tape machine, from dictating machines and compact cassette recorders, through to the high-quality reel-to-reel recorders found in recording studios. What varies is the amount and the quality of the information recorded, the speed at which the tape is pulled past the recording head, and the width and thickness of the tape used.

Multi-track Recorders

It is possible to record more than one magnetic 'stripe' or track on to magnetic tape; routinely, stereo cassette recorders are able to record two tracks side by side, on half the width of the tape. When the cassette is turned over, the other half of the tape can also have two tracks recorded on it.

Professional recorders use the full width of the tape and normally record in one direction only. Cassette tape is $\frac{1}{8}$in wide and, allowing for a space, or guard band, between tracks, each track occupies less than $\frac{1}{32}$in. Cassette tape speed is $1\frac{7}{8}$ inches per second, and the resulting quality of the recording is often poor, although great advances in tape manufacture, transport mechanisms and record and playback head design have been made in recent years, and many high-quality cassette machines are available with a wide frequency response and, using the Dolby system, low noise.

Professional two-track machines use $\frac{1}{4}$in tape, although this tape width is also used for some four- and even eight-track systems. The more common professional formats are: four tracks on $\frac{1}{2}$in, eight or sixteen tracks on 1in, sixteen or twenty-four tracks on 2in tape.

Standard reel-to-reel tape speeds are $3\frac{3}{4}$ ips, $7\frac{1}{2}$ ips, 15 ips and 30 ips. For many years, the preferred tape speed in theatres has been $7\frac{1}{2}$ ips (19 cm/s) following the somewhat misguided principle that this would give greater economy. The gains in quality from recording and playing back at 15 ips (38 cm/s) far outweigh any slight savings that can be made in tape costs. The higher speed is the standard for broadcast and studio recording and there is no reason that theatre should be any different.

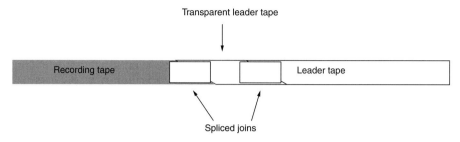

Figure 22 *Automatic stop for tape replay.*

Reel-to-Reel

Reel-to-reel analogue tape recorders were, for many years, the standard play-back device for sound effects and music in most theatres. The advantages were that sounds could be edited quickly and efficiently using the most basic tools: an editing block to hold the tape, a Chinagraph wax pencil to mark the edit point on the rear of the tape, a single-edged razor blade or surgical scalpel to cut the tape, and dry-adhesive splicing tape to rejoin the cut pieces. Cues could be easily identified with a title written on to special spacing tape, called leader tape, available in many different colours for fast identification.

Providing a high recording and playback speed is used, noise can be kept to a minimum and the quality of the recording of a reel-to-reel analogue recorder is reasonably high. To reduce noise even more, most recording studios and some theatres use noise-reduction systems, most commonly those produced by Dolby Laboratories, or the dbx Corporation.

Some machines are fitted with optical or foil sensors which will stop the tape transport when either transparent tape or metallised tape pass them, thus cueing up the machine for the next effect or piece of music.

In order to provide a fast start-up time for theatre use, the pinch wheel was normally pulled into place by means of a solenoid, and the resulting 'clunk' immediately preceding an effect could easily destroy a carefully created atmosphere. Consequently, theatres either modified their machines for as silent a start as possible, or placed their machines in soundproof cabinets, remote from the operating position, using remote controls to operate them.

The alternative to this was to use a system previously utilised by the broadcasting industry to play in station idents, sound effects, jingles and commercials. Developed for the American broadcast industry, these are known as NAB Cartridge (or 'cart') machines.

NAB Cartridge Machines

Although these machines are almost obsolete now, they represented a considerable advantage for theatre work over their reel-to-reel counterparts, and the system of operation, if not the actual recording medium, has been retained by a number of manufacturers offering a digital version. Cart machines are compact,

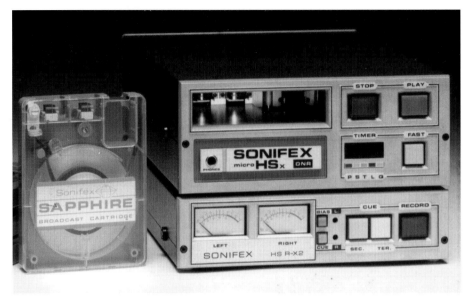

Figure 23 *NAB cartridge player.*

silent in operation and offer instant start. The tape is contained within a plastic housing and is arranged in the form of an endless loop. Special audio tones, known as cue-tones, are recorded on to the space between the audio tracks and allow the machine to stop automatically at the cue point, fast forward, or trigger other machines or effects via a relay closure. These are known as the primary (stop) tone, the secondary (wind) tone and the tertiary (auxiliary) tone. Once a cue has played, the tape loop simply continues to pass the playback head until the next primary or secondary tone is sensed, then either stops, ready to play the cue again, or fast forwards until either another cue or a stop tone is found. In some machines it is possible to disable or erase the stop tone so that the loop plays endlessly. This can be useful for long background effects.

The need to use a special, lubricated tape in the cartridge, and the high wear rate on the tape caused by the endless loop system, made the preparation of shows using NAB carts time-consuming and expensive, and it was not uncommon for several sets of cartridges to be prepared for a long-running production.

Conclusion
Although analogue reel-to-reel tape machines are still common in many theatres and recording studios, the advantages offered by their digital alternatives have meant that their use is steadily declining. Cartridge machines, in particular, are rarely encountered in their analogue format, with the digital versions, or computer-based playback and recording systems taking their place in both theatre and broadcasting situations.

The compact cassette survives as a convenient means of providing material for a director to listen to, or for use in rehearsal rooms, but as it is now less expensive to purchase blank recordable compact discs than it is to purchase compact cassettes of the same length, this situation is also changing rapidly.

In short, the days of the analogue tape-based recording and replay system are numbered, and although it is a system that we will sometimes encounter, it cannot be long before it has all but disappeared as a medium for theatre playback.

Digital Systems

The most common forms of two-track digital replay system are as follows.

R-DAT (Rotary-head Digital Audio Tape)

Usually simply referred to a DAT, this is a small tape cassette-based medium, originally developed for the consumer market but wholeheartedly embraced by the pro-audio industry. Cassette lengths available are from a few minutes up to two hours, although the tape in the latter is very fragile and prone to snapping. Digital information is recorded on to the small tape area in a series of diagonal tracks laid down by a rotating head, similar to that found in video recorders. In fact, the earliest low-cost DAT recorders were simply video recorders with an adapter that allowed them to record digitally-encoded audio information rather than video signals.

The start of each piece can be identified by a track marker, or index point, and the playback machine can search for these points very rapidly. The recordings are linear, however, and the time taken to move from one track to another can be anything from a few seconds to over a minute.

Because of their small size and the intricacy of the tape-handling mechanism, DAT machines can be problematic in a hostile environment, with the ingress of dust and moisture causing system failures. Consequently, they are rarely used as a performance playback device, but more often for master recording and archiving purposes. The information on the cassette can be erased and the cassette used again if required.

Tape-based Digital Multi-Tracks

Alessis, Tascam, Sony and other manufacturers all make digital multi-track recorders that can be used as playback devices if required, although these machines cannot be recommend as instant-start devices unless the tape is cued up and the system put into pause mode. These machines do have their place in theatre, usually as a convenient source of music playback in shows that do not use a live orchestra but require a live balance of multiple sources.

Compact Disc

This medium will be familiar to most readers: a $4^{3}/_{4}$in (12cm) diameter disc which holds audio information in digital form. The information is held on the disc as a series of pits radiating out from the centre of the disc in a spiral, and

Figure 24a *Digital media: MiniDisc, DAT Tape and CD-R.*

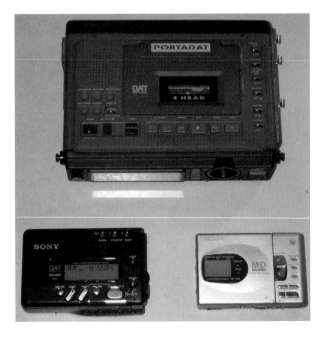

Figure 24b
Top – Professional Portable DAT recorder.
Bottom left – miniature DAT recorder.
Bottom right – portable Mini-Disc recorder.

the varying reflections from the surface of the disk from a low-power laser beam are received by an optical pickup that tracks across the disc as it rotates, and are retranslated into digital audio information.

Although not, as originally claimed, indestructible, the medium is resistant to damage, and playback machines offer instant start, fast track access, track programming and the ability automatically to pause at the beginning of each track and wait for a further 'play' command. The standard length for a CD is 74 minutes, but more can be squeezed on in certain circumstances. Once the information is recorded, it cannot be erased or added to, so this medium is suitable for the final master of an effects or music track for a show.

Special CD recording machines have recently become widely and cheaply available, both as stand-alone units and as add-ons to computer systems, and the cost of blank recordable CDs has also fallen dramatically. When I started writing this book, a blank CD cost around £7.50; now they are available in bulk for less than £1.00 for a 74-minute version.

A Note on Recordable Compact Discs

CD-R systems work by using a layer of heat-sensitive dye between the outer surface and a reflective inner surface. A laser is used to change the transparency of the dye layer, corresponding to the digital representation of the input signal, thus changing the degree of reflectivity from the laser in the playback machine. Experiments have shown that it is important to keep CD-R discs away from strong light and heat sources, and disc boxes should carry a warning to this effect.

First-generation CD-R machines required the user to prepare a detailed list of track timings on a computer which could then be written to the CD as a sub-code, allowing the CD player to display accurate timing information for each track. The currently available machines allow this sub-code to be written automatically at the time of recording, and track and index markers may be added 'on the fly'.

The latest recorders take the output of a DAT or MiniDisc recorded at the CD mastering standard of 44.1 kHz and transfer the contents to CD-R, with the index points recorded on the DAT being converted to cue points on the CD-R. As there is usually a slight delay between the start of the audio and the presence of the track index on the DAT, high-quality digital delays are included to enable the user to ensure that the CD-R cue point comes at exactly the right place.

Preparing a disc with the latest type of CD-R recorder is simply a matter of lining up the source material and then hitting the record button at the same time as starting the effect. Once the effect has played through, the machine is stopped and the next effect is added. At this stage, sounds can be added to the disc until it is full, but the disc cannot be played on a conventional CD player. Once the disc is fully loaded with all the required material, a table of contents (TOC) is generated.

The recorder then writes the TOC to the disc, allowing it to be played on a conventional CD player but preventing any further sounds from being recorded. This process is known as fixing up the disk. If you decide that you want to add an effect at a later stage, you will have to remake your original disk, add the extra effect and music, and then rewrite the TOC.

Computer programs are also available, such as Adaptec's JAM, which allow sounds prepared and edited on computer-based Digital Audio Workstations (DAWs) to be written to a low-cost internal or external CD writer. These programs allow the user to specify the order of tracks, gaps between tracks, index points, and fade-in, out or cross-fade times. By using one of these programs, theatre sound designers have access to a comprehensive and low-cost method of producing music and effects CDs for use in shows.

At the time of writing, advances are being made in the area of rewritable CDs, known as CD-RW. However, these devices will only play on the same type of machine that they were recorded on, and are not compatible with standard CD players. Also in development are the Super Audio Compact Disc (SACD) which utilises a higher sampling rate, and Digital Versatile Disc (DVD) which can handle multiple audio tracks as well as high-definition video, but there are still some matters of standardisation of these formats to be sorted out.

MiniDisc

The Sony MiniDisc system initially appears to be the most successful of the new generation of digital two-track replay systems. Like DAT, this system was aimed at the consumer market, but was soon adopted by the broadcast and theatre industries as a replacement for NAB cartridge machines, with many other advantages.

Data is stored on a tiny magneto-optical disc packaged in a protective plastic cartridge, just over $2\frac{1}{2}$ inches square, and is capable of storing up to 74 minutes of audio using a data compression system called ATRAC (Adaptive TRansform Acoustic Coding). The recording system makes use of a property of magnetic materials that results in a change in their ability to retain a magnetic field when subjected to heat. A laser heats up the surface of the disc to a point where it is easily magnetised, and a coil produces a magnetic field that varies in relation to the current produced in the coil by a digital data-stream. As the surface of the disc is constantly rotating, and the laser and coil track across the surface, the heat and magnetic field are removed from the immediate area of the disc surface, and as this cools down, the magnetic pulses are 'frozen'. In this way, the necessary 'on-off' digital pulse train can be written across the entire surface of the disk in a spiral.

On replay, the power of the laser is reduced and the beam reflected from the magnetised surface of the disc. Slight changes in the polarisation of the reflected beam are caused by the magnetised surface of the disc (a phenomenon known as the Kerr Effect) and these changes are translated by an optical pick-up back into the digital data.

The ATRAC compression system is far too complicated to examine in depth; simply put, it examines the audio spectrum of the incoming signal, and in response to a set of parameters arrived at by computer modelling the workings of the ear, throws away some of the audio information that it regards as unnecessary. At the time of writing, the system is being refined constantly, and is now in its fourth generation. Some audio engineers can detect the effects of this compression, but the convenience of the MiniDisc system far outweighs the slight disadvantage caused by the use of the data reduction method.

Like CD and DAT, the start of each audio band can be marked with a track identification. The difference is that a data sub-code can also be written that allows each track to be identified by name, with the title available to the user on an alpha-numeric display. The disc itself can also be titled, allowing for easy identification of both disc and individual tracks. Because the disc can be erased and rerecorded, either as a whole or in sections, editing is also possible to an accuracy of $^1/_{75}$th of a second – accurate enough for most purposes. Tracks can also be reordered on the disc, allowing for alternative takes to be stored out of order.

Several manufacturers make professional MiniDisc recorder/playback machines, either free-standing or rack-mounting, and software is available to allow titling, editing and copying via a computer interface.

It must be said that since the adoption of MiniDisc as a replay device in theatre, many users have experienced problems with the reliability of both the media and the machinery. The problems appear to come from the fact that MD players need to be kept relatively free from dust and dirt, and need to be maintained on a far more frequent basis than was initially considered necessary. There are also an increasing number of low-cost domestic units on the market that are, unfortunately, finding their way into theatres unable to afford the higher price of the professional models. Invariably, the build-quality of these units is inferior to their professional counterparts and the connectors are unbalanced. Because of the low cost, however, some theatre sound designers treat these units almost as disposable devices, arguing that they can purchase seven or eight domestic units for the price of one professional unit.

Digital Cartridge Machines

There are a number of manufacturers making digital alternatives to the tape-based NAB cartridge machine. So far, they have failed to agree a standard amongst themselves, and only two seem to have made an impact on the UK theatre market. The Sonifex DX10 Discart uses high-capacity (4 Mbyte) floppy disks to store up to a maximum of 81 seconds of stereo audio at a sampling rate of 44.1 kHz, and the Fidelipac/ASC DART Recorder offers similar audio, but with the option of using high-capacity magneto-optical drives or the removable 100 Mbyte ZIP disks from Iomega as the storage medium.

The 360 Systems DigiCart offers similar facilities to the DART machine, including the option of high-capacity drives.

These machines offer all the advantages of their tape-based predecessors with none of the problems, and also offer the advanced programming, track-naming and editing features of MiniDisc, with a number of additions specially tailored for the broadcast industry, such a date-stamping and variable-bed looping. This last feature has some place in theatre, but is mainly used for music played under news or traffic reports. A piece of music is recorded that has a start, a short middle section and an end. Markers are placed at the beginning and end of the middle section and the machine can then be programmed to start playing the track at the beginning, continuously looping the middle section until the play button is pushed again. At this point, the middle section will play until the end of the current loop and then continue to the end section. The effect can be heard on almost all broadcast stations that use music as a 'bed' under news reports, and is useful in some sound effects work (see Chapter 6).

Hard-disk Recording Systems

Stand-alone Systems

These systems use large, computer-type hard-disks as a storage medium, often coupled with advanced editing features, either by front panel controls or by using software front-ends on desk-top computers. Many of these systems offer more than two tracks, with Akai having four-,eight- and sixteen- track versions available. Although they are mainly aimed at the recording and film/video in-dustry, the versatility and comparatively low cost of these systems makes them attractive to some theatre sound designers. However, in order to make them usable in a live performance, it is often necessary to obtain third-part modifica-tions to allow the systems to accurately cue up at the beginning of each effects or music track.

Such a device exists for the Akai recorders, manufactured by MM Productions in the UK. It performs like an electronic optical stop on a reel-to-reel recorder, with the user having to program in the start-time of each track. The box reads the time-code information transmitted by the recorder and automatically stops the machine when the two times match.

The speed with which these machines start up, and the high quality of the audio make them ideal for certain aspects of theatre, but the relatively lengthy set-up procedure means that planning must be done well in advance of a tech-nical rehearsal. However, they are a very real alternative to multi-track digital tape recorders in recording studios.

Computer-based Systems. (Digital Audio Workstations (DAWs))

At the time of writing, there is a proliferation of digital audio recording cards for personal computers. The cheapest make use of the so-called 'Soundblaster' cards fitted as standard to many Windows/Intel- (abbreviated to Wintel) based

Figure 25 *Akai DR16 hard disk recorder.*

PCs, and at least one software company, SFX, is offering a package specifically directed at theatre use, although as only a single stereo output is offered, more than one 'Soundblaster' card is required for multi-output work. Given the limited card space inside the average PC, and the problems frequently encountered with setting up multiple cards within a PC, this must be regarded as something of a disadvantage. However, at least one company has addressed this problem by providing a professional multi-channel interface for use with the SFX system. The SFX program is discussed later in this book.

Higher up the range, companies such as Soundscape, and Avid-DigiDesign's SADIE Protools have immensely sophisticated multi-track systems available on both Wintel PC and Apple Macintosh platforms that offer stereo and multi-track recording and playback from internal or external hard-disk arrays. These systems are finding popularity in the recording and editing rooms of many theatres, but they lack the simple interface and fast start that could make them useful in live performance.

The Richmond Sound Design AudioBox Digital Playback matrix is discussed later in this book, but contains the means to play back audio from an internal or external hard-disk in response to MIDI Show Control commands generated by computer.

Versions of this type of system are available to the broadcast industry, both as

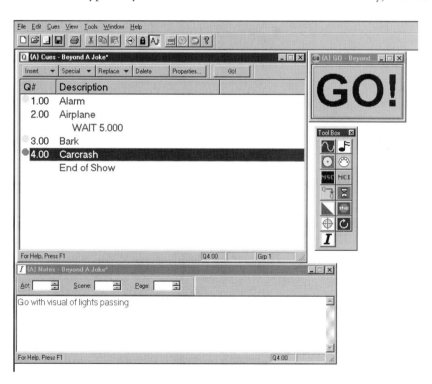

Figure 26 *The SFX show-control programs.*

a replacement for cartridge machines, and as a fast and convenient way to edit speech for news and current affairs programmes.

Solid-state Storage Devices

This system uses computer-type memory either in the form of specially-built modules, or the industry-standard PCMIA cards, to store mono or two-channel audio information in digital form. The information is read out from the memory in response to a trigger command produced either by dedicated hardware or by software on a controlling computer. The use of solid-state playback devices is much favoured in theme-parks and exhibitions, where low-maintenance requirements are often an overriding factor in the decision-making process.

Samplers

A sampler is a device that is able to store a collection of audio signals in digital format and play them back from an internal solid-state memory, or from a hard-disk drive, in response to commands from a MIDI (Musical Instrument Digital Interface) controller. This may be a keyboard, but is more commonly a computer-based music-sequencing or show-control program.

Samplers were originally intended as a way of imitating musical instruments, but their versatility and the wealth of options available to the user in terms of manipulating sounds has made them extremely popular with many sound designers. Their use is discussed at length in Chapter 6.

Which System to Use?

In order to decide which type of system to use, the designer needs to examine a list of pros and cons for each, based on the following criteria.

(1) Ease of Use

Can the system be operated easily and instinctively under show conditions? Reel-to-reel systems and cartridge machines, both analogue and digital, score highly here, as do CD and MiniDisc. A few simple controls are all that is needed for operation. Instant or near-instant start is easily achieved and each can be operated via a simple remote control. Samplers, DAWs and R-DAT machines can be more complicated to operate, often requiring complex additional controls and/or computer programs to function usefully under show conditions.

(2) Resistance to Failure

How robust is the system? Is it prone to failure under intense operating pressures? Remember that the equipment has to function day after day, very often in a hostile environment. Many pieces of equipment that seem at first sight to be suitable for theatre use are in fact designed for the domestic hi-fi or semi-professional music market, and will not stand up to the sort of use that they will meet in theatres.

Once again, old technology seems to score heavily here. Broadcast-standard cartridge machines and recording studio-quality tape recorders are built for intensive use, and some theatres have analogue tape systems that are many years old, but still perfectly serviceable.

Now that compact disc is the accepted standard for carrying music and sound effects commercially, a number of professional-quality CD players are manufactured, notably by Sony, Tascam, Denon and Studer, which are engineered to the high standard required for intensive use.

The MiniDisc system has its problems, as detailed on page 60, but provided the players are thoroughly maintained on a regular basis, few problems should occur, and manufacturers are working hard to improve the disc transport system to make it less susceptible to dust and dirt pollution.

Both samplers and computer-based hard-disk/solid-state systems can be rendered inoperable by a temporary power failure and may require reloading or rebooting once power is restored. Uninterruptible power supplies are essential items of equipment on shows where no other form of back-up can be used. Heat and static electricity can also have a disastrous effect on these systems. Having said that, I have used samplers extensively with only isolated problems.

(3) Durability and Exchangeability of the Medium

Magnetic tape is reasonably durable as a medium, provided certain storage considerations are met. Tapes produced since the 1960s have a binder/base/oxide combination that is largely stable, although problems have been encountered with some brands of tape that have been stored under damp conditions. Remedies, albeit rather drastic ones, do exist to alleviate such problems for long enough to allow a copy to be made. Formats, speeds and track standards for professional tape recorders have been in place for many years now, and a common working practice has ensured that it is relatively easy to exchange tapes and be sure that they will work with your equipment. The same cannot be said of the digital domain at present.

Although a common standard is supposed to exist for the R-DAT system of digital recording, numerous cases of machine/cassette incompatibility have been reported. In the exchange of digital audio information between systems, once again two standards exist – S/PDIF for consumer equipment and AES/EBU for professional equipment – but problems have occurred, with a degree of incompatibility being experienced as manufacturers cut corners to save money. When such problems arise in the digital domain, the result is usually a complete failure of the system to replay the stored sound.

A CD recorded to the Red Book Standard (the international standard for CDs carrying audio information) should play back on any machine, from the cheapest portable to the most expensive studio machine, but the latest generation of CD-Read/Write (CD-RW) systems tend to be machine-specific and will not play back on ordinary CD players.

The MiniDisc standard is also world-wide, but there are still some problems of compatibility, with discs failing to play back on different machines.

Most high-quality samplers will accept sample disks recorded to the old

Akai/EMU standard (the newer models use the computer industry-standard .wav format for recording samples), but will not read performance data for different manufacturers' systems.

The digital cartridge machine manufacturers have so far failed to find much common ground for interchangeability in their systems, and there is therefore little use of these machines in theatre within the UK.

Conclusion

All of the systems outlined have their advantages and disadvantages and many sound designers use a combination of equipment for their playback sources. In any event, it is always good practice to have a back-up system in case of problems with the primary system. Most of my shows now run on a combination of hard-disk and sampler playback systems, with a CD player or a MiniDisc for back-up purposes.

Mixing Desks

Terminology

Before I commence this section of the book, I should clarify the differences in terminology between the UK and the USA. In the UK, the standard term for the device used to collect and blend or balance audio signals, either for recording, broadcast or live sound reproduction, is a mixing desk or mixer. The person who operates this equipment is either a balance engineer, recording engineer or a sound operator. In the USA, the device is known as a mix(ing) board or console. To add to the confusion, the operator is sometimes known as the mixer. For the purposes of this book, I shall use the terms 'mixer' or 'desk' and 'balance engineer' or 'operator'.

The Controls

The heart of all theatre sound reproduction systems is the mixing desk. All mixing desks have a number of inputs to which incoming audio signals can be connected, and a number of outputs to which groups of inputs can be mixed and routed. Often these are arranged as sub-groups, which allows the operator to adjust the level of mixed groups of inputs. The sub-group outputs can be accessed directly, or routed to the main stereo outputs. Mixers are often described by the number of inputs, sub-groups and outputs that they are fitted with; thus a desk with sixteen input channels, eight sub-groups and two main outputs is known as a 16-8-2 desk.

In a multi-track recording studio the mixing desk has two functions. In the recording process, the desk serves to match the levels of all signals wanted in the recording, from microphones, electrical musical instruments or other external sound sources, to provide a degree of tonal correction if required, and to route each signal to a particular track of the recording machine, either directly or via the sub-groups. A studio multi-track recorder may have as many as forty-eight tracks and may use analogue magnetic tape, digital magnetic tape, or one of the computer-style hard-disk mediums currently available.

The engineer will try to maximise the level of the recording on each track, regardless of how loud the signal will be in the next stage of the process, in order to reduce the amount of noise in the final recording. Once all the signals have been recorded, the desk is then reconfigured to balance the audio signals recorded on the multi-track, further process them if necessary, and then combine them into a smaller number of mixed signals (one for mono systems, two for stereo sound, three or more for surround-sound systems) for distribution either by radio broadcast, commercially available CD, vinyl disc, MiniDisc or compact cassette, or film and video soundtracks.

In the theatre, the mixing desk is required to perform a slightly different task in addition to those needed in the recording studio. Audio signals from a variety of sources still need to be collected and processed, but we then need to send different mixes of these signals to any number of outputs, then to amplifiers and loudpeakers located around the auditorium and stage, as well as to small amplifiers feeding headphones for actors and musicians in locations remote from the stage. Often, all available sub-group and master outputs are used – with each feeding an amplifier/loudspeaker combination in a different part of the theatre. Desks designed to be used for sound reinforcement on large-scale musical productions may also have additional functions not considered vital by theatres that use their desks mainly for replay of sound effects or pre-recorded music.

In some systems, a further set of outputs is available, often greater than the number of sub-group outputs. In desks specially designed for theatre, this output system is incorporated in the form of an output matrix, where each sub-group can send its mixed signal to any combination of the matrix outputs (see Figure 16). Stand-alone output matrix systems (sometimes called console fanouts, particularly in the US) are also used, and are now also available as digital units where the various routing levels can be stored and recalled using a computer control program. Two of these units, particularly suited to theatre, are discussed at the end of this section.

Desks specially designed for the on stage monitoring requirements of rock bands may have as many outputs as they have inputs, and may lack the conventional linear fader familiar to most mixing desk users, relying on rotary faders instead.

Nearly all conventional mixing desks have the same basic set of controls for input and output functions; only the degree of control offered will vary, usually in direct proportion to the cost of the desk. Separating the input section of the desk from the output section, let's look at the controls that are common to each input or output channel of a mixing desk. For convenience, I have located the controls and connectors as they are most often found, but desks vary in their layouts. Specialist functions, such as those found on desks that have Voltage Controlled Amplifier (VCA) facilities are covered later in this chapter.

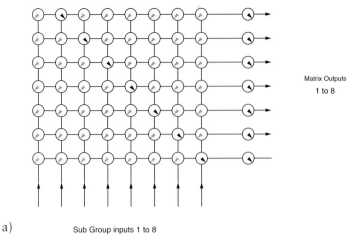

Matrix Outputs
1 to 8

a)   Sub Group inputs 1 to 8

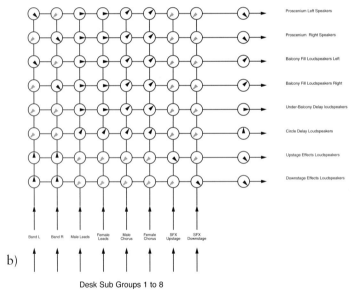

Proscenium Left Speakers

Proscenium Right Speakers

Balcony Fill Loudspeakers Left

Balcony Fill Loudspeakers Right

Under-Balcony Delay loudspeakers

Circle Delay Loudspeakers

Upstage Effects Loudspeakers

Downstage Effects Loudspeakers

Band L   Band R   Male Leads   Female Leads   Male Chorus   Female Chorus   SFX Upstage   SFX Downstage

b)

Desk Sub Groups 1 to 8

Figure 27 *These drawings show desk subgroup outputs 1 to 8 being routed via an output matrix. Each sub-group output can send all or part of its signal to any-one or combination of matrix outputs by means of the 64 'send-level' controls. The master output level for each matrix send is set by a master level control for each matrix output. In a) each sub-group is being sent to its corresponding matrix output. The black arrows show a send at maximum level, the grey arrows show a send at minimum level. In b) a much more complex routing plan has been applied, with sub-groups being named as groups of microphones, and the matrix outputs designated as amplifier/loudspeaker groups.*

Input Section

Front of Desk
Input Channel
Input Gain Control – Controls that match the incoming signal with the mixing desk inputs.

Mic/Line Switch – Selects either the microphone input or the line input and routes the selected audio either to a microphone pre-amplifier or direct to the main input stage.

Gain Control – Allows the incoming signal to be set at an optimum level for the mixing desk. Input levels are often set using a combination of the gain control, the pre-fade-listen switch and the desk's metering device. Some desks may have individual channel meters alongside the fader, which may be set to show the incoming signal level.

Pad or Attenuator – Switch to reduce signal levels that are too high for the desk input stage. Used in conjunction with the gain control.

Phase Reverse – Reverses the polarity of the incoming microphone signal in order to compensate for minute time differences encountered in multiple-microphone set-ups, where the signal from one sound source may enter the microphone for another (see page 52).

Phantom Power – Used to power capacitor microphones that do not have internal or local power sources (see page 44). This switch may sometimes be found on the rear of the mixing desk.

Equalisation Controls – Controls that allow the frequency response of the incoming signal to be modified. In basic desks, these may be limited to High Frequency (HF), Middle Frequency (MF), and Low Frequency (LF) boost and cut only. On more complex desks there may be more than three sections and the frequency bands may overlap. These controls are usually known as EQ controls.

High Shelf – Reduces the high-frequency content of the signal, starting at a stated frequency and by a fixed amount per octave for all frequences above that point. May be used to remove unwanted hiss from a signal, for example.

HF Boost/Cut – Increases or decreases selected high-frequency content by a variable amount. The centre frequency and bandwidth (sometimes called Q) may either be fixed by the manufacturer or selectable by the operator using secondary 'parametric' controls.

Figure 28 *Mixing desk channel strip – top section.*

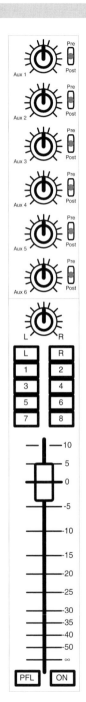

HF Parameters – Selects the centre frequency and bandwidth at which the HF boost/cut control operates.

MF Boost/Cut – As HF controls but affects middle frequencies, for example 500 Hz–5 kHz. Sometimes called a 'presence control' in older equipment.

MF Parameters – As above.

LF Boost/Cut – As HF controls but affects low frequencies, for example 80 Hz–600 Hz.

LF Cut – Reduces the low-frequency content of a signal, starting at a stated frequency and by a fixed amount per octave for all frequencies below that point. Sometimes called a 'rumble-filter', and may be used to reduce wind noise or foot-fall noise on float microphones.

EQ In/Out – Bypasses the entire equalisation section to allow comparison with the treated signal. May also be used to switch in severe equalisation on a signal that does not normally require treatment, for example a music or voice recording that needs to sound as if it's coming from a small transistor radio, or through a telephone for a particular cue.

Auxiliary Sends – Controls that send a part of the input signal to a separate mix buss – the auxilliary buss – frequently shortened to aux. buss. There can be as few as two or as many as sixteen, depending on the design of the desk. The signal may be sent to the aux. buss before or after the main channel fader (pre- or post-fade), and before or after the equalisation section (pre- or post-eq). Selection of the aux. buss attributes may be via a switch mounted on the channel, or by a jumper on the channel circuit board. Typical use of an aux. buss is to send a part of the signal to an external effects processor, such as a reverberation or echo device, in which case the send will normally be derived post-fade, or to an amplifier/speaker combination for foldback or monitoring purposes, in which case the send may be sent pre-fade. On older desks, it is not uncommon to find controls marked 'Echo Send' and 'Foldback Send'.

Routing Controls – Controls that determine which output or combination of output the signal will be sent to.

Pan Pot – An abbreviation of 'Panoramic Potentiometer', this rotary control routes the signal between odd- and

Figure 28b *Mixing desk channel strip – lower section.*

even-numbered sub-group outputs and the left and right master mix outputs, as selected by the routing switches. A centre position sends the signal
equally to left, right, and odd and even outputs. Increasing degrees of rota-
tion away from the centre point sends more of the signal to either the left
or right mix buss, and the odd or even sub-group busses. On some mixing
desks, the pan pot may be switched out of circuit, allowing for direct selection of sub-group outputs.

Routing Switches – These switches direct the incoming signal to the available sub-groups and master outputs, depending on the position of the pan
pot. A typical theatre sound desk may have eight sub-groups and a left-
right master output, giving ten possible destinations for the input signal.
On some desks, each output is accessed by a dedicated switch, on others,
the outputs are selected as pairs (L/R, 1/2, 3/4, 5/6, 7/8) and the pan pot is
used to determine which output the signal is sent to. This can be particularly annoying if you want to send a signal to sub-groups 1 and 4 only, for
example. In order to send the signal to output 1, the pan pot must be rotated fully to the left, but in order to send the signal to output 4, the pan pot
needs to be rotated fully to the right! Desks designed specifically for the
theatre tend to go for the 'one button per output' mode of construction
with a switchable pan pot control.

Channel fader – Determines the amount of the signal that will be sent to
selected outputs and to any aux. buss that has been selected as post-fade.
Usually marked with a decibel (dB) scale of amplification and attenuation,
with the 0dB point indicating that the signal will be passed with no attenuation or amplification. Typically, a channel fader will allow up to 10dB of
signal amplification (marked as +10 at the top of the fader travel) and infi-
nite (maximum) attenuation (marked as ∞ at the bottom of the fader travel), with further amounts of amplification and attenuation marked in
between. A normal range might be: ∞, -60dB, -50dB, -40dB, -30dB, -20dB,
-10dB, -5dB, 0dB (unity gain), +5dB and +10dB.

Pre-fade Listen – This switch causes the signal to pass to the monitoring
section of the desk before the channel fader, so that the signal can be
checked without having the fader open. (It is also known as the solo or
monitor switch). The signal is also usually routed to one of the desk's level
meters to allow for accurate gain-setting. In musicals, this switch is invaluable for checking the state of individual wireless microphones so that any
faults can be reported to the on stage wireless mic engineer.

Channel Mute – Turns the input channel off. May be part of a 'programmable mute' system, where groups of channel mutes are assigned a master
on/off switch.

Output Section

Front of Desk

Sub-group Fader – Acts as a master controller for groups of input channels that are routed to that particular group output. In some desks, the sub-groups can themselves be routed to the L/R output of the desk, and a pan pot and L/R select switch may also be fitted to facilitate this.

Stereo or L/R Fader Acts as a master fader for groups of input channels routed to the L/R outputs, and/or for the sub-group faders, which may also be routed to the L/R outputs. May also control the level sent to the headphone monitoring section.

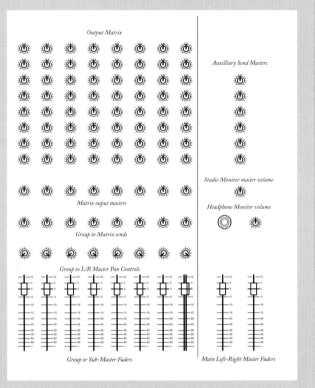

Figure 29 *Typical mixing desk 8 x 2 output section with 8 x 8 matrix.*

Auxiliary Masters – Master output levels for each auxilliary channel on the desk.

Monitor Master – Controls the level of the desk headphone monitor output and/or a separate output on the rear of the desk that can be connected to an amplifier/loudspeaker set up in a control room, for example.

Matrix – Allows each sub-group to send a variable amount of its signal to one or any combination of further outputs from the mixing desk. See Figure 16.

Matrix Masters – Act as master level controls for the matrix outputs.

Headphone Socket – Socket for connecting headphones for monitoring purposes. If the PFL button is pushed on any channel, group or master, the listen signal will be routed to this output to allow individual sections of the desk to be monitored individually.

Input Section

Rear of Desk
Input Channel
Microphone Input – XLR3F connector for balanced microphone input.

Phantom Power On/Off – Used to power capacitor microphones that do not have internal or local power sources (see page 45). This switch may sometimes be found on the desk input channel.

Line Input – XLR3F/Balanced three-pole jack connector for balanced line input.

Insert – Usually combined input/output connector (A or B gauge three-pole jack). Breaks the audio path for each input channel and allows the connection of extra processing equipment.

Direct Out – Provides a direct output from each channel, after the channel fader. Useful for making separate multi-track recordings, for example.

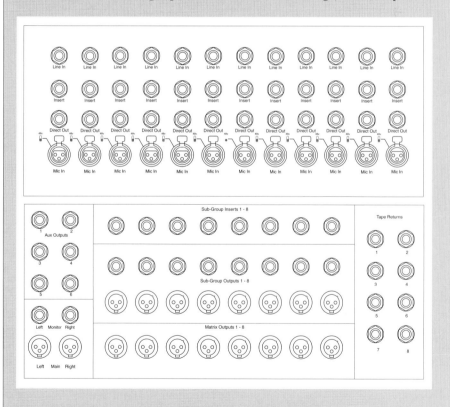

Figure 30 *Rear of typical small mixer.*

Output Section

Rear of Desk

Sub-group Output – XRL3M connector for balanced audio output direct from sub-group mix busses.

Sub-group Insert – Usually combined input/output connector (A or B gauge three-pole jack). Breaks the audio path for each sub-group output and allows the connection of extra processing equipment.

Matrix Output – XRL3M connector for balanced audio from sub-group/master matrix busses.

Auxiliary Sends – Usually either three-pole jack or XLR3M connector fed from auxilliary master controls. Allows auxilliary mixes of input signals to be sent to external processing devices or to amplifier/speaker combinations for foldback or monitoring purposes.

Auxiliary Returns – Usually either three-pole jack or XLR3F connector accepting return signal from external effects device.

Master LR Outputs – XLR3M connector for balanced audio output from main left/right mix busses.

Monitor Outputs – Separate audio outputs, selected by the operator and normally connected to monitor amplifier/speaker combinations when the console is used in a control room or other remote location.

Tape Returns – Separate audio inputs allowing the playback signal from a recording device to be returned to the mixing desk for A/B comparison with the outgoing mix signal. Usually selectable to the desk monitor outputs. More than one set may be provided, allowing multiple devices to be auditioned.

VCA

In some mixing desks, there is another form of grouping which utilises a device called a Voltage Controlled Amplifier, or VCA.

In a VCA controlled desk, the input signal passes through an special amplifier whose gain is controlled by a variable voltage. This voltage is supplied via a further set of faders and each input channel can be assigned to any one of these VCA faders. When the VCA master is raised or lowered, the signal level of any input channel assigned to that fader will also be raised or lowered. This method of grouping has distinct advantages over the use of sub-groups, as sets of input channels may be controlled by a master fader without the need for them to be routed to the same output groups. This feature is most often found on mixing desks used for musicals where the operator may need to control a large number of microphones which may be routed to separate outputs. In more advanced desks, such as the CADAC series, computer control allows the operator to assign different combinations of channels to VCA control and to store these combinations as cues that can be recalled as the show progresses. A further sophistication provides a simple dot-matrix display above each VCA master which the operator can program to show the function of that particular fader. By using a

VCA system in this way, the operator of a musical can considerably reduce the amount of adjustment of individual channel faders during a busy musical production.

Recent Advances in Mixing Desk Technology

In 1981, the RSC developed a computer-assisted audio switching matrix with four inputs and ten outputs. Each of the four inputs could be sent to any one or any combination of the ten outputs, which were in turn connected to amplifier/loudspeaker combinations. These combinations could be recorded in the memory of a simple home-built computer and recalled as cue states when necessary. Because the RSC ran a repertoire system with, typically, five shows running at any one time, five 'show' memories were available, with each show capable of storing ninety-nine cues. The shows were held in Random Access Memory (RAM) which was powered by an on-board battery, with a cassette tape interface for storing and reloading shows that came out of the repertoire. It was possible to plot the show in 'preview' mode, without affecting the live status of any of the switches, to link cues out of sequence, and to copy the contents of one cue into another, if required.

At the same time, for the main Barbican Theatre, Strand Sound, a division of Rank Strand Lighting, developed a far more complex computer-assisted sound mixing desk, The Sonnet, only one of which was ever produced. Unfortunately, although the computer-assisted routing section of this desk was fairly stable, the operation of the system was complex and confusing, and the audio performance of the desk was often unreliable.

In 1984, frustration with the Strand Sound desk and the success of the home-built system led the sound team to contemplate the design of a system that would do all that the two existing systems did, and much more. They envisaged a desk that could memorise input and output routing, gains, eq settings, auxiliary send levels, pans and channel levels as a series of snapshot cues that could be recalled as needed. It must be said that such systems already existed for recording and broadcast organisations, but their implementation was very basic, relying more on providing the operator with a graphical display of the desk, with all control settings shown on a VDU (Visual Display Unit). The balance engineer would be able to reset the controls according to the screen display for each piece being recorded, rather than relying on paper plots or wax-pencil markings on the console itself. Motorised faders were also available on some consoles, with their relative positions being recorded on a computer running in synchronisation with a time-code recorded on one track of the master tape. Playing the tape back resulted in the faders moving to their correct positions as the time-code was fed into the computer memory.

The RSC team examined all these systems, but found them totally unsuitable for live performance for various reasons, the most obvious being that actors, except in certain circumstances, do not synchronise their performances to a soundtrack, rather, it is the other way around.

Having made their observations, the RSC team decided that the ideal system would consist of an equipment rack containing all the necessary parts of a mixing desk, such as microphone amplifiers, equalisation modules, auxiliary output sections, pan controls, input and output routing switches and level controls. There would be a sufficient number of these to service the most complex shows, and they would be analogue devices that were capable of being controlled digitally from a remote control surface. In short, the system would be a digitally controlled analogue mixer. Once this decision had been made, the next step was clear; because the actual signal processing modules were physically remote from the control desk, it could be made much lighter than conventional desks and moved easily into the auditorium for balancing. Also, as each 'channel' could be controlled digitally, it made sense to centralise the controls that were not often used in performance and give the operator the option of 'assigning' these central controls to any input or group of inputs, or any output or group of outputs, thus drastically reducing the size of the desk and the number of knobs, switches and faders needed in its construction.

Changes in desk function could be made via software, audio upgrades could be made by module swapping, as could running repairs; major system changes would involve retooling just for the control surface rather than the entire desk, thus reducing manufacturing costs. It would also be possible to reassign unused parts of the signal processing chain to other areas of the system, so that a spare input equaliser section could be patched into an output. The team found a manufacturer willing to implement the design, Ted Fletcher of Alice (Stancoil) Ltd, and an enthusiastic electronics engineer, Steve Dove, who assured us that our dreams were technically possible.

In short, we had designed an assignable theatre sound console. We even had a name, DAISY (Digitally-controlled Analogue Interface System). What we didn't have was the necessary financial backing from the RSC, who, quite rightly, pointed out that they were a publicly-funded theatre company, not an electronics development company. Neither did we have the necessary enthusiasm from our colleagues in the industry. I remember vividly a meeting of the Association of British Theatre Technicians Sound Committee at which I outlined our plans. The chorus of disapproval and dissent was deafening: it couldn't work, even if it did work, it wasn't the way balance engineers were used to operating. What would happen if the computer controlling the system crashed? (We'd thought of that – each channel had its own microprocessor capable of handling the operations of a number of channels in the event of the failure of another, and the main processor would be run in tandem with a back-up processor. All of which was standard practice in industrial automation systems at the time – multiple redundancy, I believe it's called.)

Interestingly, another UK manufacturer came up with a digitally-controlled analogue mixing console, the Trident Di-An, developed by the respected audio systems designer Malcolm Toft, and it was with some degree of hope that I went to see this desk at an exhibition. Alas, responding to the recording studio world imperative of 'If I'm paying this much for a piece of kit, it has to look impressive', the Di-An was an enormous beast and totally unsuited to theatre work, as well as being far too expensive.

It soon became obvious that our dream was to remain a dream, and reluctantly we resigned ourselves to many more years of using conventional mixing desks that got bigger and bigger, eating up more and more space in the control rooms that were necessary to house them, or leading to the removal of more and more seats in theatres where they were being used for balancing musicals.

It is, therefore, with a deep sense of satisfaction, and without resisting at all the temptation to say 'I told you so', that I introduce you to the ongoing adoption by the theatre sound industry of the assignable mixing console.

In 1989, the Vienna State Opera invited tenders for a sound control desk much along the lines of the one described above, and the contract was won by a Japanese audio company called TOA. The resulting desk was large and complex to operate but was the first digitally controlled assignable console to be built especially for theatre. Its high price put it out of reach of most theatre companies, but it was a beginning, and, significantly, it showed that the Japanese audio manufacturing industry was prepared to listen to customer input and to design accordingly. A number of other manufacturers, notably Euphonics in the USA, came up with consoles that offered a degree of assignability, but these were aimed far more at the recording studio world than at the theatre. The UK manufacturer, Soundcraft, also arrived at a design for an assignable console in the late 1980s, but this early design did not see the light of day, transforming instead into one of the more promising assignable console designs of the late 1990s, the Broadway.

The first assignable console to be adopted by the theatre sound world was the Yamaha ProMix 01, a small sixteen-input desk with inbuilt effects and fifty scene memories that can store every desk parameter and be recalled via MIDI program changes. Additionally, all major desk functions such as channel mutes and level, panning, auxiliary sends and equalisation can be assigned to MIDI

Figure 31 *Yamaha Promix 01 Digital Desk.*

controllers and altered on cue using either a show-control program or a music-sequencer. Once the analogue signal enters the desk, the signal path is entirely within the digital domain and all internal processing and routing is carried out digitally, with conversion back to the analogue state occurring at the main and auxiliary output stages.

The desk layout is uncluttered, as all major channel controls are centralised and accessed via a keypad and assignable rotary controller. Information is displayed on the small LCD screen located at the top centre of the unit which changes to reflect the controls that are accessed. A graphic display of input and output levels, and of the equaliser section of the desk, is also a function of this panel.

Complete desk states can also be transferred via MIDI to a controlling computer and stored ready for recall, thus allowing as many desk states to be used as are required, without relying on the on-board memory. The desk also features motorised faders which transmit MIDI data, allowing real-time recording and replay of fader movements using a standard MIDI sequencer package, and giving a real display of the current state of the faders, unlike automated desks using Voltage Controlled Attenuators, which normally rely on either VDU or LED displays for fader position information.

Although aimed at home and project studios, the ProMix became a valuable tool in theatre, not least for automating complex music and sound effects sequences, allowing the operator to concentrate on the overall mix of the show. Part of the appeal of the desk was the combination of small size and almost unbelievably low price, which put it within the often limited budgets of many theatre companies.

The ProMix was followed a year later by a second product from Yamaha, the 02R Digital Mixing Desk. This desk was a stunning development on the ProMix 01, featuring forty balanced inputs, ten outputs, two on-board effects processors and assignable dynamic and equalisation controls for all channels. Once again, the desk is compact and affordable, although the MIDI implementation is somewhat reduced from that available on the ProMix 01, due to the vastly increased number of variables available on the desk. However, it is still possible to recall complete desk states via MIDI and, using a number of commercially available control programs, to use a computer to get at every desk function remotely. Additionally, it is possible to assign fade times of up to ten seconds on each input channel so that a high degree of system automation can be achieved.

The biggest problem with using the 02R for theatre work is that the eight - sub-group outputs do not have physical faders associated with them, although spare input faders can be so assigned if required. This makes using the desk for musicals, where it is common for a show to be balanced using mainly the sub-group faders, fairly problematic, though not impossible. A more important omission for theatre work is the lack of an output matrix, but this can be addressed either by adding a stand-alone analogue matrix, or by the more complex method of adding one of the increasing numbers of digitally controlled output matrix units. These units are discussed at the end of this section.

Figure 32
Yamaha 02R
Digital Desk.

At the time of writing, the Yamaha 02R is being adopted as an effects and playback desk by an increasing number of theatres, where its small physical size and wealth of features coupled with a relatively low cost make it highly desirable. In particular, commercial theatre producers are far more likely to allow the installation of such a console in an auditorium where only a small number of seats need to be removed.

With the introduction of the Yamaha products, many other manufacturers were spurred into producing their own assignable desks, and almost at the same time Soundcraft announced their long-planned assignable theatre desk, the Broadway.

The operation of this desk is so similar to the original idea discussed by the Royal Shakespeare Company design team that it made me wonder if our discussions had been taken seriously after all. The main audio components, still analogue, live in a card frame-based rack remote from the main control surface,

Figure 33 *Soundcraft Broadway Assignable Desk.*

which consists of a number of fader banks and a central assignable section for routing, panning, auxiliary sends and equalisation. The control surface is small and portable and can be configured in a number of ways depending on customer requirements. The Broadway was originally supposed to make its West End debut on the Schoenberg/Boubil musical Martin Guerre, but a number of problems forced the manufacturers to redesign the system interface, and at the time of writing, the first system is in use as the front-of-house mixing desk for a tour by the Canadian singer, Celine Dion.

In mid-1999, Yamaha announced their own large-scale assignable desk for theatre work, the PMD1, which has been designed for use on musicals and which should soon be in regular use in many theatres. This system also uses an assignable console with remote equipment racks that may be sited remotely from the mix position.

Each time that I have discussed the principle of an assignable console for theatre sound, and now that we have accepted that computers are a necessary and integral part of the business, I have been met with the same argument: an operator on a major musical needs to have every desk function instantly available in the event of a problem. This need has been expressed by all the operators that I have talked to, and remains a very real problem for the wholesale adoption of assignable desks in theatre. To me, this problem is addressable, but only through the manufacturers talking to the operators, not the designers, to find out how this perceived problem might be addressed. Personally, when I watch an operator controlling a musical on a sixty-input desk, it seems more likely that, with a properly laid out assignable console with intelligent display options, an operator stands a much better chance of identifying and rectifying a problem than with a conventional analogue desk that may be three metres long and in semi-darkness.

The advantage of software-based systems is that they can be altered relatively easily without involving major structural retooling, and manufacturers are listening to users of the equipment and endeavouring to include user-requested variations in system software updates.

All assignable desks work in much the same way: a single set of controls that

Figure 34 *Yamaha PM1D Assignable Mixing Desk.*

correspond directly with those found on an analogue desk are assigned to each input channel as required, and the resultant settings are saved in a scene memory. These memories are then recalled, either manually or via MIDI program changes, as the show progresses. Controls may still be altered, but a lack of 'global' alteration in the current crop of desks means that they will reset to their stored state as soon as the next memory is recalled. It is sometimes possible to 'lock-out' certain controls so that they remain unaffected by memory changes, and this can be helpful in shows where hands-on control of microphone channels is required.

Digital Output Matrix Systems

Closely following the assignable digital desk comes another major innovation for the theatre sound designer. Digital output matrix systems are similar in many of their functions, but each has a different way of implementing these functions, and two, the Richmond Sound Design AudioBox and the LCS LD88 include an on-board sixteen-track replay system that allows the unit to be used as a stand-alone system for exhibitions and theme parks. There are three major players in this market at the time of writing, although a number of other manufacturers such as Peavey, BSS and Allen and Heath produce systems that can be configured in similar ways, but are not specifically geared towards the theatre sound market.

Outboard Electronics TiMax System

This system features an 8 x 8 matrix and has the unique ability to vary delay times and levels at all inputs, outputs and matrix crosspoints. Thus complex sets of delays can be set up which rely on the psycho-acoustic effect known as the 'Haas Effect' to precisely position a sound using different time delays from separate loudspeakers. The use of digital delay systems to locate sounds is not new and is discussed in Chapter 5, but the TiMax system is the first to address this in a way that allows precise positioning of a sound in a three-dimensional soundfield, and has proven to be extremely useful in setting up discreet sound reinforcement. In addition, systems can be expanded to 8 x 16, or 16 x 16 matrix layouts.

Control is via proprietary software running on a Windows-based PC, and the system is comparatively expensive.

Richmond Sound Design AudioBox

This system is more likely to appeal to designers of straight plays, exhibitions or theme parks, although many of the functions available make it suitable for use as a console fan-out for musicals as well. The unit is a 16 x 16 matrix, with eight of the matrix inputs being available for analogue signals and the remaining eight being sourced from the internal hard-disk-based sixteen-track replay system. Input, output and crosspoints levels can be set and recalled, as can fade-up, fade-down and crosspoint fade times. Additionally, inputs and outputs can draw from a library of user-definable equalisation and delay settings. Audio tracks can be prepared off-line, in either WAV or AIFF formats and then downloaded to the

AudioBox via a host computer and played back via the output matrix, with all the equalisation, delay, level and fade functions available to the analogue inputs. Complete sequences of events, including MIDI sequences, can be stored on the internal hard-drive and the system can be programmed to operate as a stand-alone replay and distribution system without any need for a controlling computer.

What makes this system rather more flexible than the other two is the fact that control is via MIDI Show Control System Exclusive commands, and thus any computer program or peripheral device capable of producing these commands can be used to control the AudioBox. Special software with which to load audio tracks into the AudioBox is available for Windows and Apple Macintosh computers, and users running BeOS and Unix operating systems and proprietary control software is also available for both Windows and Macintosh computers. In addition, a number of software developers are producing software that is capable of controlling the AudioBox as a part of an overall show-control system.

Level Control Systems SuperNova

The two main components of this system are the LD88 matrix and the CueStation controller software, running on the BeOS operating system. This unit is similar in many respects to the Richmond Sound Design AudioBox, the main difference being that up to sixteen units can be chained together to provide a 128 x 128 matrix. Playback of sounds from a hard-disk is by means of an add-on expansion card, and control can be from MIDI or serial connections. The CueStation system controller has some similarities to the TiMax front end and the user can 'fly' sounds around a complex speaker map.

I have no doubt that these systems are just the beginning of a new approach to playback and distribution of audio in theatre, and I look forward eagerly to the forthcoming advances in this field.

Amplifiers

The next part of the system to be considered is the power amplifier. As the name suggests, this piece of equipment is used to increase the relatively small audio signal that comes from the mixing desk to a level at which it can usefully provide the power to drive a loudspeaker.

Most power amplifiers used in theatres are two channel devices; that is, they can accept two completely separate input signals and feed two completely separate loudspeakers, although in some cases they are used in bi-amplified systems to drive the middle- and high-frequency loudspeakers in a single loud-speaker cabinet (see page 88).

Choosing the right amplifier can be a confusing business. Most professional power amplifiers do exactly the same thing – increase the level of the audio signal to a greater or lesser degree, depending on their power rating – but there are a bewildering number of different makes of power amplifier available.

A professional power amplifier should have most of the following attributes:

- balanced inputs, on either an XLR or balanced jack connector, although some manufacturers still use a connector strip, which can be a nuisance for touring rigs
- outputs available on binding posts, or 4mm banana plugs, or better still both
- captive or lockable mains power connector, for obvious reasons
- fan-cooling or cool-running electronics and power supplies. Amplifiers tend to be placed above one another in equipment racks and can generate large amounts of heat. Fan-cooling will usually mean that the amplifiers have to be located remote from the stage to avoid fan noise becoming intrusive
- frequency response of between 20 Hz and 20 kHz, with a deviation of +/- 1dB or less. The last thing you want is an amplifier that is selective about the frequencies that it amplifies
- low distortion. Most amplifier manufacturers will quote a Total Harmonic Distortion (THD) of less than 0.1 per cent
- if the amplifier is a two-channel model, then there should be little or no crosstalk between the channels – a signal fed to one input should not be audible on the other output. Look for a figure of –75 dB or better at middle frequencies. Amplifiers with separate power supplies for each channel usually have better crosstalk specifications than those in which the power supply is shared between the two channels
- the ability to drive into low impedances – as low as 4 Ohms is good, but some manufacturers, such as Amcron, claim that their amplifiers will drive loads as low as 2 Ohms

The more powerful the amplifier, the bigger and heavier it is likely to be. This is due to the size of the power supply – the more current the amplifier has to deliver, the more power it will consume and the larger the transformer will be.

Many loudspeaker manufacturers will recommend specific amplifiers to match their loudspeakers, and it is true that loudspeakers will behave differently when matched with different amplifiers, although in a perfect world this would not be the case. When specifying amplifiers for a sound system, it is always sensible to have too much power on hand rather than too little. Attempting to drive an amplifier beyond its capabilities will almost always result in distortion, and distortion is what kills loudspeakers. It sounds pretty horrible, too.

Loudspeakers

Loudspeakers are the final component part of the equipment chain in any audio reproduction system. They convert the mixed and processed sounds that you have collected at the mixing desk from your various sources and sent to the amplifiers as an electrical signal, into acoustical energy, i.e. sound-waves, thus completing the process.

What type of loudspeaker you use, how it is connected and where it is placed in the theatre can drastically affect how an audience perceives the sound or music in a production, and yet it is common to find that choice and placement of speakers is the most compromised aspect of theatre sound design. The reasons for this fall into two main categories: cost and appearance.

A good loudspeaker is expensive; there is no getting around this. It needs to be built from high-quality materials and components that won't distort or otherwise affect the quality and dispersion of the sounds played through it. The cabinet itself must be strong enough to withstand rough handling, and be fitted with robust connectors and well-engineered mounts to allow safe suspension from flying-bars or boom arms.

In order for a loudspeaker to move efficiently the large amounts of air needed to create the high sound pressure levels required in many theatre productions, it has to be fairly large, especially if low frequencies are required. A single loud-speaker cabinet, capable of reproducing all frequencies from 30 Hz to 20,000 Hz accurately and at a sufficiently high level to fill a 1,500-seater auditorium, would need to be far bigger than could be tolerated in most theatres. In the past, when speaker design was not as advanced as it is today, amplified musicals used a small number of large speaker cabinets to fill an auditorium, and the end result was often not pleasing to the eye. Speaker rigs were shrouded in black gauze in the hope that, once the house lights were dimmed, the audience would not notice them, but the sheer bulk of these systems also meant that they could not be placed where they could do most good.

Today, we are considerably more fortunate in that loudspeaker design has improved and we have a wide range of cabinets to choose from, each fulfilling a different requirement. Speaker systems are divided into separate sections, with the low frequencies being handled by large cabinets that can be concealed at the sides of the stage, or even built into the set. The middle- and high-frequency speakers, usually contained in the same cabinet, are therefore able to be much smaller and can be mounted on the proscenium arch or flown above the stage without taking up much more space than a luminaire. In addition, it has become common practice to use a large number of even smaller loudspeakers placed within the auditorium and fed via delay lines so that the main loudspeaker system does not have to produce so much power. The use of delays and the positioning of loudspeakers and multiple loudspeaker arrays is covered in depth in Chapter 5.

We need to look briefly at how a loudspeaker works, concentrating on the moving-coil loudspeaker design that is most commonly used in theatre. Other types of loudspeaker exist, but their main use is in hi-fi or recording studio monitoring systems where they do not need to produce the sort of sound pressure level that is typically required in a theatre.

A loudspeaker unit consists of two parts: the driver, which is the actual device responsible for converting the electrical signal from the amplifier into an acousti-cal signal, and the cabinet, which supports the driver, gives the loudspeaker its directional properties and tailors its frequency response and power-handling capabilities.

Without a cabinet, a loudspeaker is a bi-polar device; that is, it produces

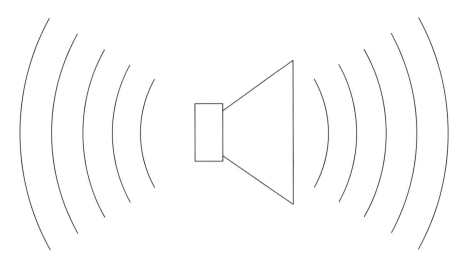

Figure 35 *Loudspeaker as a bi-polar radiator.*

sound in two directions only: in front and behind. There is little or no radiation of sound to the sides of the loudspeaker (see Figure 35). Some theatre sound designers have made use of this fact in musicals by utilising full-range loudspeaker drivers in a mounting-frame, with no cabinet. As the speakers do not radiate sound to the sides, there is less chance that the amplified sound will leak into the performers' microphones, causing distortion or feedback. However, this technique does not work for all productions as a loudspeaker without a cabinet does not necessarily produce sufficient power for use in, say, a rock musical, and phase cancellation occurs at the lower frequencies.

Once the driver is placed in a cabinet, the two items interact in a way that can change the characteristics of the driver in many ways.

The Driver

The construction of a full-range, direct-radiating moving coil loudspeaker is shown in Figure 36. A coil of fine copper wire is wound around a hollow former, and the ends of the coil attached to terminals on the body of the loudspeaker. The coil, known as the voice coil, is suspended within a magnetic field created by a circular permanent magnet and attached to a diaphragm, which may vary in size depending on the frequency band that the loudspeaker is designed to handle. An alternating current from an amplifier is passed through the coil, causing the coil and hence the diaphragm to move, in turn causing the variations in air pressure that create sound-waves.

In the case of a loudspeaker designed to handle high-frequency (short wavelength) information, the diaphragm will be small, and may be at one end of a megaphone-like construction called a horn (see Figure 40). This type of speaker, which is also common for mid-frequencies, is called a horn-loaded speaker and

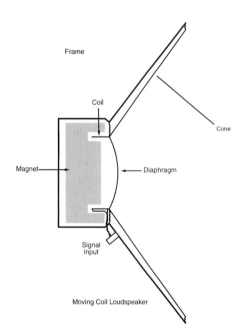

Figure 36 *Moving coil loud-speaker.*

Frame

Coil

Cone

Magnet

Diaphragm

Signal
Input

Moving Coil Loudspeaker

is constructed to maximise the coupling of the diaphragm to the air, in the same way that a megaphone will increase the efficiency and directivity of the human voice. Changing the length and shape of the horn can affect both the efficiency and directivity of the unit, and much detailed research is carried out into optimising flares and methods of coupling the diaphragm to the horn. Horn-loading of low-frequency loudspeakers is very often used in rock and roll-type PA systems, but the physical size of the horn tends to limit its use in theatre. In such a system, the horn is usually incorporated into the design of the cabinet, with the flare following a complex path, and this type of system is known as a folded horn (see Figure 37). Such systems are more efficient, needing less power from their amplifiers to achieve the same sound pressure levels as their direct-radiating counterparts.

It is common to find loudspeakers in theatre that use a combination of horn-loaded and direct-radiating components as an effective compromise between size and efficiency, and speakers of this kind are made by many companies, including Altec, JBL, ElectroVoice, Meyer and Renkus-Heinz.

An example of the combination of horn-loading and direct-radiating units in a particularly compact loudspeaker is the range of units manufactured by Tannoy in the UK, called Dual Concentric speakers, where the horn-loaded, high-frequency part of the speaker is mounted in the centre of the direct-radiating mid/low-frequency unit (see Figure 38). Such speakers have found equal favour as recording studio monitor loudspeakers and compact full-range speakers for use in theatres.

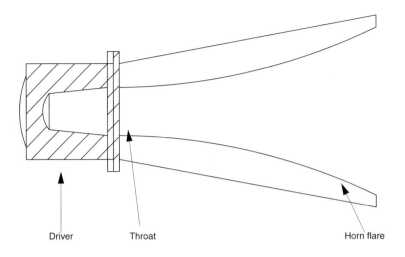

Driver   Throat   Horn flare

Figure 37 *High-frequency horn loudspeaker.*

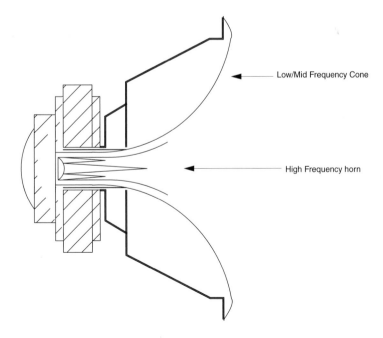

Low/Mid Frequency Cone

High Frequency horn

Figure 38 *Tannoy dual concentric loudspeaker.*

The Cabinet

The science of loudspeaker cabinet design is the subject of much debate, although considerably less so in theatre than in the arcane world of hi-fi. However, there are a number of constants which apply in all cases.

When a direct-radiating moving-coil loudspeaker is fitted into a simple baffle, sound-waves produced from the rear of the unit are prevented from interacting with sound-waves from the front of the unit and thus causing phase cancellation. The bigger the baffle, the lower the frequency at which it is effective, and the better the low-frequency response of the system. However, given the wavelength of lower frequencies, the simple baffle has to be unmanageably large to give an effective increase in bass response. The answer is to extend the baffle to the sides, top and back, totally enclosing the rear of the loudspeaker, and, at the same time, producing a volume of trapped air which effectively stiffens the motion of the loudspeaker cone. By providing ports in what we can now call the cabinet, which are carefully and precisely constructed, the loudspeaker manufacturer can tailor the way in which the loudspeaker behaves at certain frequencies, and, hopefully, remove any colouration or distortion created by the effect of enclosing the driver (see Figure 39b).

The physical construction of the cabinet is extremely important. It must be constructed in such a way that it does not vibrate and thus produce unwanted

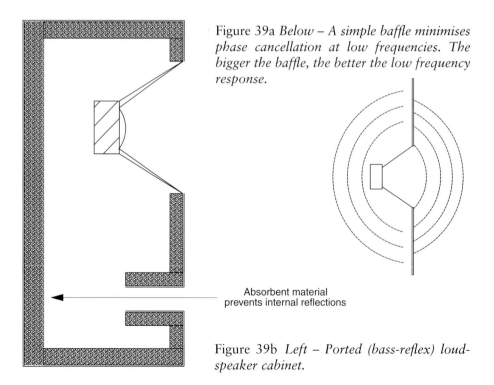

Figure 39a *Below – A simple baffle minimises phase cancellation at low frequencies. The bigger the baffle, the better the low frequency response.*

Absorbent material
prevents internal reflections

Figure 39b *Left – Ported (bass-reflex) loudspeaker cabinet.*

resonances when high levels of amplification are used, and the rear and sides of the cabinet should not act as extra radiators of sound-waves. This almost always means that good loudspeaker cabinets are heavily braced internally, and the panels are damped with absorbent materials to prevent any unwanted vibrations. By taking these measures, loudspeaker manufacturers have been able to produce extremely high-quality loudspeakers with predictable frequency responses and directional characteristics that are especially suited to use in theatre.

Crossover Networks and Bi-amplification

Whilst it is possible for a single loudspeaker to reproduce the full audio frequency spectrum, loudspeaker designers prefer to split the spectrum into bands and to assign to each band a loudspeaker that is specifically designed to reproduce it efficiently, hence the use of more than one speaker in a cabinet. In order to split and control the frequency bands two methods are used: passive crossover networks and active crossover networks. Passive crossovers use the frequency-sensitive properties of capacitors and inductors, and the current controlling properties of resistors, to form frequency dividing networks which act on the composite signal from an amplifier.

Active crossovers are placed in the signal chain before amplification takes place, and split the signal into different frequency bands at a low signal level, hence a separate amplifier/speaker combination is required for each frequency band. This is commonly known as bi-amplification where only one frequency split takes place (low/high), and tri-amplification where a three-way split occurs (low/mid/high). Frequencies at which these systems crossover vary from system to system, but a typical split might be low frequency up to 200 Hz, mid-frequency from 200 Hz to 5,000 Hz, and high frequency from 5,000 Hz to 20,000 Hz.

The advantages of bi-amplification are that two low power amplifiers can produce the same sound pressure level as one large amplifier that is rated at twice the power of the two small amplifiers. The combined waveform of the passive system makes more demands on the large amplifier than the two separate waveforms do on each of their respective amplifiers, thus allowing each of the smaller amplifiers to deliver its full output for its selected frequency band.

Many manufacturers produce loudspeaker systems that use a specialised controller to achieve a number of results. In some cases, the controller provides equalisation of the signal to counteract known anomalies in the loudspeaker, and also acts as an electronic crossover, splitting the incoming signal into two or more frequency bands. In other systems, the controller incorporates a sensor circuit which acts on a signal taken from the output of the amplifier. If the sensor detects an amplifier output level that is likely to cause damage or distortion to the loudspeaker, it will automatically reduce the signal level and limit the frequency response until such time as the problem is removed. It is not usually acceptable to remove these devices from the signal path.

Some loudspeakers incorporate a very simple overload limiter in the form of a light-bulb connected in series with the driver. As the power fed to the loud-speaker increases, the filament of the bulb heats up and its resistance increases, reducing the amount of power being applied to the driver. In the case of extreme overload, the filament will burn out, disconnecting the loudspeaker from the amplifier. It can be disconcerting, when contacting a service department about a non-functioning loudspeaker, to be told that the light-bulb has probably blown, but it is a simple and effective method of protection.

Conclusion

Enormous amounts of research and development go into designing and building loudspeakers for use in theatres, with units being tailored for specific frequency response and directional characteristics, often being designed to be used as part of a specially formulated amplifier/controller system. Modern loudspeaker sys-tems usually come with detailed instructions for setting-up, mounting and posi-tioning for many different types of installations. Some manufacturers supply computer programs with their products to allow a degree of acoustic modelling, with the user inputting data regarding the dimensions and acoustic properties of the space, and the program coming up with suggestions for placement of loud-speakers.

It is something of a mystery, therefore, as to why much of this information is so frequently ignored, either by the system installer or by the end user of the product. In one particular venue I was informed that a new speaker system from a certain manufacturer had been installed and was a vast improvement on the system that had previously existed. On arriving at the venue to open a show, I was puzzled by the lack of power, particularly in the lower-middle part of the audio-frequency spectrum, available from the system, which, in theory, should have been perfectly well able to cope. It took some time to work out that the main part of the speaker rig, arranged in an array, had not been hung in accor-dance with the manufacturer's recommendations, and that a large and unpleas-ant increase in the lower-middle frequency range had been encountered as a result. Instead of changing the rigging arrangements, the theatre's sound techni-cian had inserted a graphic equaliser in the feed to the amplifiers and filtered out the troublesome frequencies, simultaneously removing most of the low-end power from the system.

In another highly prestigious venue, the main front-of-house reinforcement loudspeakers are permanently mounted in concrete recesses in the proscenium arch. The recesses are so small that they allow no sideways movement of the loudspeakers, which are firing directly into the wooden surround of the balcony rather than into the auditorium. As there is no way for these speakers to be repo-sitioned, they are unable to fulfil the purpose for which they were installed, and are rendered virtually useless.

Of course compromises have to be reached in how loudspeakers are posi-tioned, but it seems pointless to spend large sums of money on a specific piece of equipment and then not allow it to do the job that it is designed to do.

Effects Devices

The use of effects devices to alter or add to a signal is now common in many productions of both straight plays and musicals. The auxiliary sends on the mixing desk are used to send a signal to an effects device, and the treated signal is then returned to the desk, either through a spare input channel or through auxiliary returns, which add the treated signal to the desk sup-groups or main outputs.

When I first started in theatre sound, there were only two effects devices available: reverberation and echo. The former was usually achieved mechanically, either by the use of a specially constructed spring, or with a metal plate. In the former case, a coiled spring was made to vibrate by attaching a transmitting transducer directly to one end of the spring and a receiving transducer to the other. The vibrations in the spring took time to die away and the resulting decaying sound was mixed in with the original to give a semblance of natural reverberation. In the case of the plate, the transducers were placed at different points on the plate, but the principle remained the same. The metal plates were very large and gave a better sound than the spring, but were well beyond the reach of the average theatre company in terms of cost.

Echo, either single or multiple, was achieved by using either a three-head tape recorder, or by a specialist unit that also relied on the distance between a record and playback head, but that used an endless loop of tape. These devices also had a number of playback heads and switches that allowed the user to determine how many of these heads would feed a delayed signal to the output and at what level. The signal to be echoed was routed to the input of the echo-machine and recorded on to the moving tape. As it was picked up by the playback head a short time afterwards, a delay occured between the sound entering the recorder and it being played back, and this was combined with the original signal to provide an echo.

These devices were fairly crude and simple, but they were all that was on offer.

Today that situation has changed dramatically. A glance through the pages of any musical equipment magazine will reveal a bewildering array of effects devices, mostly digital in operation, that can alter sounds in many ways. How useful most of these effects are in theatre is a point of debate.

Most theatres will have at least one multi-effects device available to the sound designer. The Yamaha SPX 1000 is one such item. The user can choose from a number of pre-set effects, echo and reverberation amongst them, as well as filtering and pitch-changing and a whole host of other treatments. Whilst these items are a useful tool, many designers prefer to use dedicated devices, particularly to add reverberation, as the sounds produced are much more complex and therefore more realistic. A recent innovation comes in the form of a reverberation device that uses acoustic modelling to synthesise reverberation characteristics and allows the user to specify the exact dimensions of a reverberant space to model. Some of these systems even come with pre-programmed reverberation patterns for well-known performance spaces.

Figure 40 *Yamaha SPX1000 Multi-Processor.*

The use of effects devices for treating recorded sounds is covered in Chapter 6, and many of the procedures described there are equally applicable to live sound work. In this section, we'll look briefly at the most common units and their possible use in a sound system.

(1) Reverberation

These units are mostly used to add character to a voice or an instrument, especially if the theatre has a dry acoustic. They can also be used as a means of making groups of instruments sound bigger than they actually are, and to iron out any tonal inequalities. Too much reverberation will simply muddy the sound and serve to confuse the listener. The sound designer will often use differing reverberation times for different instruments, as well as for singers. It's not uncommon to have three or four reverberation units on a large musical, with each dedicated to a different part of the orchestra or different sections of the cast.

(2) Echo/Delay

This device can have a number of applications, depending on the control settings available to the user. In its simplest form, it's used for producing a single repeat of the original signal after a specific period of time, which can be anything from a few milliseconds to three or four seconds. With a short repeat setting, it can be used to produce an effect pioneered by Ken Townsend at Abbey Road Studios for the Beatles, and now universally known as Artificial Double Tracking, or ADT, where an exact copy of the original sound is added to the mix with a very short delay. The mixture of the original and delayed track gives a similar effect to that which used to be obtained by the artist singing a second vocal track alongside the first. Small changes in the delay time can make this effect sound more realistic.

Longer delay settings, and feeding part of the delayed signal back into the unit for repeat processing, will give a simulation of tape-echo as described above, and even longer delay times will allow whole words or phrases to be repeated. Sometimes a 'repeat hold' function is provided, whereby a word or phrase can be repeated indefinitely until the user cancels the hold facility.

Units which are designed to allow small changes in delay time for time aligning multiple loudspeaker set-ups are covered in Chapter 5.

(3) Phasing/Flanging

Once again, a legacy of the pop music recording engineers of the 1960s, and once again originating from the fertile brain of Ken Townsend. This technique employs very small time delays which can be varied to provide a phenomenon known as 'comb filtering'. As the original and delayed signals are mixed, the varying time delay causes phase cancellation of different component frequencies in the original sound, resulting in a sound treatment that will be instantly familiar to those who grew up during the psychedelic 60s, but which has since rather gone out of favour. It's still worth experimenting with, particularly to provide an 'other world' type of sound.

(4) Pitch Transposing/Harmonising

Modern digital effects devices are able to change the pitch of a sound without affecting the duration. In the past, with the exception of a rather strange mechanical device used in novelty records, the only way to change the pitch of a sound was to record it on to tape, and then play it back at a faster or slower speed. Today, digital pitch-changers achieve their effect by varying the sample rate at which the sound is played back. This can be used to thicken a bass line, for example, but extreme changes of pitch still give a rather artificial effect, particularly with low cost units. Most units will allow the user to set musical intervals for the pitch change, allowing a single instrument or voice to automatically harmonise with itself, and a new generation of 'intelligent' harmonisers has considerably increased the usefulness of these devices. Their use in theatre is probably limited, although they can provide an additional texture to a music or effects track.

(5) Noise Gates

A noise gate is an electronic switch inserted into an input channel on a mixing desk. The user is able to set a level, known as the threshold, at which the switch will close and allow the signal to pass. Once the signal level falls below the threshold, the switch opens and the input channel is effectively muted. This can be extremely useful with electronic instruments that generate excess noise, or with microphones that are in noisy environments. Careful setting of the threshold will ensure that the microphone or instrument channel on the mixing desk only becomes 'live' when the input signal is over a certain level, i.e. when someone is talking into the microphone or playing the instrument.

(6) Compressors/Limiters

These are used to control excessive dynamic range, and are, effectively, automatic gain controls, triggered by the signal input. For example, a singer may tend to vary wildly in the level that he or she sings at, and the operator then has to maintain a constant check on the level of the singer's microphone. This can be overcome by inserting a compressor in the signal path, and setting a threshold point at which the compressor takes over. When the threshold point is passed, the gain control inside the compressor starts to reduce the output level in line with a 'compression ratio' set by the operator. In a 2:1 setting, a rise in input level of 6 dB would result in a rise in output level of only 3 dB, and with a 4:1 setting, a rise of 12 dB would result in an output level change of 3 dB. The higher the compression ratio, the more severe the gain reduction, until the unit effectively becomes a limiter, when any increase in input level over the threshold results in no increase at the output. Limiting can be seen as a fail-safe gain control to prevent unexpectedly loud sounds from causing distortion or damage to the system's loudspeakers.

Compressor/limiters can be extremely useful tools in a musical, but setting them up can be a complex and time-consuming process if they are to be used successfully. Setting the proper reaction time of the gain controller, known as the 'attack time', and the speed at which it returns the gain to normal, known as the 'recovery time', depends very much on the content of the audio signal, and improper settings can cause the sound to pulse, or 'pump'. Setting the attack time too slow on speech inputs can allow an initial high-level sibilance or plosive content of a sound to pass through and subsequently reduce the level of the word that follows, resulting in a sound that seems to be all sibilance or pop.

(7) Equalisers

These devices are the big brothers of the equalisation controls found on the mixing desk. Broadly speaking, they come in two types: graphic equalisers, which have a number of boost/cut controls at set frequencies and bandwidths, and parametric equalisers, where the user is able to set the frequencies at which boost and cut will take place, and the bandwidth, or Q, of the frequencies affected. The higher the Q number, the wider the band of frequencies either side of the selected frequencies that will be affected; the lower the number, the smaller the band will be, until a Q setting of .08 will affect a frequency range of around one-twelfth of an octave.

Equalisers are used in two ways. Firstly, to allow the user to remove any frequencies that may be causing problems in a sound system. It may be that a combination of room resonance and a particular microphone/speaker application causes acoustic feedback, or howl-round, at a particular frequency when the microphone is turned on. Identifying this frequency and using either a graphic or a parametric equaliser to reduce its content in the system is an acceptable method of using an equaliser. Secondly, to make up for deficiencies in the system over which the designer has no control, by increasing or decreasing the level at selected frequencies to ensure that the system has a smooth response. The use of equalisers to achieve this end is fraught with problems as boosting or cutting on part of the audio frequency spectrum often causes a perceived change at another

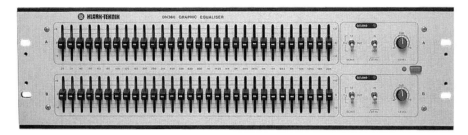

Figure 41a *Graphic equaliser.*

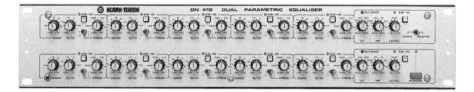

Figure 41b *Parametric equaliser.*

part of the spectrum and the need to make more changes to the equaliser to compensate. All too often, the controls on a graphic equaliser end up looking like a row of rotten teeth and the system still sounds awful.

The analogue versions of these equalisers are rapidly being replaced by their digital equivalents; units that can offer storage of many different settings as well as a combination of graphic and parametric operation, and may well incorporate other facilities such as time delay and multiple outputs. The most flexible of these units are intended for use in complex sound reinforcement applications, and are sometimes referred to as speaker management systems.

In a well-designed and set-up system, equalisation should be regarded as the final tool that a designer turns to to iron out the few remaining system anomalies, and in most straight plays that I design, graphic or parametric equalisers do not feature at all. Parametric equalisers, however, can be a very useful tool in fine-tuning complex loudspeaker set-ups, when used in conjunction with an audio analyser and a good pair of ears, but the inexperienced user should treat them with a degree of caution, rather than relying on them to make a poorly designed system sound good.

Conclusion

The range of effects devices and signal processors available to the sound designer today is huge. They won't necessarily make your show sound great, and they have the potential to make it sound dreadful, but they can, when used in moderation, enhance and control sound in a way that enhances the final production. By all means experiment with them and understand what they can do, but please do not become fixated by their use.

Cueing Systems

It is important in any dramatic production that the sound effects arrive at the right time and at the right level. In order for this to happen effectively, the responsibility is given to a stage-manager who will call cues for all the effects required in the show. The method of communication between stage-manager and operator will vary from theatre to theatre, but two common methods are the cue-light and the intercom system.

The Cue-Light

This is a simple system of lights and switches via which the stage-manager can tell effects operators to perform an action. In the UK, a red light tells the operator to stand-by, and a green light to perform the cue. Some systems use electronic means to flash the red light until the operator responds by pressing a reply button, and some have a third light which is used to show that a stand-by has been acknowledged. In the United States, the system is even more simple. A red light is illuminated for a stand-by and extinguished for the go.

In some theatres, no cues are given during the performance. The operator is expected to follow the script and to take his or her own cues. The stage-manager may warn the operator of large blocks of cues, but even this is omitted in some theatres. In many ways, this is a satisfactory arrangement as it involves the operator in the production in a positive way, but very often the stage-manager needs to call sequences of cues very precisely, and in these circumstances the operator must take his or her cue as called.

Ring Intercom Systems

Wired intercom systems are relied on in situations where it is necessary for the stage-manager to identify particular cues or actions to the effects operators, or where it is essential for the operator to be able to respond verbally to the stage-manager.

Each person who requires one is issued with an out-station consisting of a belt-pack or a desk unit that connects to all the other out-stations on the system in a daisy-chain, ring or radiating pattern. See Figures 42a and 42b.

For a sound operator this can be restricting, as it usually requires the wearing of a microphone/headset combination and should therefore be avoided if at all possible during performances. Sometimes, a telephone-style handset may be used so that the operator has a means of communication that does not have to be worn continuously. Another convenient compromise can be reached by using cue-lights until it becomes necessary for voice communication, at which point a flashing light on the intercom unit can attract the attention of the operator.

Each department will normally require a two-channel intercom out-station; one for private use, say between the lighting designer and the board operator, and one for communicating with the stage-manager. Ideally, each person on the

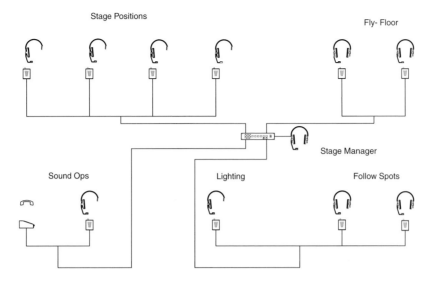

Figure 42a *A simple intercom cueing system layout, using both daisy-chain and radial configurations. Shown for show operation – no designers.*

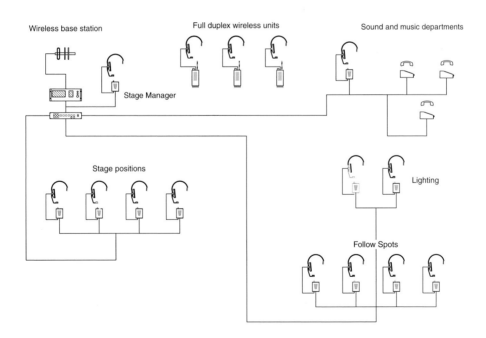

Figure 42b *More complex communications layout with a wireless connection to walkie-talkies and separate circuits to sound and lighting designers.*

system will be able to talk to and listen to either or both channels.

The system may also provide an override facility whereby the stage-manager can mute all microphones on the system except his or hers and force all channels to receive from the s.m. position only. This can be extremely useful in making sure that important information gets to all out-stations on the intercom system without interruption.

Once again, correct use of a ring intercom system can make life easy for all concerned in a production, but constant and irrelevant chatter, or a microphone left live whilst the user coughs, eats, or drops the headset, can cause havoc during a technical rehearsal or a complex show. The simple rule is: don't talk unless you have something relevant to say, and always make sure you turn your microphone off after you have finished speaking.

It is becoming more common on shows that involve complex scene changes for a wired intercom system to be interfaced with a wireless system, giving stage-crew complete freedom of movement around the stage. In the UK, radio transmission licensing regulations make the adoption of a wireless system that allows the simultaneous reception and transmission of information, known as full duplex, rather complex. More common is the half-duplex system whereby the stage-manager's voice is transmitted constantly, and a crew member is able to reply by pressing the transmit key on the wireless belt-pack, releasing it at the end of the message. With this system, only one person at a time may transmit, and correct operation requires strict adherence to this rule, otherwise interference from the two transmitters will obscure the content of the transmission.

Some theatres also have a point-to-point intercom system, which is independent of the ring intercom. These units are similar to a private telephone system so that two locations can be connected with complete privacy and with full duplex communication. The system may also be voice-activated so that hands-free operation is possible. Such systems can be integrated into the ring intercom and the internal telephone network if required, although the complexity of such systems often defeats the purpose of having a communications system in the first place.

Whilst cue-light systems are extremely simple to construct and set up, communications systems, especially if they involve wireless transmission, can be immensely complex to set up, and very difficult to troubleshoot if the need arises.

Two typical intercom systems are shown on page 97.

Setting Up the System

Having looked at the various parts of the sound system, from signal source to loudspeaker, and at the cable and connectors that are used to connect all these items together, we need to take one further complication into consideration to enable our system to perform efficiently. Simply connecting all the elements together, opening up the desk faders and turning up the power amplifiers is a sure way to provoke noise and distortion problems. In order to avoid these, we have to be aware of the gain structure of a system.

Electrical Gain

If a device in a sound system chain can produce a higher level at its output than was present at its input, it is said to exhibit gain. If the level at the output is less than that present at the input, the device is said to exhibit loss.

In general, active devices, i.e. those that have powered electronic circuitry, such as amplifiers, active equalisers and mixing desks, exhibit gain, unless they are specifically designed otherwise.

Passive devices, such as some equalisers, crossover networks and mixers, that do not use powered electronic circuitry, but rely instead on the passive quality of their components, exhibit loss. It's fairly rare to encounter passive elements in a sound system, except in loudspeakers that have passive crossover networks, and those are taken into account by the loudspeaker manufacturer in their specifications. However, all cables exhibit loss to a greater or lesser extent, and it's important to take this into account, especially when dealing with the cables that connect wireless microphone aerials with their receiver units. See Chapter 5, page 135.

When setting up a sound system for the first time, it is important to make sure that the electrical gain structure of the system is correct. Simply, each piece of equipment in the chain must have gain characteristics that allow it to connect to the previous and following items in the chain. For example, connecting the output of a microphone directly to a loudspeaker will not achieve any useful results; the output of the microphone is far too small to produce any movement in the voice coil of the loudspeaker. Simply adding a power amplifier will not improve matters much, because the input of the amplifier needs a larger signal than that available from the microphone in order to drive the loudspeaker. Adding a microphone amplifier into the chain, either via a mixing desk or a stand-alone microphone pre-amplifier, provides the missing gain element of the chain and will allow the system to function properly. However, to avoid the noise and distortion problems mentioned earlier, it is vital to make sure that all the variables in the system are properly set.

If the gain on the input channels of a mixing desk is set too low, then the amplifier connected to the system will increase the noise generated by the mixing desk and you will hear system hiss and power supply noise through the loudspeakers. If the gain is set too high, then the input stage of the mixing desk will not be able to cope with the signal and will distort it. A distorted audio signal which is then amplified is one of the best ways of blowing up a loudspeaker that I know.

If the gain on a power amplifier is set too high, then the mixing desk faders will have to be set at too low a level to allow proper control over the signal, and the slightest movement of a fader or auxiliary send control will result in huge variations in level at the loudspeaker.

Getting the gain structure right depends on a whole series of variables. If microphones are involved, then gain setting for each microphone should take place once the rest of the system has been set up. If the system deals only with line-level signals, i.e. signals from playback machines where the maximum likely output is predictable, then the simplest, if not the most scientific way to set up the system gain is as follows:

1. Set all mixing desk gain and level controls to minimum – (∞).
2. Set all equalisation controls flat (centre position).
3. Set all amplifier and controller levels to minimum – (∞).
4. Connect a sound source to the mixing desk. This can be an external signal generator, the desk's own oscillator, providing it has a separate output, a pink/white noise generator or a source of recorded material that produces maximum output from the playback machine. If you are using a signal generator, make sure that it is set for a nominal 0 dB output.
5. Select the Pre-Fade-Listen switch; this should have the effect of routing the incoming signal to the mixing desk's metering system. If the desk has no PFL function, you must set the input channel fader and master output faders to 0 dB. As the amplifiers are set to minimum, you will not send a signal to the loudspeakers. Any audio monitoring that you want to do will have to be carried out with headphones, but make sure that the headphone volume control is set to a low level before you start, otherwise you risk damaging your hearing.
6. The desk meters should be showing a signal level of some sort; slowly turn up the input channel gain control (not the channel fader) until the desk meters show a constant level of 0 dB if the signal is constant, or reach a maximum of 0 dB for the loudest part of a varying signal from a CD or other playback device.
7. Repeat steps 4 to 6 for all input channels.

Don't forget that if you then add equalisation to the input signal, you are effectively increasing the input signal gain at the selected frequency and distortion may result. If large amounts of equalisation are to be added for effect, then it may be necessary to reduce the input gain control to compensate.

Once each individual channel has been set up properly, any other processing equipment should be connected to the mixing desk outputs. If this equipment has gain controls and/or level indicators, then these should also be set to show 0 dB. Once again, if the device is a graphic or parametric equaliser, then boosting the signal will increase the signal level and affect any other piece of equipment that follows in the chain. Some equalisers allow for adjustment of the output level to compensate for this, and others allow the user to switch the level indicator between input and outputs so that any change in level can be determined.

The next step in setting up the system involves the power amplifiers and is pretty straightforward. It is probably best at this stage to use a music signal, rather than one produced by an oscillator or a pink/white noise generator, particularly if you are attempting to set the system up whilst other people are working in the auditorium. If the amplifiers are remote from the mixing desk, you will need a colleague and a communications system to help you.

With an audio signal passing through the mixing desk and the output faders set at -10 dB, increase the amplifier input gain controls until you feel that the level in the auditorium is as loud as you might require it. Then slowly raise the output faders to 0 dB and check to see if any distortion is evident. In a well-planned system, there should be none; the extra 10 dB available on the output faders gives you a margin for increasing the level should the director ask for it, or other circumstances dictate it. As mentioned before, many things can affect the perceived sound level in an auditorium and you may find that you need to increase the overall level of the system once a balance has been set.

Much the same procedure can be used to set up for a recording session, with the recorder being the last link in the chain.

Setting Microphone Gains

Assuming that you have been careful in choosing your microphones, and have not specified an extremely sensitive capacitor microphone for the kick-drum, and an insensitive dynamic microphone for the flute, you should have no trouble with either noise or distortion at the output of the microphone itself. Problems occur when you try and match the microphone output with the mixing desk input using a signal that varies wildly from musical number to musical number. In a recording session, time is invariably money, and the setting of microphone gains is something that most experienced recording engineers carry out almost instinctively; they know what to expect from a combination of instrument, microphone and player, and will make the necessary adjustments almost automatically, using rehearsals to carry out the fine tuning.

In theatre, there is usually a period during the rehearsal process when the orchestra is available for a sound-balancing session which is solely for the benefit of the sound designer. It is at this point that any gain and equalisation settings can take place. Some sound designers like to listen to each instrument in turn, asking each musician to give an example of his or her loudest passage of music and setting the input gain accordingly. If a musician is doubling, i.e. playing more than one instrument in the same family, such as clarinet and bass clarinet, or flute and saxophone, then it will only be possible to set a compromise gain level if a single microphone is being used. This can lead to all sorts of problems during the performance, with the operator having to make large adjustments, either at the fader or at the gain control, to cope with the different levels produced by each instrument. It is far better to have a separate microphone for each instrument, and to mute those that are not used in each number.

My own preferred method is to ask the musical director to play through a selection of numbers from the show, and to make the adjustments during the rehearsal. I find that this also helps to address any problems of spill from one musician's microphone to another and gives me a feel for the way that the orchestra sounds as a whole, rather than as individual instruments. It is also far less tedious for the musicians, who have a further opportunity to rehearse rather than having to play their sections solo. Kit-drummers and percussionists present their own set of problems, however, and almost always need to be the subject of an extended gain and equipment setting session. Their wide dynamic range and extensive repertoire of 'toys', such as bell trees, mark trees, gongs, ratchets, castanets, woodblocks and Vibra-Slaps, as well as any tuned percussion, such as timpani, xylophones, marimbas and vibraphones, all contribute to a sound that can easily overpower even the most experienced operator.

Conclusion

Once the gain structure of a system has been properly set up, the system should exhibit minimum noise and distortion and the operator should be able to make control changes to input faders, equalisation and auxiliary controls within a sensible range to achieve the desired results. Badly set up systems will cause the operator extensive problems, either with very small changes in desk controls causing large changes in the system, or with insufficient gain to cope with large dynamics and a system that hisses and buzzes unpleasantly. It's worth spending the time to get this right.

Chapter 4

The Production Process

Script Analysis

The first part of the process of mounting a production involves reading and analysing the script for the show (assuming that a script exists). Some productions evolve from improvisation throughout the rehearsal process, and the role of the sound designer in shows such as these can become extremely complex, with requirements changing on a daily basis.

Script analysis is more than simply skimming through the script and making notes as to where any sound or music is mentioned, although this is a sensible first step. After an initial perusal of the script, it should be read again with a view to determining other factors, such as period, mood and settings. Although no director will expect you to come to a first meeting fully informed about the piece, you will be expected to have some views as to how sound might help the production, and a thorough knowledge of the structure of the play.

Some plays can be extremely difficult to read. Unless you are familiar with the style and content of Shakespeare's plays, for example, making sense of the language can be a problem. Many published versions of period drama come with explanatory notes that can help the reader through most of the more obscure passages, and it is often an easier way in to the play than struggling with a text that is not annotated. It is always worth persevering, however difficult the play might be, because without an informed understanding of the production it is very difficult for a designer to offer constructive suggestions during the rehearsal period. If in doubt, ask; no decent director will be upset at explaining sections of a production that you don't understand, and many actors come to a first reading of a play without a clear idea of what the production they are in is about.

At the first meeting with the director, it is likely that you will discuss the way in which the director intends to stage the play, and other factors that need to be taken into consideration that are not obvious from the script. If the show is complicated, the director may also want to talk about the way that sound is to be handled throughout the rehearsal process, and whether you will be required to attend rehearsals and add effects and music as rehearsals progress.

It is sensible to make notes of all discussions, with dates if possible, so that as the rehearsal period progresses you will have a written record of all the director's requests. Those that are not mentioned again in subsequent discussions may not have been discounted; the director may simply feel that they do not need to be discussed again.

Research

In any production that uses realistic sound effects, or music of a particular period, the sound designer will, like other members of the design team, need to undertake research into the various aspects of the sound and music to be used.

Audiences can be disturbed by anachronisms in sound and music – modern instrumentation in a piece of baroque music, for example, or a British telephone in an American play. Research can take a great deal of time and ingenuity, particularly as we live in an age where, although the amount of information that we can access is increasing, the quality of that information seems to be decreasing. Without a degree of background knowledge of the subject under research, the information available can often be sketchy.

Apart from helping to add authenticity to a production, research often helps to engender an understanding of the period that the play is set in, and the social and economic conditions prevailing at the time. I'm not suggesting that you spend a week in rural Italy analysing the exact rhythmic patterns of the insect sounds, but making sure that the basis of your choice of sounds or music is correct is an excellent starting point from which to then use your imagination.

Some past research projects have taken me to: a working transport museum in an abandoned quarry, the Museum of Broadcasting in New York, a bell foundry in the east-end of London, a private collection of Jewish children's music, frequently to the natural history department of the Sound Archive at the British Museum, and to a manufacturer of wooden clogs in a remote Yorkshire village. All these visits, and many others, have not only provided me with useful source material, but have widened my horizons on any number of related subjects.

Music research can also be fascinating, and just as time-consuming. The Internet has made finding obscure pieces of music and exact dates of composition much easier and faster than was once the case, and sourcing rare items for use in shows has also become far less complicated. I used to have a number of record shops that I visited on a regular basis, buying anything that I thought would be useful in some future production. Sadly, many of these shops have now gone, and I rely on Internet searches to find the more obscure pieces. However, browsing the Internet is not the same as browsing through a record collection, where sleeve notes can provide an enormous amount of information.

Newspaper archives are also an excellent starting point for research on historical shows: vaudeville and music hall playbills will give an indication of which show tunes were popular at the time, details of road or rail connections for a particular area, and many other items of information that the sound designer can use to create the correct ambience for a show.

Once again, filing any such information can form the basis of an excellent resource for the future. My vinyl collection of some 500 weird and wonderful discs is still in regular use, and often provides long-since unavailable tracks for myself and other sound designers to use in shows. My phone book also has details of contacts who are expert in such diverse areas as bell-ringing, beekeeping, military history, broadcasting history, steam-railways and farming. All have been useful to me over the years, and the phone book continues to grow.

Whilst research is often vital for a show, it should not be the be all and end all of your design; it is simply the foundation for the rest of the work that you do, and the jumping off point for your imagination. If a director tells you that a particular sound doesn't fit in with the production and he wants a different bird call, for example, launching into a long explanation of how that type of bird is simply not found in that particular country at that time of year will not be regarded as helpful. You will need to find a way to give the director what he or she wants, and it may well mean that you have to be inaccurate in order to make the sound work. That's when you start to exercise your skill as a designer.

Planning and Inter-departmental Co-operation

As rehearsals progress, a series of production meetings will be held at which matters arising from the rehearsals are discussed. Production managers use these meetings to keep track of expenditure on the show, and to try and foresee any problems that might crop up during the technical period. Directors use them to ask about progress on particular technical aspects of the show, and to bring up any points not covered in rehearsal notes. Designers and heads of department may also bring up points that need to be clarified, as well as matters relating to budget, staffing and planning. A member of stage-management will usually take notes of the proceedings which are then circulated to all members of the production team. Production meetings are an excellent way of resolving matters that relate to more than one department, and designers should attend whenever possible.

As a part of the creative team, you will be expected to raise questions of your own at these meetings. Normally, these questions will arise out of the work that you have been doing on the production, and may be related to purely practical matters, such as where a loudspeaker is going to be positioned on stage, or whether a particular prop such as a telephone or a radio needs to ring or produce sound.

This is also the point at which problems that are going to involve other members of the team should be aired. If the show is a musical, then the question of where radio microphone transmitters are going to be placed will involve the costume designer and the wig department; special pouches may have to be sewn into costumes, and time will need to be set aside for the miniature microphones to be concealed in the hair or wigs of the actors.

The placing of loudspeakers in the auditorium will involve the set designer and the lighting designer, and they will expect a measure of compromise from you if they feel that their part in the production is being threatened by your stated need to hang large, black loudspeakers from every point on the proscenium arch, and position a row of unsightly microphones across the front of the stage. Most of the time, there is little point in taking a confrontational attitude; it simply hardens the resolve of the other members of the team not to let you destroy their carefully thought-out plans, although there are occasions where it is important to point out the problems that might result from your not being allowed to do what you want. A particular problem arose on a musical where the set designer, director and lighting designer were all adamant that they didn't want to see any loudspeakers at all. The compromise solution was to conceal as many of the loudspeakers as possible within the set, and to disguise them with acoustically transparent material that was lightly painted to match the surroundings.

Keeping others informed of any special requirements is vital to avoid a series of unpleasant surprises at the technical rehearsal stage, all of which could have been avoided by some careful pre-show planning and co-operation.

Rehearsals

In most cases, rehearsals will happen away from the stage, in a room in which the basic set has been marked out by stage-management. In the first few days, the director will usually be involved in 'blocking' the play, or working out how the actors will move from place to place during the course of the show. Once this process is finished and the actors begin to gain command of the text, the director may want to introduce some elements of the show into rehearsals. This will usually involve the provision of props and, in a period piece, rehearsal clothes so that the actors can get used to the feel of wearing long skirts, top hats or armour, but the director may also want to start using both sound and music to give the actors a feel for what will be happening during the actual performance. This can be helpful to the sound designer, as many of the glitches that would normally be encountered in the technical rehearsal can be overcome in the rehearsal room, but it also presents the very real problem that attendance in the rehearsal room means less time in the studio, particular in a short rehearsal period. On a show with a six- to eight-week rehearsal period and a complex sound plot, I would expect to have the last week or two set aside for attending rehearsals, but on some shows it can be necessary for a member of the sound team to be in rehearsals for most of the time.

One example of this was Michael Frayn's play *Alarms and Excursions*, one section of which needs the cast to interact with a whole variety of noises from domestic appliances such as smoke alarms, telephones, car alarms, cookers and burglar alarms. For this production, the operator was in rehearsals almost from the first day, and became an integral part of the cast. I, as the designer, made frequent visits to the rehearsal room, adding sounds and music as soon as I had finished creating them in the studio.

Where this is not practical and where a director wishes to have sound in rehearsals, I will often set up a small portable studio in the corner of the rehearsal room and work on the show using headphones whenever I'm not needed to play effects and music for rehearsals. Over the years, I have acquired enough portable equipment to allow me to do this at a level which produces acceptable results, both for rehearsals and for final performance. Needless to say, computer-based Digital Audio Workstations (DAWs) play a large part in this process, as do samplers, MIDI sequencers, keyboard controllers and a large collection of portable CD players, DAT recorders and MiniDisc machines. The programmable mixers mentioned in Chapter 3 are also invaluable for rehearsals, allowing temporary mixes to be set up and recalled at a moment's notice.

Attending rehearsals can be an extremely useful way of becoming familiar with a production, and can help the sound designer a great deal. However, some directors and actors do not feel comfortable with unfamiliar faces during the rehearsal period and do not welcome loud bursts of music or sound effects when they are grappling with a particularly difficult piece of text. The sound designer needs to have a well-developed sense of when his or her input is going to be useful and – far more importantly – when it is going destroy a morning's work.

Plotting and Cue sheets

The process of transferring a play from rehearsal room to stage can be both lengthy and complex. A typical schedule will involve the striking of the set for the previous show, derigging any sound equipment used on stage and front of house that cannot be reused, hanging any sound equipment that needs to be flown before the new set is built, installing any extra speakers or microphones after the set has been built, testing the system and then having a plotting session.

The plotting session is time given over exclusively to the sound team, during which they listen to any sound effects or recorded music involved in the play, run complex sequences, and try to set accurate levels with all the set elements in place. This session takes place without actors, but with the stage-manager responsible for calling the show, and with the director, sound designer, sound operator and composer, if one is involved. Ideally, all other work is suspended for the duration of the plotting session, but experience shows that that is rarely the case, and plotting sessions can take place against a background of set construction, the focusing of lanterns and the sound of massed vacuum cleaners.

In a plotting session, each sound cue or set of cues is played as if during an actual performance. Adjustments are made to the source of the sound, level and tonal quality until the director, composer and sound designer are all happy. The operator then makes a series of notes so that the sequence can be replicated during technical and dress rehearsals, with modifications as required.

Most operators will use some form of cue sheet, detailing the level and location of each effect or piece of music, the point in the script where it should occur, and any extra notes on the operation of the cue, such as whether the sound is to be brought in at a specific level, faded in or out, and over what duration. A cue sheet can be as simple or as complicated in design as the operator wishes to make it, but it must contain all the relevant information to allow a person other than the operator to replicate the settings if needed (see Figures 43a & b). Sometimes, if

Name Box			Plenty Initial Cue list			
A	B	C	D	E	F	G
Scene	Page	Music	Effects	Scene Time	Notes	
1	377	MQ1	Rain, Doorslam & Footsteps	2:26		
	379		Clock chimes 6			
	379		Distant plane			
2	379		Plane builds & crosses onto stage	9:02		
			Announcer			
			Night noises through scene & wind			
	380		Bird flies off		French is not good	
	384		Plane flies over		You know who I am	
	384		Dog barks		Get down	
	388	MQ2	Music under		Mackerel sky	
3	388		Music builds	13:32		
	388		Announcer into Victor Sylvester			
	399	MQ3	Music under		I've decided to lie	
4	400		Music builds	16:11		
	400		Music Ends – Radio Announcer			
			Distant traffic – 1947			
	404		Car horn?		Really make a splash	
	410		Slight traffic build?		The entire world	
5	414	MQ4	Light traffic – water lapping – ships' hooters			
	420		Music under		Great Sky	
6	420	MQ5	Music builds	7:02		
	420/1		Fireworks			
			Charlie Parker			
			Record off & Autochanger			
	428		Back-up gunshots			

Figure 43a *Initial cue-list.*

| | File Edit View Insert Format Tools Data Window Help | | | 3:39 am | Microsoft Excel |

Cue No	Page	Description	Cue point	Source	Routing/Channel Level
		Pre-show – set John Ramm's Radio Mic and turn it on			LR & All groups @ –10
1	1	Play-in When Day Is Do	Top of show	Akai 7&8	Mix @ –0
1A	1	Fade out	For Charles' speech		Fade to out
2	1	Chasing Rainbows	My mood	CD 1	Mix @ –10
2A	1	Dip Rainbows	Dr. Halder?		Dip to –20 then restore to –5
2B	1	Further fade down	Self-pity		Down to –30
3	2	Fade Rainbows	Serve lunch		Fade out
4	9	Star of Eve – Piano	Playing Wagner	Akai 7/8	At –15 & route to Group 7 only
8	13	Tauber	Heart's Delight	Akai 7/8	Mix at –10
8A	13	Drop – **Not called**	After "Delight"		fade to –35
8B	13	Out	"probably was Tauber"		F10
9	14	Tauber	Visual on touch.	Akai 7/8	Mix @ –20 f/on drop to –35 Visual
10	13	Snap out	I admit that.		F10
11	15	Doorbell	Myself a bit	Akai 5/6	Group 7
12	15	Tauber again	After doorbell	Akai 7/8	Mix @–25 drop to –37 Visual
12A	15	Snap out	Her coat, soaked through.		F10
13	18	Falling in love again	Bloody terrified	Akai 7/8	Mix @ –25
13A	18	Reduce Marlene	fancied her, anyway		Drop to –35
13B	18	Fade Marlene	Anxiety neurosis		Slow Fade out
14	20	Yodel & Band	Written from the heart	Akai 7/8	Mix @ –125
14A	20	Reduce band	Bavarian Mountain band		Reduce –30
14B	20	Birdsong	My beloved	Akai 1/2	1&2 @–10
14C	21	Music snap out	Bavarian Mountain Ensemble		F10
15	23	Jewish Wedding	What do you think?	Akai 7/8	Mix @ –10
15A		Music Build	Rug goes off		Build to 0
15B	23	Music Dip	Hitler		Drop to –30
16	24	Fade Jewish wedding	End of Hitler Dance		Snap out
16	24	RF			RF to –5
17	25	RF Out	Have to see her		RF to –5
18	28	Drinking Atmos	As soon as you have it	Akai 3/4	–25
19	29	Drinking Song	Student Prince	Akai 7/8	Mix +5
a		Reduce level for lines	After 2nd Tankard raise		Drop to –175
b		Build for Drinks & press	"1916"	Akai 7/8	Fast build to –10
c	29	Reduce for text	2nd "Drink"	Akai 7/8	Drop to –225

Figure 43b *Show-running plot sheet.*

a sequence of cues is particularly fast or difficult, the sound operator will write relevant details in the script, or on specially designed action sheets that simply show the changes that have been made to a master cue sheet set up at the beginning of the sequence. This allows fast access to important information, without having to produce a detailed cue sheet for each event.

If a show is part of a repertoire, it is often necessary to make a complete plot of how all the controls on the desk are set at the beginning of each performance of each show in the repertoire. As mentioned in Chapter 3, some desks allow the memorising of all controls, either as a graphical representation on a computer screen, or as a series of scene memories that set all controls to the right state automatically on recalling the memory.

Although plotting sessions rarely lead to final decisions on level and position of cues, they can be an extremely useful point of reference for the sound operator, the stage manger and director, and a chance for mistakes to be rectified before the next stage of the production process.

Once the plotting session has happened, a set of cue sheets made and any changes made to the sound effects or music, the next stage in the process is the technical rehearsal.

Technical Rehearsal

This is the time period set aside on the set, for actors and technicians to work slowly through the play, with the right props and costumes, and with lighting, sound cues and scene changes happening in sequence. On complicated shows, the technical rehearsal can occupy many sessions spread over many days, with sequences being repeated over and over again until all concerned feel comfortable with them. Any changes that need to be made can be done so during the technical rehearsal, or noted for alteration before the dress rehearsal.

Technical rehearsals can be immensely tedious when the problem being overcome is not one that concerns your department, so a good book is often essential to alleviate boredom. However, when you are involved, the director will expect a quick response to requests to reset and try a sequence again, and intelligent anticipation can often save a great deal of time and frustration on these occasions.

A notebook, sufficient cue sheets, pencils and erasers are essential for all rehearsal sessions. Never write up a cue sheet in ink until you are absolutely sure that it will never change again, unless you want to spend the entire rehearsal period rewriting cue sheets when the designer or director changes one aspect of a cue. A good operator will make a note of the previous setting when a cue is changed, so that should the designer change his or her mind, the original setting can be restored quickly. A good designer will also keep copious notes so that he or she is always aware of how each cue sequence should be set up. Once each section of the play has been rehearsed technically, and all modifications have been made, the next stage in the production process can begin.

The dress rehearsal is simply a run-through of the play with no audience present. The director may stop the performance and repeat sections that have not worked well, or, more usually, copious notes will be made of aspects of the production that are not working, either artistically or technically, and these are discussed at a notes session after the dress rehearsal. The dress rehearsal is usually the first time that the play has been run at speed, and it is common for the operator to find that there is simply not enough time for some complicated sequences to be set up and executed. In this case, the designer and the operator will have to work through the problem until it can be solved satisfactorily.

A notes session can feel very intimidating, particularly if the operator has made a mistake, but it serves no useful purpose not to admit to mistakes. As long as the director knows that the problem was caused by human error, and the human concerned has recognised the error, the result is normally a direction to get it right in the future. Trying to transfer the blame, no matter how worried you might be at being shouted at, is a waste of everyone's time and does not help to solve potential problems. If a mistake is made repeatedly, a good designer will often find a way to modify a sequence so that it is more logical for the operator.

If time allows, a second or third dress rehearsal may take place, and the director will expect far fewer problems, or none at all by a third dress. Changes will almost certainly still be being made to the show, and many theatre companies will have a preview period in which the audience are sold seats at a reduced price on the understanding that what they are seeing is work in progress.

Previews are very useful to all members of the company as they provide audience reaction and allow performances and technical details to be refined before the official first night, when the critics are invited to review the show. Very often, a commercial production bound for the West End or Broadway will tour to a number of venues, with alterations being made depending on audience reactions, and it is not unknown for the producers of a show to decide that it will not work as a commercial venture and that it should therefore be closed whilst 'out of town'.

Personally, I hate first nights as they all too frequently have a false atmosphere. The audience is almost totally composed of friends, relatives and critics, and reactions are quite likely to be completely different from any other performance. High levels of anxiety and adrenaline can also cause dramatically different vocal performances in musicals, and an operator needs to be especially vigilant on these occasions.

Possibly the only good thing about first nights is the party after the performance, at which the sound designer on a successful show can bask in the compliments and get very drunk; or, on a less successful show, can rage at the injustices of the world, blame everyone else and get very drunk. Please note that this is not obligatory.

Musical Theatre

The most common forms of musical, apart from opera, are the traditional musical, in which staged musical numbers punctuate spoken text, and the sung-through musical, in which there is little or no spoken text and the music is continuous from start to finish.

In the early part of the twentieth century, when amplification in theatre was unknown, musicals tended to star a certain type of performer who could sing well enough to fill a theatre without the need of a microphone. Composers and arrangers were careful to provide orchestrations that left a place for solo vocal lines to sit, ensuring that the lyrics could be heard. Large numbers of chorus singers meant that a high level of sound could be achieved where necessary, and the musical director in the orchestra pit maintained strict control over the dynamic range of the musicians. Musicals were, in effect, self-balancing, without the need for a sound designer to help out. Composer, arranger, director, musician and performer all contributed to making sure that the show was audible to the audience. It is also true to say that the lyrical content of many of the songs delivered in these shows was not exactly demanding, and the endless repetition of phrases almost certainly helped audiences to understand the words.

When amplification systems became more commonplace in theatres, microphones and loudspeakers were used simply to enhance the voices of the singers, so that they did not have to sing quite so hard for every number. The major changes in the use of sound in musicals started in the late 1960s and early 1970s, most noticeably with the Stephen Sondheim show *Company*, then took a major leap forward in the mid-1970s with Andrew Lloyd-Webber and Tim Rice's *Jesus Christ Superstar*, and reached a wild crescendo in the mid-1980s with *Cats*, *Time*, *Les Miserables* and *Starlight Express*.

The American musical *Company*, with its then-contemporary band arrangements involving electric guitar, rock percussion and jazz-based brass and woodwind, and its complex lyrical construction and multi-level set, meant that the cast were not always best placed to deliver a song without the need for amplification, and small microphones were concealed in the set and used along with rifle microphones to allow the lyrics to be heard more clearly.

In the UK, the musical *Jesus Christ Superstar* started life as a recording, and only after the success of the record was it presented at the Palace Theatre in London in 1972, where it ran for many years. What was unusual about the show was the fact that, as well as the traditional band in the orchestra pit of the theatre, a rock band was on stage next to the performers. The pit musicians were amplified to bring them up to a similar level to that of the on stage band, and so that the performers could be heard, hand-held microphones were used. After each song, the microphones were either placed on the stage to be picked up by the next singer, or hauled into the wings by their cables. The sound system, designed by David Collison for Theatre Projects, used a custom-built forty-channel mixing desk to control all the microphones, feeding a number of loudspeakers mounted on the proscenium arch. The overall effect was more that of a rock concert than a traditional musical, but the show started a rise in the tide of amplification in musical theatre that has only recently begun to recede.

The use of cabled hand microphones was obviously not appropriate for all musicals, and sound engineers started to exploit the availability of miniature wireless transmitters coupled with small electret-condenser microphones. The development of the miniature transmitter and the parallel advances in miniature microphone technology have made an enormous difference to the way that sound designers work in theatre, and especially musical theatre. In the original production of *Jesus Christ Superstar* only one radio mic was used; as the actor playing Christ was 'crucified', his final words were picked up by a Sony ECM50 microphone connected to a transmitter pack concealed on the cross.

As musical arrangements and lyrics became more complex, and the actor who could sing took over from the singer who could act, a wireless mic for each leading actor became standard practice, with a few extra sets available to be swapped around the supporting cast as musical numbers demanded. An extra member of the sound team armed with a complex plot dealt with this duty, and with any other problems that might have arisen, such as defective microphones and transmitter aerials. In the UK, Lloyd-Webber's *Cats* was probably the first production in which each cast member was individually miked, and this has been the norm ever since.

Strictly speaking, until the early 1990s the use of multiple sets of wireless microphones in the UK was in contravention of the Wireless Telegraphy Act, which allocated limited bandwidth to theatre productions. To circumvent this problem, sound designers 'borrowed' frequencies from broadcasting organisations and film companies, on the basis that the West-End theatres were far enough away from most film and television studios for the frequencies to be used without the danger of interference. This state of affairs continued until the press night of another Lloyd-Webber show, *Starlight Express*, when a high-powered wireless microphone transmitter being used by a television company reporting on the show outside the theatre, caused severe interference with the transmitters inside the theatre operating in the same frequency band.

The resulting debacle led indirectly to a major revision of the radio frequency bandwidth allocation for theatre, although not without long and complex discussions with the theatre sound rental companies, the wireless microphone manufacturers and the government body responsible for frequency allocation. The result was a commercial enterprise set up to allocate radio-frequencies to theatres and entertainment venues on a much more rigidly controlled basis, but with many more frequencies being made available.

With the ability to individually amplify every member of a musical, and the tendency of composers and arrangers to score for a much more complex mixture of instruments – including the synthesisers that were being used to provide thickening for depleted string, brass and woodwind sections – overall sound levels began to creep up. Increasingly, the theatre-going public were becoming used to hearing recordings of musicals created in the studio, and in an attempt to realise this style of production in the theatre, composers were requesting higher levels of music reinforcement, with musicians often located away from the orchestra pit. So that vocals could still be heard, sound designers were forced to use recording studio techniques such as compression to reduce the natural dynamic range of the human voice. The result was a period in which musicals became, in some cases, almost unbearably loud, and where it was often impossible to work out which character was singing, as all directional information from the stage was being swamped by the sound from the loudspeaker system. Thankfully, advances in technology and the realisation that louder is not always better have meant that many sound designers now strive to achieve as natural a sound as possible, using a combination of sophisticated time delay networks and small loudspeakers positioned at strategic points in the theatre auditorium (see Chapter 5).

The production process for a musical is slightly different from that of a straight play. There may be three sets of rehearsals going on at any one time. Music rehearsals, so that the cast can learn the songs; dance rehearsals so that they can learn the musical staging; and full rehearsals so that the entire piece can be fitted together by the director. Many changes will be made during the course of a rehearsal period for a musical, and it is vital that the sound designer and the sound operator keep up to date with any alterations to the production.

Towards the end of the rehearsal period, the designer and operator will attend more frequently so that a running plot for the show can be devised. This will detail which actors are singing in which musical numbers and will enable the operator to plan the best way to arrange the microphones on the mixing desk. If there is a need to economise on the number of transmitters used, suitable swaps can also be plotted at this time.

In the last week or so, the orchestra will be assembled and will start to run through the musical numbers, with the arranger and composer making alterations as required. The sound designer will also want to attend some of these sessions to see if there any problems arising from the orchestrations. This is also the opportunity to discuss arrangements for members of the orchestra who are playing electric instruments. Electric guitar and bass players (including double-bass players) will often want to bring their own amplifiers, and keyboard players may need to have separate personal mixing desks to balance the large number of sounds that they are required to produce at source.

Part of the sound system will need to be dedicated to a function known as foldback. Most members of the band will want to have access to some form of audio monitor so that they can hear the on stage vocals or other members of the band. The musical director will also need an audio monitor of the cast vocals in order to keep the cast in time with the orchestra. Similarly, the cast may need to hear the orchestra relayed to speakers on stage, and some singers like to hear their own voices in the monitor speakers. In some musicals, a separate monitor engineer is employed just to look after all the various monitor levels. In this case, separate audio feeds are sent to a special mixing desk known as a monitor mixer. Depending on the requirements of leading actors, foldback levels can be crucial to the smooth running of a musical, and can often take a long period to set up correctly. The use of vocal foldback, or monitoring, is discussed on page 116.

In some cases, when the cast is not able to see the musical director, for example when the band are remote from the stage, a closed-circuit television camera (CCTV) is pointed at the musical director, and video monitors are mounted close to the stage so that the cast can see a picture of the musical director. The musical director will also need a video feed from a camera pointed at the stage so that he or she can keep a visual check on the action. As it is important that the sound operator and the stage-manager calling the show should be able to see the musical director, they will also need video monitors, and in addition the stage-manager may require a video feed of the stage. Finally, any cast members required to sing off stage will also need audio and video monitors.

As well as audio and video relay of the performance, all technical staff will need speech communication circuits so that information can be circulated between departments. It is not uncommon for there to be three or four separate communications channels, for lighting, sound, flying and stage crew, as well as sub-circuits for follow spot operators, wireless microphone operators and stage-management, and it is also likely that one or two communications circuits will be dedicated to wireless headset systems for members of staff who need to cover the entire stage area without being tied to a cabled communications pack.

All of these requirements need to be noted and installed along with the main show audio system, before the cast and the orchestra move into the theatre, so that the technical rehearsals can progress smoothly. On the largest musicals, the sound installation crew may start work in the theatre many months before the cast are due to rehearse on stage.

The final part of the rehearsal process for a musical is the sitzprobe. This is a German term, borrowed from the opera, and usually means that the orchestra and cast will gather in a rehearsal room to play and sing through the musical numbers. This gives the actors an opportunity to hear the arrangements and to sort out any musical problems before they get into the theatre. It also gives the sound designer and operator a chance to hear how the vocals and band arrangements fit together and to spot any sections that might cause difficulty.

It is often sensible to provide a simple vocal reinforcement set-up at the sitzprobe, so that the cast do not have to force their voices in order to be heard above the sound of the band in an enclosed space. Three or four microphones on stands, and a simple mixing desk, amplifier and speaker set-up is normally sufficient for these rehearsals.

When the cast move into the theatre for the technical rehearsal, they will all need to be fitted with their microphones and transmitter packs, with the wireless microphone engineer making sure that the packs are well concealed but comfortable, and that the microphones are sited correctly. Small variations in the positioning of a microphone can make a tremendous difference to the sound, and it may take some time to find a position that is both comfortable for the actor and acceptable to the sound designer. The fitting and concealing of wireless microphones is covered in greater detail on page 135.

Technical rehearsals for a complicated musical may take many days, and to reduce costs, most shows will not have the musicians in the theatre for this period, relying on a piano to provide the musical accompaniment. This also provides the sound team with the opportunity to achieve the best possible vocal balance without having to worry about band levels, so that by the time the orchestra arrives in the theatre, the operator and designer have sorted out all the vocal problems and can concentrate on achieving a good musical balance.

Microphones and Foldback

Once the performers have been fitted with their microphones and transmitter packs, it will be necessary to check the settings of each transmitter and to ensure that an acceptable signal is being received at the mixing desk. Typically, an equipment rack containing all the wireless microphone receivers will be located close to the stage, with the shortest possible distance between the rack and the receiving aerials to minimise radio-frequency problems. The engineer responsible for the wireless microphones will work with the sound operator to ensure that each microphone and transmitter is set up correctly.

All wireless microphone transmitters can be adjusted so that the level at the microphone does not overload the audio section of the transmitter and give rise to distortion, and many transmitters are fitted with limiters to prevent accidental overload. During rehearsals, the wireless mic engineer will need to set each transmitter to achieve maximum output level and will usually monitor all transmitters during performance to make sure that both audio and radio-frequency signals are good. A number of wireless microphone manufacturers, including Sennheiser, Shure and and Trantec, produce computer software programs that give a visual display of audio and radio-frequency levels on the computer monitor.

At the mixing desk, the sound operator will ensure that the channel input gain of the desk is set correctly for each microphone, and will then adjust equalisation, auxiliary sends to reverberation and other effects devices, and any foldback systems, at the request of the sound designer and the performers. It is worth mentioning that no two performers are alike with respect to the balance of the foldback system. Some singers like to hear their own voices in the monitor system, as it can be difficult to judge how much level to give when singing within a group. Some leading performers will require reverberation to be added to their voices, and what might be considered an unnaturally high level of their own voices in the foldback mix, and the sound operator often has to provide different foldback mixes for each musical number. In addition, the performers will also expect to hear a mix from the orchestra pit so that they can keep in time and in tune with the orchestra, on any occasion when the staging dictates that they are not in the ideal position to see or hear the orchestra. With the freedom that individual wireless microphones give to directors in modern musicals, this can be for much of the production. Positioning of the loudspeakers for foldback is a crucial part of the sound design process, and it may be necessary to conceal speakers in the set in order to allow performers to hear all over the stage.

Over-loud foldback systems can cause severe problems for the sound designer, as sound from the foldback loudspeakers can easily enter the performers' microphones, giving rise to unpleasant colouration of the vocal sound and also causing acoustic feedback, or howlround. Unfortunately, it is often singers with the weakest voices who ask for the highest foldback levels, usually as a confidence booster, and who are therefore most prone to the problems described above.

In order to combat these problems, there has been an increasing use of personal in-ear monitoring systems in musical theatre. These systems, pioneered by Garwood Communications, are a development of the talk-back systems used extensively in television; the performer is fitted with an earpiece that is moulded to the shape of the individual's own ear, and constructed of transparent or flesh-coloured plastic so that it is almost invisible to the audience. Systems are manufactured either for single-ear use, or for both ears, although this is far more common for performers in rock music concerts. The earpiece is connected to a small radio receiver that picks up a signal from a transmitter fed from the fold-back section of the mixing desk. As each performer may require a different mix, there have to be sufficient auxiliary sends and transmitter channels to cater for each performer fitted with a receiver. Although this system works extremely well for rock musicians, substantially reducing colouration, some performers find that the earpiece has the effect of reducing the feeling of ensemble with the other members of the cast, and that they would rather not use it.

Achieving a foldback mix that is acceptable to all members of the cast is usually a difficult process, involving a degree of compromise on the part of the performer, and enormous amounts of tact and diplomacy on the parts of the sound designer and operator, and it has been my experience that musicals with minimal use of vocal foldback tend to sound much cleaner and more natural. Obviously, in certain cases such as rock musicals, the vocal monitoring requirements will be very different, but the audience's expectations will also be different, allowing a greater use of the monitoring methods described above.

During the rehearsals, the operator will assign groups of microphones to desk sub-groups and/or voltage controlled amplifier (VCA) groups, to allow the control of a large number of microphones at once. Very often, it is possible to use computer control for these assignments, changing them for every musical number as the score demands. If this is the case, the designer and operator should have planned the changes during the rehearsal process and programmed the computer accordingly. Computer software developed for the CADAC range of mixing desks also allows for an alpha-numeric display to be mounted above each VCA master so that the operator can see at a glance which group of microphones is being controlled at any one time.

With shows that use such systems, the majority of the balancing during the performance is carried out using the VCA controls rather than individual microphone faders, these being set to maximise the signal sent to the mix busses, thus maintaining a high signal-to-noise ratio. Even with the aid of computer-controlled systems, the operator's job is extremely complex and requires a great deal of skill, manual dexterity and musical sense.

Dealing with the Orchestra

When the orchestra arrives at the theatre, time will need to be allowed to make sure that each member is seated in such a way that they have enough room to

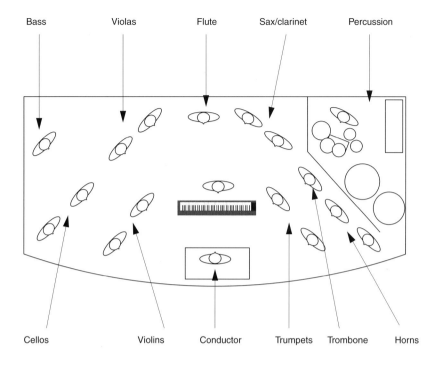

Figure 44a *Typical orchestra pit layout for a musical.*

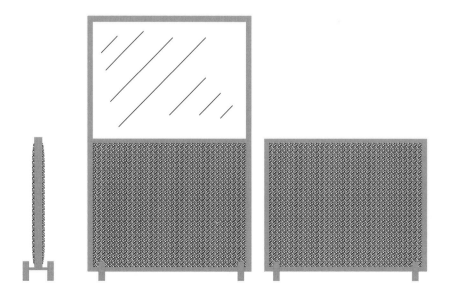

Figure 44b *Acoustic screens.*

play and that they can all see the musical director. Many theatres have orchestra pits that are small and cramped, and much care must be taken to work out a seating plan that is acceptable to all concerned. At this point, the musicians' microphones should also be roughly positioned, although they will almost certainly need to be adjusted at the balancing stage.

The musical director will want to be positioned in such a way that he or she can be seen by all the musicians, and also by the cast, although the use of CCTV systems is employed in many musicals.

A typical orchestra pit layout is shown in Figure 44a, with the strings to the left of the pit, keyboards left of centre, woodwind and brass right of centre, and percussion at the extreme right. It may be necessary to use screens to separate sections of the orchestra, particularly the percussion, so that the sound does not leak into the microphones of another section. Special sound-absorbing acoustic screens with perspex panels are often used for this purpose, so that the musicians can still maintain eye-contact with the musical director (see Figure 44b).

Once the orchestra is seated and comfortable, the process of creating a musical balance can begin. Once again, this will be a collaborative process involving the composer, arranger, musical director and sound designer, and can (in some circumstances) take a very long time.

All sound designers have their own methods for achieving an acceptable orchestra balance, but each will go through the basic process of setting the correct microphone channel gain and equalisation for each instrument.

As previously mentioned my own preferred method is to ask the orchestra to play through a selection of pieces of the score with all instrument faders set at 0 dB, then to adjust individual microphone positions if necessary, and make fader adjustments at the desk as required. My ideal is to achieve a self-balancing mix, where the arrangements and the musicians dictate balance, rather than trying to impose an artificial balance. Obviously, such a method is only feasible where the arrangements permit, and scores that utilise a large number of electronic or electric instruments and require severe processing of acoustic instruments will need an approach that is more akin to that used in multi-track recording studios, with multiple effects processors, compressors and limiters being brought into the signal chain via auxiliary sends and channel inserts. A great deal of time can be saved by planning the use of external processors before coming into the theatre, and the sound design and musical team may usefully spend time programming effects and synthesiser sounds in the weeks before a production comes into the theatre. Once in the theatre, the composer and arranger will also become far more heavily involved with the process of balancing than might be expected with more traditional scores.

When an orchestral balance has been achieved, the first full rehearsal with the performers and the orchestra can take place. Initially, this may simply involve the performers singing through the musical numbers without any moves or scene changes so that they can begin to feel how the show is going to sound for them on stage. It is at this point that the sound operator is able to try and achieve an acceptable balance between the singers and the band, and to sort out any logistical problems that might arise.

This process often takes place before the technical rehearsal, which may then proceed without the orchestra, using a rehearsal pianist, so that the musicians are not sitting around doing nothing whilst technical problems are sorted out. The composer and musical director may also make the most of this time to run through any changes that need to be made in the scoring. Once the technical rehearsal is over, the orchestra is called back and a full-scale dress-rehearsal is undertaken. This can be a particularly testing period for the sound department, as it is the first time that the entire show has come together with all technical aspects and a full orchestra, and it is here that any major problems will come to light.

It is impossible to describe 'how to do a musical', as each production will involve a different set of problems, but the production process will be much the same in every case, with only the length of time spent on each stage being a variable. Musicals are very demanding of the skill of the operator, the talent of the sound engineering team and the overall control of the sound designer, but are also the most rewarding of productions to get right. My own aim is to achieve a musical and vocal balance that sounds as 'real' as possible, and that allows the audience to hear the complexity of the lyrics and the subtlety of the score without subjecting them to unnaturally high sound levels, but many commercial producers have a different idea, and the most frequently heard request from producers in the preview periods of musicals is: 'I want the music louder and the lighting brighter – this is a musical!'

Music in Plays

The use of music in straight plays is as old as theatre itself. We know that the Ancient Greeks used musical accompaniment for their drama productions, as well as sung choruses for dramatic effect. There are numerous references to incidental music in Shakespeare's plays, and many of the world's most famous composers have written incidental music for theatre.

Music is a very powerful tool in theatre but, used thoughtlessly, can also have the opposite effect to that intended. As I write this, I'm sitting in a park in central London, on a warm spring day. The soundtrack to this scene is as one might expect: children are playing, birds are singing, the hum of traffic in the distance can be heard, interspersed with the wail of police sirens, but every now and then a trio of new-age hippies starts drumming. It's a boring and repetitious rhythm and it serves one purpose only for me; it raises my pulse rate so that I am no longer relaxed, and it prevents me from working efficiently. For them, it's a simple musical expression; for me it's an irritating distraction that has a physical as well as a mental effect. For an audience in a theatre, with no means of reducing the effect of intrusive or misplaced underscoring, it can ruin an entire production.

It is well-known that particular types of music have an effect on the human mind and body. At London's mainline railway stations, military marches are often played over the public address system at peak times. Commuters find it difficult not to walk in time to the music and they pass through the station much more quickly than when music is not played, whilst anyone who has travelled by air will be aware of the 'calming' music that is played over the cabin sound system prior to take-off.

Producers of dance tracks for use in clubs observe how a particular rhythmic structure of a piece of music can affect the number of people dancing, and tailor the 'beats-per-minute' of their music accordingly. At the other extreme, music used as part of stress-reduction therapy is deliberately devoid of rhythmic content, and, very often, of any other stimulating content such as form or recognisable tune, acting mainly as a means of masking other, more distracting sounds.

Today, we are constantly exposed to music, either live or recorded, in every aspect of our lives: music from the radio, music from the Internet, music from film and television, music used for advertising, music used as political statement, music in religion, and our own personal choice of music, either from sound systems in our homes or from personal, portable stereo systems. We are exposed to many more types of music than our ancestors ever dreamed possible, and the range of music available to us in our everyday lives is so large that it would be impossible to have a thorough knowledge of every aspect.

The theatre sound designer, however, is expected to be able to choose music from this vast resource that exactly fits the mood of whatever production he or she is working on. Listening to and studying music is all part of the process of theatre sound design; from gregorian chants to gangsta-rap, from fifteenth-century French court dances to nineteenth-century folk dances, you're bound to be asked for it one day.

Researching music for straight plays can be a very rewarding, but very time-consuming pastime, although the presence of many music sites on the Internet has helped tremendously. For a recent production with specific period musical requirements, after a long and fruitless search of the more conventional sources, an electronic search tracked down the elusive pieces to a specialist record dealer in New York and a small music publisher in Germany. Mail-order credit-card transactions and international express mail services meant that the required music was on hand in a few days.

Curtain and Entre-Act Music

We can use music in many ways, the most straightforward being as a curtain-raising mood-setter for a play. The first thing an audience hears in many productions is music, either playing as they come into the theatre, or to start the production off. 'Go Music, fade out house lights, curtain up, stage lights up, fade out music,' is the opening sequence of cues for a large number of straight plays, and the initial impact of the music can be critical in setting the mood, particularly for an unknown piece. Similarly, if music is used in scene changes, it very often has multiple functions to perform. Not only must it continue the mood of the last scene, but it should foreshadow the mood of the next scene, and, more prosaically, it often has to distract the audience from the noise of a complicated scene change taking place on stage.

Choosing commercially-recorded music to fulfil these functions relies on a number of factors. Obviously, the music must have some relation to the production; this may be in terms of period, country of origin or mood, or it may relate directly to the play. It is not uncommon for a play to start with a piece of music played in the auditorium which, once the stage lights are up, locates to a hi-fi or radio on stage, or continues as background music to specify a location: organ music for a play set in a church, period dance music for Noël Coward's play *Private Lives*, or the piano music that starts Oscar Wilde's *The Importance of Being Earnest*, for example.

Sometimes, the choice of a familiar piece of music can be used as a 'short-hand' mood-setter to inform the audience of the mood of the piece before a word has been spoken. Obvious choices are popular songs that relate to a particular period in recent history, such as the 1960s and the two world wars. Using a Beatles, Beach Boys, Glenn Miller or Elvis Presley recording can give an audience a near-instantaneous link both to when the play is set and the opening mood. Similarly, classical music can cover a variety of moods, from light-hearted comedy to doom-laden tragedy, although the ruthless plundering of the classical catalogue by television advertisers has meant that there is often a danger of the music being associated with bread or after-shave rather than the play. Beware, however, of simply using a piece of music because it means something special to you, unless you're sure that it has a similar meaning for the rest of the audience – and a relevance to the play.

Inevitably, you will not strike the right note with every member of the audience, but with care, the right choice of music can be a decisive factor in attuning the audience to the mood of a piece.

Music as Underscore

Using music to underscore action and dialogue is a process that most of us are familiar with from film and television soundtracks, and it is a practice that is very much on the increase in theatre. However, whilst the dubbing mixer in film and TV. has absolute control over the relative levels of all the aspects of a soundtrack, the theatre sound designer usually has control over the music alone. Consequently, it is extremely important that control of underscore is in the hands of a sympathetic operator placed in the same acoustic as the audience. If this simple rule is not followed, a very real danger exists of distracting the audience and detracting from the performance of the actor.

Choice of music for underscore will obviously depend entirely on the style and period of the production, but it is wise to avoid music that has too great a dynamic range, or is too familiar, as the risk of distracting the audience is high. Very often, a single note, rhythmic pulse or held chord will be enough to suggest the mood required, and may be set at a very low level so that the audience is almost unaware of it.

The siting of loudspeakers for the replay of underscore is very important. The initial temptation is to use loudspeakers placed at the rear of the stage so that the audience cannot readily identify the source of the sound. However, in order for the music to be audible to the audience, the on stage level often has to be high, which can be a distraction for the actors. Once again, it may be tempting to insist that the performers cope with the problem because 'it sounds great out here', but such an argument is often counter-productive and leaves the actor having to adjust a performance to suit the technical requirements.

Using loudspeakers that are sited in front of or above the acting area can be a much more satisfactory arrangement. Judicious use of time-delay can help in the aural positioning of underscore for both music and effects, with the sound originating from speakers both in front of and behind the actor, so that levels can be set at which the actor feels comfortable, and so the playback level is sufficiently high from the audience's point of view. This does require immense sensitivity from designer and operator.

Using Commercially Recorded Music

Very often, restricted production budgets do not allow for the use of a composer as part of the creative team; alternatively, a director may not wish to use a composer, even if funds are available. Trevor Nunn's revival of the Kaufmann & Hart show, *Once In A Lifetime*, at the Royal Shakespeare Company, used music recordings of the 1920s to tremendous effect, and the use of a live twelve-piece orchestra was held back until the play's chaotic ending, when a ten-minute song-and-dance curtain call was embarked upon. Many contemporary playwrights specify the recorded music that they wish to use in their plays, often because of specific textual references. The playwright Doug Lucie has written a play called *Gaucho*, which draws heavily on music from a Steely Dan album of the same name, and the Irish playwright Brian Friel is specific about music in many of his productions, notably *Dancing At Lughnasa*, and *Aristocrats*, in which Chopin piano pieces are played off stage as an underscore to much of the play.

Many plays specify music as part of the action, from radios or hi-fi systems, and in these cases the designer has little to do other than find a suitable recording of the piece requested and arrange for it to appear to come from the specified device. The choice of music may be set down in the script, or it may be decided by the director. Alternatively, the director may give the sound designer an idea of the type of music required and rely on the designer to offer a series of possibilities from which one will be chosen. Intelligent study of the script with respect to period and situation will usually point towards the right style and it is then up to the sound designer to gather together a selection of music to offer to the director. If the music is to be used as an integral part of the production, for instance as a piece for the actors to dance to, then it is important that these choices are offered to the director and/or the choreographer at the earliest opportunity.

Music research for some plays can be far from straightforward. *A Streetcar Named Desire* by Tennessee Williams specifies a great deal of music, both atmospheric and specific, and there are constant script references to a piece that is heard as if in Blanche's head called 'The Varsouviana', a polka originating from Warsaw. I have provided soundtracks for this production on a number of occasions and have always used a generic recording that seems to fit the mood, rather than spend time looking for a specific piece called 'The Varsouviana'. However, if the author and/or director are specific about a particular piece, then there is no way out except to start researching. Specialist record dealers, music libraries, the Internet and university music departments can often be very helpful if you are unsure of where to begin. You should be aware that this process can take many weeks, and in the end you may not be able to find the piece that is required, but the chances are that you will have found something similar, or even better, that the director is happy to use.

Never be afraid to present alternatives. Whilst working with an actor on a one-man show, a request came through for the music soundtrack for Alfred Hitchcock's film *Psycho*, by Bernard Hermann. The actor and director wanted to use the 'shower curtain' music for one particular scene, but, taken out of context, the music was not as powerful as they remembered. We were able to substitute a piece written as a pastiche of the Hermann music in which the motifs were overexaggerated, and for this production it made a much greater impact than the original. Incidentally, many members of the audience believed that we had used the original Hermann music for this sequence.

Working with a Composer

Having a composer as part of the production team for a straight play is an option taken up by many theatre companies. The advantages are great: the composer can fit the music to the action, changing timings, content and mood as the rehearsals progress. In some cases, the sound designer will also fulfil the position of composer, producing an integrated sound track of music and effects, but often the sound designer will work alongside the composer, taking care of the practical aspects of integrating the music with the production.

If the composer requires the music to be played live, then the same considerations must be made as for a musical production, for example where the band are to be placed and whether or not there is a need for amplification and foldback for the musicians. In technical rehearsals, the sound designer will also be responsible for ensuring that the sound operator understands how the music is to be balanced against the text, and for making sure that the internal balance of the band is correct. Once again, the need for the sound operator, composer and sound designer to be in the same acoustic space as the audience is paramount.

If the music is to be recorded, the sound designer may be required to arrange recording sessions, and to either run the session or be in attendance to deal with any technical questions that may occur.

Many theatre composers use synthesisers and samplers to produce their music, and have their own small studios, in which case the designer is often simply given a finished score which will need to be edited into the final show order and transferred to the theatre's preferred playback medium. Ideally, the sound designer should be involved in the final recording stage so that a check can be made on levels, distortion and any other problems that home studios frequently present.

The biggest problem with producing theatre music in a recording studio is the difference between the studio's playback equipment and that of the theatre, particularly with regard to loudspeakers. Most commercial studios spend a great deal of money on obtaining a full-range flat frequency-response high-power monitor–loudspeaker system, which cannot be matched by the theatre's playback system. Consequently, often when decisions about equalisation, reverberation and balance are made in the studio they prove disastrous in the theatre. My own favoured method for working with specially recorded music is to record on to a multi-track system such as the ADAT or DA88 digital eight-track format, simultaneously producing a two-track mix on to DAT for use either as a reference, or, if no problems are encountered, as the final master.

Once in the theatre, if any changes need to be made it is a relatively simple matter to hire a multi-track playback machine and small mixer such as the Yamaha ProMix 01, and remix the music to the composer's satisfaction. On a number of occasions, I have used a show-control computer to control the multi-track playback, whilst the composer balances the music during a dress rehearsal, either recording the fader moves on mixing desks that allow that function, or recording the mixed output to a digital audio tape recorder in real time and feeding the resulting mixed signal to the desk. When the composer is happy with the balance, the mixed master is substituted for the multi-track playback. This allows the composer to try a number of variations each time the music is played, whilst the operation of the show is not changed for the operator, the only alteration being that the show-control command is changed to trigger playback of the master playback machine rather than the multi-track.

In some circumstances, it may be desirable to use the multi-track as the main playback machine, and have the operator balance the music during the show as if he or she were mixing a live band, in which case the sound designer needs to ensure that the playback machine is capable of a near instant start and that he or she can locate start and stop points on the machine reliably. Most digital multi-track machines are capable of being controlled either via MIDI Show-Control (MSC) commands or MIDI Machine Control (MMC) commands, and the new generation of show-control computers are more than capable of integrating such commands into show cue lists.

On Stage Musicians

Some playwrights require live musicians to be used as part of the action of a play, for example Arthur Miller's play *Broken Glass* specifies an on stage cellist, whose playing links the action between scenes. In these cases, the sound designer may have to arrange for amplification of the instruments in such a way that it does not detract from the artistic design of the show. Microphone stands, cables and a foldback speaker do not fit well into period plays, and it can often take a great deal of ingenuity to hide the essential elements of sound reinforcement within the set.

It is also important that the musicians are considered part of the cast of the play and given the same consideration as the rest of the acting company. They are as much a part of the creative life of the production as the actors, director and designers and should be treated as such. It is a sad fact that musicians working in theatre are often regarded as second-class citizens and treated accordingly, whereas many musicians have spent far longer refining their craft than other members of a theatre company. How many actors do you know who practise their Shakespearean verse-speaking on a daily basis?

Legal Matters
(1) Commercially Available Recorded Music
In the UK, the use of commercially available recorded music in public performances is covered by a series of legal agreements, confusingly involving three different fee-collection organisations and the copyright holders of the original work, usually handled by the artist's record company. (The addresses of these organisations can be found in Appendix A at the rear of the book.)

The Mechanical Copyright Protection Society (MCPS) issues licences to allow the transfer of recorded music from one medium to another, and will often grant a theatre a blanket licence, payable annually. So, unless you are going to play your music from a stack of the original recordings, you will need to apply for a licence to copy from the original on to whatever medium you are using for playback. The cost of the licence can vary and is based on a number of factors; MCPS will advise you of the likely cost for your venue or production.

The Performing Rights Society (PRS) issues licences that allow you to perform in public or broadcast music (both live and recorded) that is written and published by its members. For theatre, a different rate is charged for music used during curtain-up, scene changes, or curtain-down, from music used as part of the action of a play, i.e. music that is supposed to be heard by the characters in a play. Details of all music used in productions, including duration and number of performances, must be supplied for each production, and when a production is on tour, the information must be provided for each theatre that the show visits. Performing Rights returns must also be made for musicals and for music that may be sung or played by an actor as part of a performance, and this can add considerably to the size of the final charges.

Phonographic Performances Ltd issue licences permitting recorded music issued by their member companies to be played in public, although their main source of income is from television and radio stations and discotheques. They charge on a sliding scale depending on the amount of music used and the number of performances, with a minimum amount payable per week.

Finally, it is necessary to approach the copyright holder of the recorded work, usually via the record company on whose label the work is released, for permission to use the music at all. In most cases, this permission is granted, but in a number of high-profile cases permission has been denied as the copyright holder feels that the association of the music with the production will be detrimental to the reputation of the artist.

This problem occurs most frequently with famous and (oddly) dead pop-music artists, and in cases such as these, permission should be sought at the earliest possible time. In shows that rely extensively on contemporary music, this can take up a great deal of time, as artists frequently swap record labels, and record companies frequently merge and divide. An attempt to obtain permission to use music by Elton John in a production required five phone calls simply to establish which record company was currently managing his catalogue.

With the notable exceptions of PRS and MCPS, the amount of time and effort needed to secure the necessary licences and permissions from this profusion of license-issuing authorities and copyright holders leads many theatre companies to ignore all legal requirements and use recorded music indiscriminately and without payment. It is also a source of great irritation to both theatre administrators and sound designers, particularly when decisions are made late in the production period, but ignoring these requirements, particularly on high-profile shows, lays the theatre company open to expensive legal action.

(2) Specially Composed Music

Many directors commission composers to write original music for their productions, and this provides a further set of complications in the UK.

The Musicians' Union has a set of guidelines about the type of music that can be recorded for theatre productions, currently stipulating that music may only be recorded for curtain-up, curtain-down and scene changes, and that no more than seven minutes of recorded music may be used in any production. Musicians who take part in unauthorised recording sessions for theatre productions can be penalised by their union, and theatre companies who use unauthorised recordings may find that they appear on a black list of organisations issued by the MU to its members.

These rules, although mainly aimed at preventing the use of pre-recorded backing tracks in musical productions, are also intended to ensure that the artistic status of musicians is recognised by theatre managements, and to provide work for musicians in a related branch of the performing arts.

The Musicians' Union is working hard to accommodate the musical requirements of straight plays and is happy to discuss these requirements with producers in order to make sure that the end product is to everyone's satisfaction. It is always best, however, to make your approach at an early stage in the production process.

Chapter 5

Advanced System Design

Multiple Speaker Systems

In any theatre production, either straight play or musical, the sound designer will need to put together a loudspeaker system that will serve the needs of his or her design.

In a straight play, the sound effects must seem to come from the correct location, scene change music may need to be routed to the auditorium, whilst underscore music must not interfere with the dialogue. Sound effects and music may also need to be played at the sides and rear of the auditorium, and in some cases vocal reinforcement may be necessary to overcome the problems of a difficult acoustic. Small loudspeakers are often mounted below an overhanging balcony, or on a bar suspended above the auditorium and angled to cover audiences in the top sections of the theatre.

In a musical, the dialogue, lyrics and musical accompaniment must be heard clearly and intelligibly by all members of the audience, and the members of the cast and orchestra must hear as much of each other as is deemed necessary. All elements of the music need to be reproduced faithfully in accordance with the wishes of the composer and the director with respect to both frequency and dynamic range.

In both of these cases, the designer will have to put together a system in which a large number of loudspeakers are used to achieve a desirable end result. In previous chapters, we've looked at the siting of individual loudspeakers for effects playback, the use of foldback speakers for musicals, and the positioning of loudspeakers for general cover of an auditorium, but there are a number of factors that need to be taken into account when designing complex systems.

Firstly, the designer must calculate the coverage of each loudspeaker or loudspeaker array in the system and produce a plot showing where coverage starts to fall off. The speakers are then mounted in the theatre and focused to cover the main areas of the auditorium. There will be many other areas, at the sides and under balconies, where the direct signal from the loudspeaker is not high enough to counteract reflections and reverberations, or where acoustic shadows occur due to balcony overhangs, and so extra loudspeakers will need to be positioned. It is important that there is minimal overlap of the coverage areas, or wave-fronts from different loudspeakers will combine at certain frequencies and give rise to

Figure 45 *Delay loud-speaker rigged under balcony front.*

anomalies in the frequency response of the system, known as hot-spots, Once the designer is happy that all areas of the auditorium are covered with minimal over-lap, the next stage of the process needs to be considered.

Compared to an electrical signal through a cable, sound through air travels relatively slowly. In Figure 46, the audience member sitting at the rear of the auditorium will hear the amplified sound from the secondary loudspeaker around 60 milliseconds before the actual sound arrives from the stage, a situation which gives rise to two main effects.

1. Loss of localisation: the ear is unable to use a phenomenon known as the precedence effect to determine the left/right source of the sound with any degree of accuracy, as the sound arrives from a number of different sources, including the original, at different times. If there are many sound sources on the stage, for example various singers with microphones, it can be difficult to determine who is actually singing a particular line.

   The brain uses the tiny differences in level and time of arrival of a sound at each ear to determine the direction that a sound is coming from. If a sound originates from the right of the listener, the first wave-front will reach the right ear, and then, a fraction of a second later, and with various changes in timbre introduced by the shape of the head, it will arrive at the left ear. The brain compares these differences and determines from them the direction of the original sound. This is known as the precedence effect. If the sound from a loudspeaker reaches the left ear before the direct sound reaches the right ear, then the brain will translate this into directional information and locate the apparent source of the sound to the left. In the 1940s, Helmut Haas investigated this effect more thoroughly and discovered that the ear clamped on to the first signal arriving and effectively ignored the delayed signal until the level had been increased by up to 20 dB. This effect, known as the Haas effect, holds true up to a delay of around 50 milliseconds, after which the delayed signal is perceived as an echo.

2. Loss of clarity: because the amplified and direct sounds arrive at the ear at different times, the wave-fronts combine to give a diffuse overall impression. At any distance over about 10 metres, this becomes extremely disturbing and interferes greatly with the listener's ability to comprehend what is being said or sung. This effect is most clearly experienced with poorly designed public address systems in large, reverberant areas such as railway stations and airports, where multiple loudspeakers are used to cover large areas. The same announcement arrives at the listener from a variety of speaker locations and reflected from walls and ceilings, and the end result is usually a confusing mess of sound, with the announcement being rendered unintelligible. At smaller distances, the effect is to muddy the sound and reduce clarity, and sound designers have to prepare systems to overcome this problem.

The simplest way to deal with the latter problem is to use a number of loud-

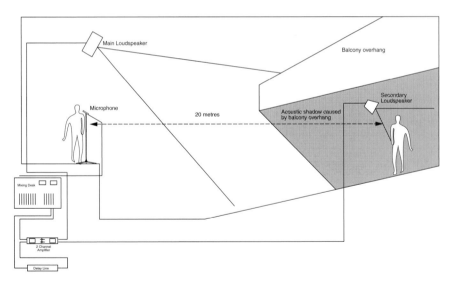

Figure 46 *Simple under-balcony delay system.*

speakers at a variety of locations in the theatre, and then to use a device called a digital delay line to time-align the system in relation to the distance of the loudspeakers from the stage.

The digital delay line has a single input which is split, often three ways, and sent to a time-delay processor where the output signal can be delayed in very small increments, often as small as one-tenth of a millisecond. Each output from the delay unit is sent to a separate set of loudspeakers in the auditorium with a delay time set to match the distance of the loudspeakers from the source, and the level of the delayed loudspeakers is set so that it is below that of the main loud-speaker set-up. The listener then perceives the main signal source to be the stage and the loudspeakers around it; the amplified sound does not reach the listener before the direct sound from the source. This sounds very simple, but can be fairly difficult to achieve, since the practice of simply measuring the distance and dialling in the corresponding delay time does not necessarily produce acceptable results. As a rule of thumb, most designers will start with this procedure, and then add 6–10 milliseconds to the delay time before starting to tune the system by ear. The theatre must be completely quiet, and delay setting sessions frequently happen during the night when the rest of the company have gone home.

A method used by many designers, described below, works perfectly well for me, although others have their own methods, and some rely on the use of computer-based audio analysers such as Metric Halo's excellent SpectraFoo or JBL's Smaart-Pro to determine the initial delay settings – particularly useful in touring venues when time is tight.

A loudspeaker is placed on the stage at a pre-determined central point where the bulk of the action takes place. This is called the zero point and is the reference to which all delay times are calculated. A single repeating pulse or click is then fed to this loudspeaker directly from the desk, with no delay time added, and then via the delay unit to an ear-piece worn by the designer on his left ear, who positions himself in the field covered by the first set of speakers to be delayed. The designer will hear the click directly in the left ear, and, turning sideways on to the sound source, the output from the loudspeaker in the right. Levels are set so that the direct click appears to be at the same level as the click from the loudspeaker, and the precedence effect will then cause the designer to perceive the direct click as arriving at his left ear first.

The delay time is then increased until the click appears to be coming from a central point. Increasing the delay time will fool the brain into thinking that the signal is arriving at the right ear first, and the delay time is decreased until the signal once again appears to be central. A note is made of the delay setting, and the designer then moves to the area of the auditorium covered by the next set of speakers and repeats the procedure until all delay times have been set. The times are then entered into the delay lines and the amplifier levels are set by ear, with the speaker at the zero point once again being used as the reference. Using this method, the designer can make sure that sounds arrive at most points in the auditorium at the same time.

Speaker Locations

Every sound designer will have his or her favourite way of placing loudspeakers for a musical production. In some cases, the sound designer will use an array of loudspeakers directly above the centre of the proscenium arch as the main sound source for the reinforcement system. This has the advantage of providing maximum coverage for a large part of the audience, but has the disadvantage that the apparent image will be above the stage, and that left/right localisation is lost as there is only a single source. To counteract these problems, speakers are also placed at the sides and along the front of the stage to pull the image down and to provide a source of sound for those members of the audience sitting immediately underneath the cluster.

Other designers prefer to use a left/right system without a central cluster, and rely more on extra loudspeakers mounted in the auditorium to achieve maximum coverage. The final decision depends on many factors: the size and construction of the venue, the type of music, the size of the cast, whether there is a position to mount a central cluster, whether it would interfere with lighting or design concepts, and so on, and it is not my intention to recommend any one system over another. Careful planning with the information provided by the loudspeaker manufacturer and a plan and elevation of the auditorium is essential in setting up a successful reinforcement system for a musical, and many years of experience contribute to the work of the most successful sound designers. Use every opportunity to experiment and you will soon begin to understand the systems that work for you.

Placing loudspeakers on stage for a musical or a straight play has been discussed elsewhere in this book, and many of the same criteria apply. The ideal position is rarely available so some form of compromise is inevitable.

Source Oriented Reinforcement (SOR)

This term was coined to describe the process whereby small amounts of delay and careful routing of sounds to a relatively large number of speakers are used to give localisation information to an audience. As we have seen, the Haas effect can be used to fool the brain into determining the apparent directional source of a sound by altering the time at which similar signals arrive at the ear. SOR systems use a programmable time-delay/level matrix to allow the designer to make many changes to the delay times of a number of individual signals and to use those changes to place the apparent source of the sound between a number of loudspeakers. The advantage of this system is that it can be used with two, three or more loudspeakers and the software allows the user to specify exactly where the sound appears to come from. More importantly, the field covered by these loudspeakers can be comparatively large and the effect still works.

The TiMax system developed by Outboard Electronics allows the user to prepare a virtual map of all loudspeaker points in an auditorium, and then to plot a source, or a number of sources, for a particular sound to follow. This can be a sound effect, a wireless microphone or a group of wireless microphones, and each set of moves for each source can be saved as a cue in the computer control program. Multiple cues can be triggered together to make extremely complex moving sound patterns, or to follow a cast member as he or she moves around the stage. The operator simply mimics the movements required with a mouse pointer on a computer screen and the computer works out the combination of levels and time delays that are required to achieve the desired result. A matrix with up to thirty-two inputs and thirty-two outputs is available and many excellent results have been achieved. Similar systems are available from LCS (The SuperNova system), and Richmond Sound Design's AudioBox can also be utilised in this way using software available on either the Windows NT or Apple Macintosh platforms.

Source Independent Measurement (SIM)™

Source Independent Measurement was developed by The Meyer Corporation to assist sound designers in equalising and delaying multiple speaker systems. High-quality measuring microphones are placed around the auditorium and connected to the SIM computer-based analyser. The output from the mixing console is also fed to the analyser and the system allows the user to compare the source material with the signal picked up by the microphones. Any resulting differences between the two signals produced by room resonances, delays, echoes or loudspeaker abberrations can then be corrected by the SIM operator with the use of equalisers and/or delay units. SIM is not an automated equalisation system; the equipment allows the designer to switch between the various measuring microphones and to adjust equalisers and delays as required. The final decision as to how the system sounds is left to the designer's own discretion.

Originally, the system was designed to be used once during the system set-up, but advances in the design of the system have meant that many designers now specify the later model of SIM, SIM System II, as a permanent part of a sound reinforcement package. It is possible to achieve similar results using either SpectraFoo or Smaart-pro software.

Wireless Microphones

It has always been desirable for a performer using a microphone to be able to move freely around a studio or a stage without being constrained by the cable carrying the audio signal from the microphone. The possibility of carrying a personal radio transmitter to which a microphone could be attached was explored many years ago, with a degree of success. Early transmitters were physically large and unsightly, and could not be carried without some difficulty. Battery technology was not what it is today, and the reliability of these systems was not good.

As technology advanced, smaller and smaller transmitters were produced, until today it is possible to hide a powerful sub-miniature transmitter virtually anywhere on a performer.

Initially, such systems were used in cinema and television sound, where their narrow dynamic range and relatively high background noise were regarded as acceptable.

They were, however, used sparingly in theatre sound. Amplification levels in musicals were relatively low, and actors' voices did not need to be reinforced to overcome the high levels of music that we encounter today. The musical *Jesus Christ Superstar* effectively raised the loudness threshold via the use of handheld microphones to allow the actors to overcome the use of an on stage rock band as well as the traditional pit orchestra.

Why Do We Need Radio Mics?

Gradually, composers began to write musical scores as though they were to be recorded under studio conditions, and individual instruments were miked up so that they could be controlled by a balance engineer in the auditorium. Another LloydWebber/Rice show, *Cats* took theatre sound to new heights in terms of the number of personal radio microphones used, but the apotheosis was reached with *Starlight Express*: twenty-one radio microphones were in use, and the band were in soundproof booths playing electronic instruments and listening to each other through headphones.

The USA is suffering from similar problems and radio microphone users are experiencing a number of problems due to the recent introduction of digital broadcasting. I can recommend Jim Brown's excellent information site on the Internet at www.audiosystemsgroup.com for a full insight into the frequency range problems currently being experienced in the USA.

Problems

There are many problems involved in using a radio microphone, the biggest being that the transmitters are limited in power. Theoretically, a well set-up transmitter should be able to transmit over a distance of around two or three kilometres, but this assumes outdoor usage, an absence of large buildings or electricity pylons, and a properly equipped receiver.

Multiple sets of radio microphone transmitters may have problems with intermodulation; that is, one transmitter may cause interference with another transmitter due to interaction of transmission frequencies. The resulting sound is unpleasant and sounds like a poorly tuned transistor radio. The manufacturers and rental agencies of this type of equipment are keen that there should be as few problems as possible, and they will work out the frequencies that are effective in multiple sets. Always ask advice when using more than one radio transmitter. At least one service provider in the USA, Comtek, has a computer program that will calculate 'safe' sets of frequencies. The program runs on the Windows platform and is available via the Internet at www.comtek.com

Other problems result from the siting of receiver aerials. Radio-waves are reflected from metal surfaces, and the use of a single aerial and receiver system in a hostile environment (i.e. any theatre) can result in phase cancellation and loss of signal (see Figure 47).

When the direct and reflected signals are in phase, they combine, with no ill effects, but when the direct and reflected signals are out of phase, due to a

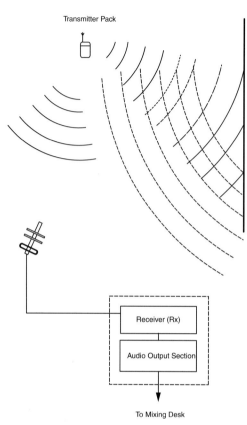

Transmitter Pack

Receiver (Rx)

Audio Output Section

To Mixing Desk

Figure 47 *Time delays between direct and reflected radio frequency signals can lead to loss of signal in non-diversity systems.*

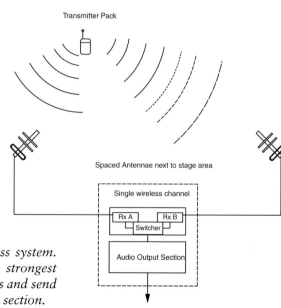

Transmitter Pack

Spaced Antennae next to stage area

Single wireless channel

Rx A   Rx B

Switcher

Audio Output Section

To Mixing Desk

Figure 48 *A diversity wireless system. Whichever receiver gets the strongest signal will trigger the switches and send its signal to the audio output section.*

combination of reflection and distance, then phase cancellation will occur, giving rise to distortion or noise; in extreme cases the signal may disappear completely. By using two completely separate receivers, two aerials and an electronic switching device sometimes known as a 'voter', the strongest signal is automatically selected and sent to the receiver output (see Figure 48). This type of system is known as a true diversity system.

There are other types of diversity system that use two aerials and a single receiver, and these may be adequate in some circumstances, but a true diversity system tends to be far more reliable.

Siting the Aerials

There are a number of simple rules to apply when siting receiver aerials for wireless microphone systems:

1. Keep the aerial at least one metre away from metal structures. This includes sets constructed from metal, lighting bridges and structural reinforcements.
2. Keep the distance between the transmitting and receiving aerials as small as possible, but a minimum of three to four metres.
3. Use special co-axial cable with an impedance of 50 Ω; for long runs use thicker cable to minimise attenuation of high frequences. Standard cable RG-58 is acceptable for medium-length runs, but the higher standard RG-213 is recommended for longer cable runs.

Placing the Microphone and Transmitter pack

There is no problem with a handheld wireless system, other than ensuring that a fresh battery is in use and that the aerial connection is sound.

For a body pack system, there are certain rules that should be followed. Ideally, the transmitter aerial should be free from any clothing, and hanging down from the transmitter pack. It should not be in contact with the skin. Neither should the aerial be twisted around the microphone cable, or touching the metal case of the transmitter pack. The pack itself should be in a pouch that insulates it from the wearer's body and that is not susceptible to the absorption of sweat from the performer's body; water and electronics do not mix.

Most sub-miniature microphones are omni-directional, and it is therefore helpful to keep them as close to the sound source as possible. With the new generation of sub-miniature microphones from Sennheiser, Sanken and Danish ProAudio, it is now possible to hide the microphone in the hairline of the performer, preferably towards the centre of the forehead. Skilful use of paints, false hair and near-invisible wig-clips can make the microphone all but disappear in this position, and it is usually possible to find a place in the hair to hide the microphone. Actors with short hair or no hair at all can present a problem, but a reasonable alternative is to place the microphone just over the ear, using a special mounting clip known as an ear-clip. Surgical tape such as MicroPore from 3M can be used to fix down the cable to the nape of the neck, and make-up can be applied to the tape or to the cable to help it blend with the performer's flesh-tone.

The fitting of this type of microphone is a skilled and time-consuming job, and may involve the theatre's wig-master or mistress, particularly if elaborate period hairstyles are not to be ruined.

For rehearsal purposes, it is generally a good idea to make temporary headbands from thin elastic so that it is easy for the performers to remove their microphones, and for the sound designer to experiment with different placings.

If a head-mount is not possible, then the only other sensible place is in the centre of the breastbone. This will ensure that the microphone is placed in an arc, more or less near the mouth, and will avoid problems associated with the head being turned to one side or the other. Various clips are usually supplied with a microphone of this sort to enable it to be attached to ties, lapels or other articles of clothing. A microphone mounted on the body may be susceptible to clothing noise, or resonance from the chest cavity, and may need considerably more equalisation than a head-mounted version.

All sub-miniature microphones are prone to damage from sweat and make-up and they should be kept clean at all times. Some designers like to mount the

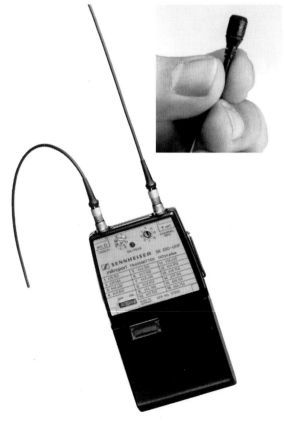

Figure 49 *Sennheiser SK50 Transmitter pack with Sennheiser MKE2 Microphone shown in insert.*

microphone on a small pad of material to insulate the capsule from the worst of the sweat that an actor invariably develops during a performance. Similarly, it may be sensible to insulate the transmitter pack from sweat, either by using the small plastic ZipLoc bags that are often used to pack electronic components, or by using an unlubricated condom, although these can sometimes be hard to locate. Avoid lubricated super-thin condoms as these are unpleasant to handle, contaminate the transmitter and are likely to tear.

The photograph on page 136 shows a typical modern miniature body pack transmitter by Sennheiser, with a sub-miniature MKE2 microphone.

Monitoring the Signal

In most musicals, it is common to employ a person whose only job is to look after the distribution of the transmitters, and to make sure that all batteries, aerials and microphones are in good condition. This person is also responsible

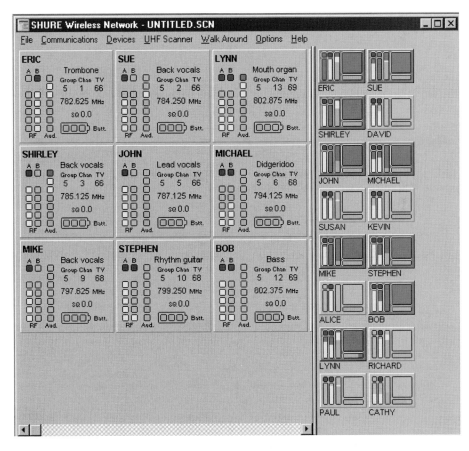

Figure 50 *Shure computer program for wireless microphone monitoring purposes.*

for collecting and reallocating transmitter packs when there are too few for all performers to have one each for the duration of the performance. He or she is sometimes known as a radio-mic runner, and in most musicals has the receivers in a position where they can be observed so that a running check can be kept on the signal and battery strength. (Most modern transmitters are able to send out a coded signal when their internal battery is getting weak.)

Sennheiser, Shure and Trantec produce computer software that allows the monitoring of both audio signal level and radio-frequency strength, and this can make monitoring much simpler. It isn't a good idea to rely on these systems entirely, and a good-quality audio monitoring system is essential (see Figure 50).

The radio-mic runner will keep a kit of spares and will also be expected to make running repairs to faulty units during the course of the show. Often, such repairs will have to be made 'on the fly', in the brief moments when a performer is not on stage and conditions are not ideal. A torch, a steady hand and an unflappable temperament are all pre-requisites for a radio-mic technician when confronted with an angry, sweaty performer who has to be back on stage in a few seconds and needs to have a transmitter rebatteried or replaced. It is not a fun job.

Licensing

The laws governing the use and licensing of wireless transmission equipment in the UK are complex, and the frequencies available for use in theatre are constantly changing. The full list of frequencies available for theatre use in the UK is also extremely complex and depends both on the town in which you are planning to use the equipment, and on whether the production is at a fixed site or touring. It is neither possible nor desirable to devote space in this book to the enormous number of rules and regulations pertaining to the use of wireless microphones in the UK, and as the situation changes rapidly, the only sensible solution is to apply to the organisation charged by the Radio Communications Agency with allocating and licensing frequencies for wireless microphones.

Current information is available from: the Joint Frequencies Management Group Ltd, (JFMG Ltd), 72 Upper Ground, London SE1 9LT, UK. Tel: 020 7261 3797. Their website at www.jfmg.co.uk contains information on using wireless microphones and which frequencies are currently available.

Conclusion

Modern transmitter packs incorporate sophisticated circuitry to ensure that the dynamic range and noise levels are acceptable to an audience's discriminating ear, and a high-quality system consisting of a transmitter and diversity receiver can cost upwards of £1,000. The sub-miniature microphones are also expensive and prone to damage in any number of ways, and the hostile environment of most modern theatres and theatre sets makes the trouble-free use of wireless microphones a difficult goal to achieve.

Even if the system behaves perfectly, the requirement of balancing upwards of twenty individual microphones as well as a live band in an unobtrusive way, calls for immense skill and concentration from the operator. Slight positional shifts in microphone capsules can drastically alter the sound from a microphone, as can the ingress of sweat or make-up, and the operator and radio-mic technician must monitor the incoming signals constantly.

The fact that all major musicals and, in the USA at least, many straight plays are now amplified using multiple radio-microphones points to a further reliance on technology in general, and the sound designer in particular, to make up for what some might see as deficiences in many other parties: composers and arrangers who do not allow 'gaps' in their music for the voices to sit; audiences who have become so used to the high audio levels experienced in cinemas, rock concerts and in 'home-theatre' systems; performers who have had little or no vocal training and do not know how to project without shouting; architects who design theatres with little regard to acoustic performance; and commercial producers, whose perennial cries of 'louder and brighter' have all but destroyed subtlety in musical theatre.

It may seem odd to say this, but if you get the opportunity, try doing a musical without using wireless microphones, and relish the difference.

MIDI Show Control (MSC)

Show control systems are becoming increasingly common in theatre. Developed initially by the theme park industry to allow centralised and synchronised control of complex shows without recourse to a whole team of operators, they have slowly found their way into the theatre, chiefly through the large-scale musical, where they are frequently responsible for co-ordinating moving scenery, moving lights, pyrotechnics and projections.

Many of these systems are proprietary; that is, they work only with one manufacturer's or developer's system and cannot interact with other systems, except maybe for simple interconnects such as contact closures. In an effort to overcome this problem, a number of interested manufacturers and developers, led by Andy Meldrum of VariLite and Charlie Richmond of Richmond Sound Design, came together under the MIDI Manufacturers' Association banner to develop an extension of MIDI, using System Exclusive (SysEx) Commands known as MIDI Show Control, or MSC. The implementation was approved by the MMA and became a standard in 1991; it is currently being revised for a second standard, MSC Version 2, intended to address some of the shortcomings of the existing standard, particularly with regard to concerns about the safety aspect of MSC Version 1.

Implementation

Each device in an MSC network can have its own unique identifying number, from 0 to 112, to which only it will respond, or it can accept MSC messages which carry an 'All Call' identifier. The system allows for over fifty different generic types of equipment, from moving lights to flame and smoke machines, taking in Lighting, Audio, Video, Machinery, Projection, Process Control (Hydraulics, Compressed Air, Fog and Smoke, etc.) and Pyrotechnics, with each device being able to respond to 127 different commands, each command containing 128 bytes. How each device responds to each command is determined by the particular manufacturer, and information as to how commands are interpreted should be supplied with the device.

In its simplest form, MSC has three basic commands: GO, STOP and RESUME. The GO command simply fires the next cue in a sequence; the STOP command will halt whatever action has been started; and the RESUME command will cause the action to continue.

By adding a cue number to each command, i.e. GO 8, STOP 4, previously programmed cues can be made to start and stop in response to each MSC command.

The full set of basic commands is as follows:

GO, STOP, RESUME, TIMED_GO, LOAD, SET, FIRE, ALL_OFF, RESTORE, RESET, GO_OFF.

A second set of commands – SOUND COMMANDS – also exists, and is aimed specifically at sound control systems. These commands originated in Richmond Sound Design's Stage Manager and Command/Cue applications, but are also being incorporated by other manufacturers of MIDI-based sound control systems, particularly those running to a time-code, from either an internal or external clock.

MSC's natural home is in theme parks, exhibitions and complex theatre shows, but take-up in these areas has been slow, mainly due to resistance by equipment manufacturers to sacrifice their proprietary control systems. The command set continues to be refined, however, and a number of companies are beginning to appreciate the usefulness of a common command set.

A further development of this system by Richmond Sound Design allows MSC commands to be distributed via and Ethernet Data Network, with commands being interpreted by local MIDI outstations connected to the network, thus making the system even more versatile.

Sound designers have been in the forefront of adopting this system of show control in theatre, as it offers enormous possibilities in improving the way that sound interacts with other elements of a theatrical production, to the benefit of the show. An example of this, whilst not strictly MSC-based, is given below.

In *The Front Page* by Kauffman and Hart, staged at the Donmar Warehouse Theatre in London in 1998, the action took place in a press-room attached to a gaol where a hanging is scheduled. At a certain point in the action the prisoner escapes, and the director required that the following sequence of events occurred: a gunshot, followed by a fusillade of shots, the prison siren starts up and the alarm bell in the press-room goes off. The lead actor runs for the light switch and turns out the main lights. There is another shot, closer this time, and the window shatters. A tin coffee mug is hit by the bullet and falls to the floor as the slug ricochets around the room. Another shot hits the wall and sparks fly. Yet another shot hits the metal lampshade, and once again we see the sparks and hear the ricochet. All the while, there are shouts, running footsteps and a searchlight criss-crossing the scene outside the window. Finally, the fugitive climbs in through the press-room window, and the clamour dies down. The siren winds down and the alarm bell stops ringing.

The Donmar is a small theatre, and very often a single operator controls both lights and sound, as was the case in this instance. On examining the sequence, it became obvious that there would have to be a fair degree of automation to ensure that all events happened in perfect synchronisation. The decision was made to use a show control system, in this case Richmond Sound Design's Stage Manager 3000, in conjunction with an mm productions MIDI to Relay controller, and the MIDI control function of the theatre's lighting board.

All sounds were triggered via MIDI from an Akai S3000XL sampler, with the siren sound starting, looping, and then running down on a MIDI note-off command.

The window break and coffee mug devices were electro-mechanical in operation, involving a solenoid and compressed-air release respectively. The alarm bell used a simple electrical connection, and these three devices were triggered by sending a MIDI command to the MIDI Relay controller. Each device was controlled by a different relay that responded to a unique MIDI message from the controlling computer, as were the three pyrotechnics producing the sparks from the 'bullet-hits', with the deputy stage-manager having a 'dead man's handle' override in case of problems. The pyrotechnics would not fire unless she first armed the system with a key, and then held down the master fire-button.

The lighting cues were triggered via direct MIDI commands from the show control computer, giving the operator a single button to press for each event during the gaol break.

The sound effects of the gunshots, window break, bullet hits and richochets were all synchronised to their 'real-world' counterparts using MIDI sequences, so that each sound tallied precisely with the mechanical or pyrotechnic effect that accompanied it. Without the show-control system, at least four operators would have been required, with no guarantee of precise synchronisation. With the system, what could have been a logistical nightmare became an effective and repeatable sequence that worked perfectly night after night.

There was a good deal of speculation from various members of the creative team about how effective the system would be, which lasted until the first time we ran the sequence. Once it was seen that the system worked, and continued to work perfectly, it was interesting to note how quickly all concerned took it for granted.

Readers wanting to investigate show-control further should consult John Huntington's definitive book on the subject, now in its second edition (see the Bibliography).

Chapter 6

Sound Effects

Using Sound Effects

What are the reasons for using sound effects? We can break them down into a number of categories, but the most usual ones are as follows.

(1) Information
The audience needs to be told something about period, location, time of day, time of year, any external events that may be relevant, or the state of the weather. Modern authors have a tendency to write stage directions that read something like this: 'The play opens in a deserted warehouse near a freight yard in Seattle in 1933. It is late evening on a bitterly cold winter's night.' These details may be very important to an audience's understanding of a play, and it will be up to the scenic designer, the sound designer and the lighting designer to give the audience the clues that it needs.

(2) Textual Reference
Sounds referred to or reacted to by characters in a production. These can range from the mundane, such as toilet flushes, to the ethereal, such as the 'twang' in *The Cherry Orchard*, to the monumental, such as the avalanche at the end of *When We Dead Awaken*.

(3) Mood Creation
Any sound that creates an atmosphere that may not be suggested in the text, but complements the underlying mood of the piece. The wind whistling in a horror story, for example, or the sound of factory whistles in a gritty, industrial drama.

(4) Emotional Stimulus
Sounds that play on knee-jerk emotional, and sometimes physical, reactions from an audience, such as loud bangs, heartbeats, piercing metallic scrapings, squeal of car brakes, high-level/low-frequency rumbles, comic effects (although these must be handled with care – not all audiences share the same sense of humour).

(5) Cues
To reinforce on stage action, for example telephones, doorbells, door knocks, domestic fires, and so on.

Many plays will require effects from a cross-section of the above categories. As an example, I would like to refer to a play by Nicholas Wright, *The Desert Air*.

The play was produced at the Royal Shakespeare Company's studio theatre in Stratford-upon-Avon, directed by Bill Alexander, and was set in Africa during the Second World War. The play opens on the parade ground of a British army camp somewhere in the North African desert, and continues in and around the camp during the period of one week. There are scenes that take place indoors, outdoors, in a house of ill-repute, in a nightclub, in a car and in the desert itself, and the play has a stage direction towards the end of the first page which simply reads: 'The doors of the theatre open and an invisible Sherman tank drives onto the stage.' A little later in the text, Field Marshal Montgomery taps on the hull of the invisible tank, and holds a conversation with the (equally invisible) driver. This rather odd sequence was inspired by the fact that the Allies sought the help of an illusionist, Victor Maskelyne, to help them disguise their tanks during the fighting in North Africa.

The first scene takes place on a bare stage with the sound of soldiers carrying out parade ground drill in the background, a distant gramophone playing songs of the period, and an atmospheric track of insects. A bright lighting state reveals the stage. The audience is thus informed that the following scene is set in or near a military establishment, probably outdoors, in a hot climate during daylight hours in the 1940s. Gradually, soldiers drift on to the stage and the actor portraying Montgomery arrives to start the proceedings. His opening speech gives more precise information about the location and time in which the play is set.

In the next scene, the invisible tank comes on to the stage. This effect was achieved by the simple method of having the 'tank' start its engine off stage; a cloud of exhaust fumes from a smoke machine is blown on to the stage as the double doors leading directly on to the stage open and the sound effect is slowly panned from the external speaker on to speakers in the centre of the auditorium. The effect is played at a high level, and contains sufficient low-frequency information to affect the audience physically, i.e. they feel the sound as well as hearing it. The tank stops, the smoke gradually clears, and there is complete silence. Montgomery leans forward, raises his swagger stick and raps the air in front of him. We hear the sound of the stick hitting the tank in sync with the actor's movements. The cast applaud and Montgomery congratulates the inventor, who is driving the tank. We hear 'Thank you very much, sir' in a muffled voice from thin air, and the tank is started up and driven out of the theatre with the help of a little more smoke.

Gradually, during the course of the scene, the insects start up again and play until the next scene, which is an interior.

In the opening pages of the script, therefore, we have an example of sound effects giving the audience information about the location and period of the action, creating the invisible tank referred to in the script, providing a sound effect to correspond with an action, and intentionally making the audience laugh, which the muffled voice-over invariably succeeded in doing. During the rest of the play, many other sound effects were used in conjunction with specially composed music played by a small band, lighting changes, and the minimum of props and furniture to suggest all the other locations in the play.

Stereo

The use of stereo recordings of effects and music can enhance a soundtrack in a number of ways, even though the majority of the audience will not be in the ideal listening position. Problems may occur in the use of stereo music with a particularly wide sound stage for those sitting in extreme side seats, but such recordings are the exception rather than the norm. Stereo recordings are useful for 'moving' sound effects, such as traffic, but can also add an air of realism to many other atmospheric effects, such as wind, rain, birdsong or sea.

Effects that need to change location in response to stage action are best left in mono, and moved from speaker to speaker using desk output faders or joystick controllers. The complex helicopter sequence in the musical *Miss Saigon* is controlled by a set of automated moving faders. The operater moves the faders during rehearsals at the required rate for each part of the sequence, and the fader moves are recorded by a microprocessor-controlled memory system. Each set of moves is recorded as a cue, assigned a number and stored in a non-volatile memory until it is recalled for playback. Servo motors then reproduce the operator's fader movements in response to each cue. This system has the advantage over other fader automation systems using Voltage Controlled Amplifiers in that the operator has an instant visual check on the progress of a fade, and access to the faders should the need arise.

Experiments with surround-sound systems, such as Ambisonics, have proved to be successful under controlled circumstances, but few theatre companies have investigated their use with any degree of enthusiasm. The lead may come from cinemas and theme parks, which use enhanced stereo systems such as Dolby Surround and Roland 3D to add realism to their presentations.

Multi-tracked Effects

Multi-channel replay devices, such as multi-track tape recorders, both analogue and digital, and multiple-output samplers, are also useful in creating realistic effects sequences. A fierce storm at sea, for example, can have a large number of component parts: wind, thunder, rain, crashing waves and creaking timbers. Rather than produce a fixed mix of all the effects on one tape, it is often better to isolate each element on one track or output of the replay device, and mix the effects in situ. The designer can then vary the content and ferocity of the storm as the action of the play demands. This can save constant remixing of composite tracks when the balance needs to be changed.

Locating the Loudspeakers

A number of factors other than artistic considerations will dictate where you place the loudspeakers:

- type of theatre: in the round, thrust, proscenium arch, end-stage or traverse
- set construction: box-set, open stage, flown scenery, lifts, revolves, trucks, and so on
- Aesthetic considerations: will the appearance of modern loudspeakers seriously compromise the overall look of the piece? (One London theatre management used to insist that luminaires and loudspeakers in front-of-house positions are painted to match the decor of the auditorium.)
- safety: will the actors making a fast exit in a blackout trip over a cable or bang their heads on one of your loudspeakers?

Inevitably, you will not be able to place your loudspeakers where they will do most good, (i.e. directly in sight of the audience). You will have to place them behind flats that are all-too-commonly constructed of solid wood and metal; or amongst mass ranks of luminaires with shutters and colour-frames that rattle and buzz at the slightest provocation; or you will have to fly them to avoid trucks and moving scenery. This is why it is important to have a speaker rig designed as soon as possible, and to get into discussion with the designer and the lighting designer at an early stage. The sooner you declare your problems to them, the more chance you have of reaching a compromise that is favourable to you.

Practicals

Practicals are devices that have to work on stage, such as record players, tape recorders, radios or televisions. Wherever possible, conceal a speaker in the device and connect it to your sound system so that it is under the control of the operator. If you cannot get a speaker inside the device, then you may try and conceal it on set either above or below the item. If an item has to be moved around the stage, then a number of small speakers can be hidden at varying locations and the signal moved from one to another via the output faders on the mixing desk.

Situations often arise when a practical item is situated on a revolve or on a truck. Where there are no slip-rings or cable looms available to feed the signal through, it may be necessary to use a battery-operated wireless transmitter/receiver combination of the type used in musicals. The source signal is fed into the microphone input of the transmitter either via a special attenuator lead or a direct-injection box, and the receiver is concealed in the practical item, along with a battery-powered amplifier and small loudspeaker. I have used this technique with success on numerous occasions, most often to produce a 'crying' baby, or music from a portable radio or tape player on stage.

Similar systems have been used for 'vehicles' that need to move on stage, but use quiet electric motors. In a production of John Whiting's *Penny For A Song*, a steam-driven fire engine spluttered and gurgled very convincingly with the aid of a small receiver/amplifier combination hidden inside the firebox. A battery-operated smoke machine added realism. The Royal National Theatre also used the technique for Mr Toad's car in *The Wind In The Willows*, with additional low-frequency reinforcement from a concealed sub-woofer.

Two words of warning: always make sure that you have a back-up in the form of a local hard-wired loudspeaker in case of failure of the wireless link, and *never* put control of a practical in the hands of an actor. They have enough to concentrate on without having to judge whether they have set the volume of the radio at the right level, or remembered to turn the TV back on.

Playing It Back

As well as a way of storing and replaying your sounds, you will need equipment with which to broadcast them during the play. Playback systems are covered in Chapter 3, but at the very least you will need a means of combining your effects and music at varying levels, i.e. a mixing desk, and a means of amplifying the sounds and locating them in the right part of the stage, i.e. amplifiers and loudspeakers.

The essential elements of any system are the ability to set and vary the levels of all the component sounds of your soundtrack, and the ability to determine which loudspeaker or combination of loudspeakers each sound should be sent to. In a large theatre, many loudspeaker locations may be required. The original installation at the Barbican Theatre in London had provision for twenty-six separate loudspeaker channels; the Royal National Theatre's main auditorium, the Olivier, had twenty loudspeaker channels when it first opened; whilst the Royal Exchange Theatre in Manchester is currently equipped with over 40 loudspeaker outputs. It is unlikely that a show will require all of these to be used at once, but a breakdown of the sound requirements of a typical show in a repertory theatre will reveal that, at minimum, six separate speakers channels should be available.

I have already mentioned *A Streetcar Named Desire*, and it is a play with which many readers will be familiar. The script calls for a number of specific effects, some of which are listed:

- the sound of a jazz saxophone from down the street
- music from the on stage radio
- the sound of a shower in the next room
- the clatter of the elevated railroad
- the sound of a distant train whistle
- thunder.

Assuming that the director will want music in the auditorium at some point during the evening, we are presented with the following locations: auditorium (left and right), special for the radio, shower in the next room, street sounds, railroad sounds and thunder. It is possible that the loudspeaker location for the street sounds and the railroad sounds could be the same, though ideally it would be good to separate them. It would also be useful to incorporate some extra low-frequency loudspeakers, known as sub-woofers, to add realism to the thunder and train sequences. Most portable loudspeakers used in theatres are too small

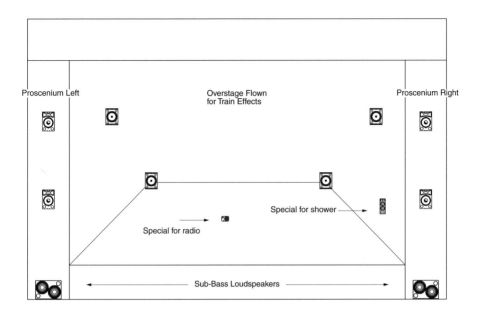

Figure 51 *A Streetcar Named Desire loudspeaker positions.*

to be able to reproduce low frequencies well. The final loudspeaker rig for the show might look like that in Figure 51.

Having designed the physical part of the system, we should now look at some of the practicalities involved in gathering and creating the effects themselves.

Creating and Recording Efftects
Effects Libraries

In recent years, a huge resource of pre-recorded sound effects has become available to the theatre sound designer. There are more than twenty extremely high-quality CD sound effects libraries on the market today, and many others that may not be quite so useful for general purpose use, but may be good for more obscure effects. These libraries are extremely expensive, but the purchaser buys the right to use the effects without further payment to the originator, and they now form the basis of most sound designers' effects source.

Single effects are available over the Internet on payment of a fee, and most record stores have a sound effects section, although the use of these without further payment is often restricted to non-professional use. For example, the BBC has a series of effects discs intended for amateur use, but also offers a library of sixty CDs for professional use. The difference is in the cataloguing of the library, in the length of the effects, and, of course, in the price. Other libraries are available from Sound Ideas, Digiffects, DeWolfe, Hollywood Edge, Warner

Bros, Universal Sudios, and many other companies. A list of suppliers can be found in Appendix F.

A designer may start off with a particular sound from a library and then mix it with others, or carry out some of the processing described later in this chapter, but it is pretty rare that an effect is used direct from the disc without some form of modification. Effects libraries are an excellent starting point, but that's all. Use them as building blocks or as somewhere to start, but if you use the same standard effects over and over again, your designs will start to sound overly familiar to directors and to audiences.

Ideally, a good effects library will consist of commercial effects and a stock of effects that you have made or recorded yourself. Creating and recording your own effects is an extremely rewarding but time-consuming business. In the next section we'll look at ways to gather your own effects.

Location Recording

In many cases, there is no substitute for getting out and recording the natural effects for yourself. A high-quality portable digital recorder, some microphones with effective wind-shields, a pair of headphones and endless charm and meticulous planning will get you a long way in location recording, but first it is essential to make sure that what you are going to record will actually be there when you arrive! I learned long ago that a phone call in advance can save time, money and sanity, although things can still go wrong. The recording session for the Sherman tank in *The Desert Air*, was carefully organised with the Tank Museum in Dorset, but shortly before I arrived, a heavy rainstorm deluged the camp, and the tank, with water in the ignition system, resolutely refused to start. Instead I have an excellent recording of a Sherman tank failing to start, and a very irate sergeant cursing fluently; not much use for the show, but it raises a laugh at seminars. In the event, a slowed-down recording of a three-ton diesel lorry mixed with a Caterpillar road-mending vehicle did the trick.

Never take permission to record for granted, and always offer to pay a facility fee, even if only a small one. In doing so, you are less likely to alienate the person on whose property you are recording, and much more likely to render them friendly for future sessions. By far the biggest problem with recording in exterior locations is that members of the public will come up and talk to you, ask you questions at critical moments, shout out their names or call out 'Hallo Mum', or just make silly noises into the microphone. They will think that this is great fun, never dreaming for a second that they have ruined what could have been several weeks' worth of planning. There is no real solution to this problem, save that of using concealed microphones or arranging to be in a location to which the general public have no access. Apart from the necessary permission, if you are intending to record on private or public property, you must also make sure that you have public liability insurance. Tripping a member of the public with a microphone cable or dropping a microphone on to a passer-by can be very expensive. The policy will cover you for most eventualities and will not cost much.

Recording outdoors also poses another problem aside from bad weather and over-enthusiastic passers-by: it is increasingly difficult to find locations where traffic and aircraft noise are not a constant problem, and I have had to undertake many sessions either early in the morning or late at night to be sure of getting long background sounds that are free of extraneous noise. It is, of course, always possible to edit out intrusive sounds, but a plane flying overhead whilst you are trying to record that perfect country clock striking twelve, or a motorcycle starting up just as you are about to record the perfect bird-call, can destroy hours of preparation. There's very little that can be done about things like this, except to start the whole process of watching and waiting over again. In thirty years of location recording, I can think of only three occasions when recording natural sounds on which I have had more than ten minutes of uninterrupted recording time.

Equipment for Location Recording

Today, portable equipment is small, light, very high quality, and not necessarily expensive. When I first started recording my own effects, I used a Uher portable reel-to-reel recorder and carried around a case full of batteries and small reels of tape. For critical work, I would hire in one of the excellent Nagra portable machines, but that meant even more batteries and, if recording at 15 ips, even more reels of tape. I now use a portable R-DAT recorder; a larger professional model for critical work, or a tiny pocket model for grabbing effects inconspicuously.

Microphones and wind-shields are a different matter. If you are planning to do a lot of your own recording, you will have to gather together a collection of microphones suitable for all types of recording work.

A high-sensitivity microphone that will capture the sound of a mosquito will almost certainly not be suitable for recording thunder or gunfire at close range. You will need to pick a model suitable for the job that you have in mind, and take into account a number of factors that would not normally be a problem. I have yet to come across an all-purpose microphone, although I do use the AMS ST250 microphone to cover many of my needs. This is a development of the Soundfield microphone from the same company, but with the advantage of being completely portable. The pre-amplifier can be powered by battery, mains, or mixing desk phantom power, and signal output can be designated as an X–Y stereo pair, a Mid-Side pair, or B-Format surround sound. The polar pattern of the microphone is variable, as is the apparent angle between the X–Y capsules, although the microphone actually uses a four-capsule design, deriving its various outputs electronically. The microphone is available with a wind-shield made by Rycote, acknowledged experts in this field. The wind-shield is an essential item for exterior recording, as even the slightest breath of wind can register as an annoying low rumble on a sensitive capacitor microphone. The complexity of this microphone gives the sound designer a large number of options for recording in difficult circumstances, and saves them carrying around a large collection of different devices.

Most capacitor microphones and digital tape recorders are badly affected by condensation; taking such equipment from a warm environment to a cold one can cause instant formation of condensation. Allow time for equipment to acclimatise to different temperatures.

There may not necessarily be a local power supply for you to plug your equipment into, or a pro-audio shop to provide you with batteries, tapes or cassettes. Always take twice as much in the way of consumables as you think you will need.

Sometimes, portable equipment can react adversely to being moved in a particular way. For example, centrifugal force can play havoc with some rotary head digital audio tape machines, as I discovered to my cost after subjecting myself to a particularly gruelling roller-coaster ride in Disneyland. Most of the recording was perfect, but as the car passed through the part of each turn where the centrifugal force was at its greatest, severe drop-out occurred.

You will almost invariably have to monitor your recording using headphones. The open type of headphone favoured by hi-fi enthusiasts may give superb reproduction, but will be almost useless in a noisy environment; closed-ear models, on the other hand, will give you the acoustic isolation that you need to check if your recordings are OK. If you are recording on to a DAT recorder that does not have confidence monitoring (allowing you to monitor the recording 'off tape'), then be sure to check your entire recording for faults; you may not be able to repeat the session at a later date.

Studio Recording

Once effects have been sourced either from a library or from real-life, there remains only one other avenue: the sound designer's own imagination. This is where the real creative work is carried out, first in the mind of the designer, and then in the recording and dubbing studio. A sound effects recording studio should have an area devoted solely to acoustic recording. It should be quiet, reasonably free from reverberation, large enough to accommodate a sufficient number of actors for a convincing crowd scene, and with a variety of surfaces available for recreating footsteps if required. A water supply and a large sink or bath can also be a distinct advantage. Few theatres have space devoted to this sort of studio, and rehearsal rooms are often pressed into use as makeshift recording areas. Unfortunately, the poor acoustic properties of these spaces can make them less than ideal unless care is taken to deal with the more undesirable elements.

The sound effects dubbing studio should contain the means for treating and mixing sound effects and rerecording the result. Our company studio currently contains the following equipment:

- 1 x 1" eight-track digital recorder
- 1 x high-speed two-track analogue reel-to-reel tape recorder
- 4 x R-DAT recorders, rack-mount, portable and sub-miniature

- 1 x PCM701/F1 stereo digital recording system
- 2 x CD players
- 3 x CD recorders
- 1 x compact cassette recorder
- 2 x MiniDisc recorders
- 1 x analogue synthesiser
- 1 x digital synthesiser
- 2 x digital samplers
- 3 x MIDI keyboard controllers
- 2 x Apple Macintosh computers with MIDI sequencer software and hard-disk recording system
- 1 x Wintel computer with MIDI sequencer software and hard-disk recording system
- 1 x 32–4–2 digital mixing desk
- 1 x 8–4–2 analogue mixing desk
- 1 x Vinyl Disc player
- a variety of miscellaneous processing equipment such as reverb units, noise reduction systems, delay lines, compressor/limiters, and so on.

In many theatres, the sound control room also does duty as the dubbing room, but this is a less than ideal arrangement, unless the theatre also has a proper operating position in the auditorium. Even if it is only a small space, all theatres should have a room set aside for preparation of sound effects so that work on a show can take place whilst the control room is in use during performances.

The recording and dubbing studios are the places where technical trickery and personal ingenuity can transform the mundane into the remarkable, mistakes can be rectified, and the disparate elements that go to make up a soundtrack can begin the process that will organise them into a coherent whole.

Every studio should have access to a supply of noise-making equipment, including some of the following items:

- bicycle bells, sleigh bells, small hand-bells, wind chimes, door-bells (regular, chime and electronic), tubular bells, alarm clocks
- miscellaneous crockery, glassware, cutlery, brooms, saucepans, dustbins (trash-cans)
- running water, wash basin, enamel bowl
- acoustic piano, side drum, bass drum, assorted Latin percussion, cymbals, finger cymbals
- electric fans, motors, mechanical toys, clock mechanisms

This may look like a formidable list, but you will find that most of the items will either be available to you at home or in the theatre. The secret is to know where you can lay your hands on them quickly!

Although many of them will be useful for effects as they stand, all can be pressed into service as a source of other sound effects. In a production of *The*

Wizard of Oz, the various clanks and creaks of the Tin Man were produced by mistreating a variety of cooking utensils. Kitchen knives and a sharpening steel have proved useful for creating sword and dagger effects; a battery-operated miniature electric drill and a metal ashtray provided a particularly nasty old-fashioned dentist's drill for a Feydeau farce; and in the soundtracks of two Peter Shaffer plays, *The Royal Hunt of The Sun* and *Equus*, a scraped piano string, bowed and reversed cymbals and a bass drum were used to great effect. In his book on theatre sound, David Collison describes how he and composer Guy Woolfenden created various effects for the Royal Shakespeare Company's production of *Henry V* in 1965, using similar methods.

Some Useful Studio Techniques

Altering the source sound to make it more suitable for use in a production involves a variety of processes in the dubbing studio. Some of these techniques are discussed below.

Looping

Many sounds used in plays are of the atmospheric variety, and can sometimes be required to play for long periods. If the sound is rhythmic or repetitive in character, the technique of looping, where an endless loop is created either by joining together the ends of a piece of analogue recording tape using a tape cartridge, or creating a loop in a sampler, can be used to create a long effect from a short one. Care must be taken to match levels so that the end of the loop perfectly matches the beginning. If this is not the case, there will be an audible and disturbing change in the level each time the loop repeats.

Not all effects can be looped successfully. Bird-song and animal noises where identifiable patterns repeat over and over again, quickly declare themselves as having been looped to even the least discerning of audiences if the loop is only a few tens of seconds in duration. Once a loop has become apparent, all concentration goes as the listener's sub-conscious waits for the loop to repeat. Creating long loops with analogue tape, particularly when recording at 15 ips (38cm/s), would often involve finding a path for the loop around the dubbing room, with microphone stands, empty tape spools and human help being pressed into service. Samplers and Digital Audio Workstations have now made this process so easy that long loops can be undertaken with ease. I will often use two- or three-minute long sections of audio in loops, cross-fading between three or four looping sections to produce the impression of a constantly changing background.

A regular crash of waves on the shore is a good sound for looping, provided the effect is used gently in the background. Wind and rain can both be looped successfully, as can fire effects, but longer loops should be used to provide some variation.

Insect sounds are by nature repetitive, and short loops can be created with ease. It should be noted, however, that insects do not make a continuous noise; the odd quiet passage will add to the verisimilitude of the soundtrack, and the audience will be reminded of the effect each time it restarts after a quiet passage.

Crowd sounds can also be looped successfully, but if the effect is to run for any length of time, a mix of several loops should be used for the sake of variety and reality. The sound of a large crowd waxes and wanes in a fairly random manner; we are all familiar with those occasions in a theatre auditorium before a show, when the audience suddenly goes quiet for no reason, and then slowly builds up to a more constant sound.

Striking clocks and tolling bells require a more careful approach to looping as the effects normally need a beginning and an end which have to sound natural. The looped chimes must contain an element of ring-on from the previous strike, but the beginning chime must be clean, and the end chime must have a long ring-on to a realistic decay. Ideally, a source effect of three chimes minimum is required for creating convincing clock chimes and tolling bells of any duration. The middle chime is looped, containing as it does the ring-on from the first chime, and the first and last chimes are edited into position after the required length of material has been recorded. A word of warning: you must use a single chime that starts from silence and decays to silence for a clock striking 1 o'clock. Trying to isolate a single chime from the middle of a group, or using the final chime from a sequence, may sound unnatural.

Horse-drawn and motor traffic effects will only loop if there are no specific sounds such as shouts, car horns or tyre squeals that will give the loop away to an audience.

Almost any indeterminate background atmosphere can be looped, but it is possible to rely too much on loops. I prefer to try and procure long recordings of natural sounds that have their own dynamic, or to artificially recreate sounds with a similar dynamic.

In a recent production of *Heartbreak House*, the director required bird-song throughout a 45-minute scene. During the course of the scene, the lighting state indicated that late afternoon was changing to dusk, then to twilight, then to darkness. Instead of preparing a 45-minute soundtrack of looped bird-song, I used a series of lengthy bird-song effects, gradually thinning them out during the course of the scene, until the only bird to be heard was a distant owl.

A frequent requirement in shows is for a background wind effect; at specific moments, the wind is required to rattle the shutters of the house, or to sound in the chimney. The spot effects are prepared separately and played in as required, but the continuous effect may be created using a mix of long naturalistic wind recordings, and often a synthesised wind. By setting up random pitch variations using a synthesizer's in-built effects generators, it is possible to create a long wind background in which no mix of elements ever appears to repeat.

Some effects libraries aid the designer in this respect by providing cuts of atmospheric sounds that are between three and six minutes long. Rather than looping, these may simply be recorded end to end and edited into a continuous track.

Close-up Recording

In the same way that extreme close-up photography can reveal unusual aspects of the object being photographed, using a microphone very close to a sound source will reveal many different aspects of even the simplest sounds. When these sounds are amplified, a completely different effect may be produced. I needed a swinging inn sign for a production of *A Tale of Two Cities*, and produced it by recording the creaking sound made by swinging a compact cassette case lid on its hinge. The sound of a crackling fire can be recreated by a close-up recording of the bubble-wrap type of packaging being gently squeezed in the hand, with the odd pop of one of the bubbles adding a great deal to the effect.

In a production of *The Tempest*, we needed a threatening drumming rhythm. Nothing that the music department could produce was quite right, but by placing a microphone face down on a table top, and then drumming on the table top with fingertips, the right sound was produced. Feeding the end result through a reverberation unit produced a convincing thunder of drums in the distance. Once again, there are no rules; if you think it might work, try it.

Speed Variation

Changing the scale of an effect can often be achieved by altering the speed at which it is replayed. A change of speed produces a change of pitch, which can alter a sound considerably. A pistol shot can become a cannon shot when slowed down sufficiently. Conversely, a speeded up cannon shot can become a truly remarkable rife shot.

For Peter Whelan's First World War drama, *The Accrington Pals*, we needed a sound that could suggest a massive industrial machine, thumping away in the distance of a small northern town. The same sound had also to suggest distant gunfire on the Western Front. No library effect was suitable, so I used a recording of a spring-loaded date-stamp thumping down on to a desk. Slowed down to an eighth of the original speed, and then looped, a satisfyingly sinister and mechanical machine rhythm was created. The slower recording was used mixed with an actual recording of distant gunfire as a background to the battle sequences in the show.

The digital signal processing devices available today offer two time domain functions not available using analogue equipment: pitch variation without speed change and speed change without pitch variation. Used sparingly, these can be helpful to the sound designer. In a production of Jules Feiffer's *Little Murders*, a window is opened and closed at various times by members of the cast. The sound effect that went with the action had all the right ingredients, but was too long. Recording the sound into the digital signal processing section of an Akai sampler allowed me to reduce the playback time without altering the pitch of the effect. Too much variation of either pitch or speed will produce unpleasant distortion, only really useful if you are producing a science fiction sound score.

Echo and Reverberation

The use of artificial echo and reverberation to alter the perceived acoustic of a sound has long been a favourite tool of the sound designer. Through the use of digital reverberation and echo units, almost any acoustic condition, whether real or imaginary, can be simulated. The designer should consider at what stage the effect is added, however, as echo or reverberation, once applied to a master recording, cannot be removed without remaking the effect. I prefer to record sounds without processing, adding this during playback in the theatre. If this is not possible, I will prepare twin-track recordings, with one track carrying the sound 'dry' and the other treated. That way, the two can be combined in the theatre to give the desired result. Generally, the shorter the reverberation time, the smaller the perceived space; most digital reverb units have controls that allow the user to set the size and shape of the 'room' with a fair degree of accuracy.

In the RSC's production of *Cyrano de Bergerac*, the play ended with the sound of a distant choir of nuns as Cyrano dies. Our recording session in the theatre early on a Saturday morning was graced by a group of singers who were not in best voice, and the resultant recording was not as sweet as we had hoped. The addition of a judicious amount of artificial reverberation, coupled with playback from a flown loudspeaker at a very low level, produced exactly the effect that was required.

Repeat echo, or slap-echo, is often used to heighten battle scenes on stage. Microphones pick up the live action sounds and the signal is then fed to a delay unit set for a repeat time of around a quarter to a third of a second. The delayed sound is then relayed to the stage loudspeakers, where it is picked up by the microphones and fed back to the delay unit. Used subtly, this effect can enhance battle scenes by adding to the general sense of confusion and chaos. Overused, it becomes as much a cliché as too much smoke or dry-ice.

Using reverberation in the same way can help to give an audience a sense of place in a production in which there are no visual cues. A small black box can become a cathedral in the mind of an audience if they hear the actors in an acoustic that represents such a space.

Compression

The ear is capable of perceiving a wide range of levels of sound; if this range was to be expressed in a non-logarithmic fashion, the ratio of the quietest sound to the loudest would be around ten million to one. To avoid dealing with such large numbers, we can express noise levels using a logarithmic scale called to the deciBel (dB) scale, where 0 dB sound pressure level (SPL) represents a sound level at the threshold of hearing, and 140 dB SPL represents a sound level at the threshold of pain. (This is a much simplified explanation of sound pressure level. For further details, consult one of the books listed in the Bibliography in Appendix E.)

The background level of sound in a theatre can be quite high, certainly reaching levels in excess of 40 dB SPL. Sound effects that contain a wide range of levels can easily have their quiet passage lost under the general background noise. A heavy sea effect is a good example; in order to hear the effect during the backwash, the operator increases the level, but then the sound of the wave breaking on the shore becomes too much and the operator has to reduce the level once more. In order to avoid this see-sawing of levels, it is advantageous to use a compressor to limit the dynamic range of an effect. The compressor can automatically reduce the higher levels of an effect or piece of music passed through it. Precise settings of the amount of level reduction will depend on the type of effect or music. Compression is particularly useful in coping with sounds sourced from digital recordings (see also Gunshots and Explosions, page 159).

Equalisation

Equalisers can be used for more than tonal correction; judicious use of a comprehensive equaliser can change the characteristics of a sound so that it is more suitable for a given application. Obvious examples are telephone conversations, transistor radios, public address systems and intercoms. I find that these sounds are enhanced by the use of a distortion box – either a setting in a multi-effects processor or a stand-alone unit as used by rock guitarists – although these can be a little on the harsh side.

Very often, a combination of treatments is required in order to arrive at the correct sound. A modern-dress production of *Timon of Athens* included a scene set at a horse racing track. The sound requirement was for a commentary that should be audible, but not coherent, alongside the sound of thundering hooves in the distance. The race commentator became more and more excited as the scene progressed, but it was important that no actual words should be audible. The answer was to record the commentary and then apply the following treatments.

1. Severe compression so that the voice level was constant. No sudden peaks got in the way of the text.
2. Drastic application of equalisation to remove all frequencies below 300 Hz and above 3,000 Hz to give that authentic 're-entrant horn' sound.
3. Application of distortion using a Yamaha SPX900 multi-effects processor. Just enough distortion was added to render the words incomprehensible whilst still retaining the sense of urgency.
4. Discrete application of slap-echo, with the echo effect being routed to a separate speaker.

The end result was convincing, and distorted enough to ensure that nobody could quite make out that the winning horse was ridden by the director, the second horse by the designer and the third horse by the leading actor.

Composite Effects

Rarely will a library effect or a location recording be exactly right for the show. You will have to massage the effect into shape by using some of the procedures outlined above, but also by editing and mixing effects together. It is often necessary to disassemble a sound, study the component parts, and then build the sound up from scratch. The window opening and closing effect from *Little Murders*, mentioned above, consisted of three sounds: first, the metal against metal creak as the jammed window started to move, next the sliding sound of the frame in its groove, and finally the sound of the frame hitting the end stop. Finding a library recording that sounded just right was unlikely, so the effect was fabricated. The metal creak came from the noise made by a spool retainer on an elderly Ampex tape machine, the sliding sound was from a greenhouse door, and the bang was taken from a library recording of an old sash window closing. In producing the final effect, it was necessary to 'think' the action of opening and closing the window, and to orchestrate the playing in of the various elements at the correct time.

A colleague, Alastair Goolden, was required to make up the sound of a drink vending machine at very short notice. His analysis of the effect was as follows: coin drops, solenoid clicks, plastic cup drops, pump motor whines, liquid drips into cup, pump stops, solenoid clicks again. He recorded the coin dropping into a metal container, the plastic cup dropping on to a metal tray, and the water dribbling into the cup, in the dubbing studio; the solenoid click and pump whine were pulled from the effects library. Most of the component sounds were recorded into a sampler in sequence, having been adjusted for level and length, and then played out as one long effect. The water into the cup sound was mixed in from a separate machine, and allowed to continue for a few drips after the mechanical sounds had ceased. This was achieved in slightly less than an hour and shows how a familiarity with both process and equipment can help to create convincing effects quickly. The effect was subsequently cut, but this is also something with which the experienced sound designer learns to cope. (The same show used short samples of sound effects in a musical score by composer Jeremy Sams. Set in the foreign exchange dealing room of a merchant bank, the music track was made up from pitched recordings of typewriters, telephones and the bleeps and hums of office quipment.)

For some composite sound effects, it may be desirable to keep the various elements on separate machines or on separate sampler outputs. Timing can change from night to night, and the ability to place the different elements in time and space precisely with regard to each performance is very useful. A play by Charles Wood called *Red Star* includes a sequence set in a Russian railway station. During the course of the scene, prisoners are loaded on to a train. We hear the doors of the cattle truck in which they are being transported slam shut, and the guard call out a warning that the train is about to depart. The train starts to build up steam, a whistle blows, and the train begins to move off, sounding its own whistle as it does so. As the train moves out of the station, we hear the whistle again, more distant, and finally we are left in the empty station with the sound of people going about their everyday business. This entire sequence was continuous (and pre-sampler) and was split up on to three two-track analogue tape machines in the following way:

Deck A: track 1 – general station atmosphere; track 2 – stationary steam train, sound of hissing steam and thumping of brake pumps.
Deck B: truck doors slam shut.
Deck C: guard announcement.
Deck B: track 1 – train builds up steam; track 2 – five seconds of silence then guard blows whistle.
Deck C: train moves off – stereo effect with whistle mixed in. Fade out **Deck A** track 2 under the sound of the train moving off.
Deck B: distant whistle.

Each of the tape machine starts were on specific line or movement cues from the actors. The stage was filled with people and props and the cue points varied each night. Trying to create a single effect of the whole sequence would have meant the actors trying to fit their lines and moves to a rigidly defined time scale, with no room for manoeuvre if things went awry on stage.

Today, I would approach the same sequence by using a sampler and a sequencer or show control program.

Live Effects

There are some effects that are always better performed live. These include glass smashes, telephones, door knocks, door-bells and gunshots and explosions.

Glass Smashes

It is unusual to see the old-style 'glass-crash' boxes in theatres these days; their place has largely given way to the use of digitally recorded effects. If it seems necessary to use such a box, two alternatives are available: either the use of real glass, in which case great care should be taken in the handling of the effect, with protective clothing, and in particular eye protection being used; or the use of thin metal plates suspended on fine nylon wire. The advantage of the second method is that it is much safer, much cheaper and easy to reset. The disadvantage is that it rarely sounds right. In order to get the scale of the effect right, multiple crashes may be necessary along with amplification through the sound system.

Telephones

Whenever possible, the ringer inside the phone should be used; it is usually possible to wire the phone so that the ringer stops as the receiver is lifted. Special telephone ringer boxes can be obtained that will ring the phone in the correct sequence for the country in which the action is happening. Few stage-managers can recreate and sustain the ringing cycle of the British telephone system manually.

It is also possible to feed audio to the telephone ear-piece so that the actor may hear the other half of a conversation if required. If the audience also needs to hear the conversation, the level at the ear-piece may have to be so high that it causes the actor discomfort. In this case, a local speaker may be used, as close to the actual phone as possible, with a suitably distorted feed from the sound desk, or the actual handset speaker may be relocated to the mouthpiece.

The source of the remote voice can either be a recording, although this will need precise operation if it is not to sound stilted, or an actor with a microphone in an off stage position. The actor will need to be able to hear what is being said on stage, so a suitable show-relay feed will be required. This method has the advantage that conversations will sound absolutely natural.

Always have a stand-by ringer available, even if this is a simple electric bell in the wings. Plays that use telephone conversations almost always use them crucially to advance the plot, and this cannot happen if the phone does not ring.

Door Knocks, Locks, Slams and Bells

Most theatres have a device known simply as a 'door-slam'. It usually consists of a full-sized door set into a sturdy, stand-alone frame, and fitted with an assortment of locks, chains and knockers. Actors can create their own effects at the correct point, unlocking and slamming the prop door as required, or a member of the sound or stage-management team can do it for them. Once again, it may be necessary to amplify and treat the sound to give the correct impression of scale. The porter's scene in 'Macbeth' will invariably involve a special session to achieve the correct level and sequence for the knocks which are integrated tightly into the dialogue.

Distant door knocks, slams and creaks will be better as recorded effects, so that there is precise control over the level and location of the effect. Door-bells and buzzers will most often be live, with the stage-manager or the actor simply pressing the bell-push at the required moment. It is easier for a director to give precise instructions about the length and pattern of any rings to a live operator, than for the sound designer to constantly remake the effect.

It is possible to use a sampler for all these effects, and for the sounds to be triggered by contact closures or pressure pads built in to the set. A number of units exist that allow this to happen using the MIDI interface, as well as one that will allow the use of wireless microphones to trigger effects remotely, using a small tone generator. Care should be taken that effects played in this way are not subject to spurious triggering.

Gunshots and Explosions

These are the most difficult effects to generate from recorded material. They exhibit a dynamic range far in excess of most reproduction equipment, and in the case of explosions, the sudden displacement of large amounts of air is difficult to recreate. Audiences are used to seeing realistic gun battles and fire-fights in the cinema, where the sound effects can safely be dubbed on afterwards. Some amusement parks with a cinematic theme also provide recorded effects as part of their live action sequences, but in these cases, distance helps to mask any obvious lack of synchronisation.

Gunshots on stage as part of the action should, as far as possible, be produced using a specially altered firearm and blank cartridges. There are obvious exceptions to this: automatic weapons with a high firing rate provide their own problems, as do situations in which one actor has to fire a gun in close proximity to another. The flash and debris discharged from the blank cartridge can do severe damage at close quarters. In this case, a gun may be fired in the wings by the stage-manager, or a recorded effect can be used. The wireless MIDI triggering device described above can sometimes be used concealed in a weapon, with the effect being relayed over a local loudspeaker. As with important telephone cues, important gunshots should always be backed up, with a recorded effect or with a standby gun in the wings. For really important gunshots, both back-up methods should be employed.

Distant explosions can be well served with recorded material. Effects can be created using the speed variation techniques described earlier, or taken from actual recordings. In the case of distant cannon fire, slowing the effect to provide a dull rumble is often effective. Close explosions are most often achieved with theatrical maroons, as described on page 6. These have a short, sharp impact that is very effective but have the side effect of making any recorded effects used in conjunction sound as though lacking in attack. It may be necessary to reproduce recorded explosions used in this way at a much higher level than might be anticipated.

Trying to record a gunshot, cannon shot or explosion without using compression will result in a very disappointing sound. If the recording level is set for the initial impact, any reverberation will be almost inaudible and the effect will sound dead and unimpressive. Digital recorders do not overload gracefully and a compressor/limiter is vital to prevent this happening and to compress the dynamic range to something more usable in a theatre.

Fights

Stage fights have to be safe, but to look and sound convincing. No actual contact is made during a fist fight; actors hit themselves to simulate the sound of a punch landing, break-way bottles made of sugar glass or brittle wax are used for bar fights, and chairs and stools are made to collapse easily. Once again, post-dubbed movie fights have lead an audience to expect realistic fight sounds, and stage fights often involve a great deal of vocalisation to hide the fact that all punches are pulled.

At the request of fight director Malcolm Ranso, I arranged a series of 'knaps' (sounds of punches landing) as well as bottle smashes and wood crashes on a sampler, with an operator following the action on stage, for a fight scene in Michael Bogdanov's production of *The Ginger Man* at the Deutsches Shauspielhaus in Hamburg. Without the sound effects, the fight was pretty terrifying; with the sound effects it was that degree more convincing. The operator was able to track the fight and spot in the effects by hitting a particular note on a keyboard at exactly the right moment. On the first public performance, the theatre's administrator was so sure that the leading man had received a bar-stool full in the face during the brawl, that he left the auditorium to go backstage and check that no serious damage had been done.

I have mentioned samplers on a number of occasions throughout this section of the book, so now would seem like a good time to look at their use in theatre in some depth.

Samplers

The advent of digital audio recording technology has changed the way that we can manipulate sound. It is now relatively simple to alter the pitch or speed of a recording, add echo or reverberation, or produce the wide range of effects familiar from the world of modern music. We can also store sound in the same way that computer data is stored, i.e. on floppy-disk, hard-disk, or in random access memory (RAM). The near-instantaneous retrieval of data held in RAM can be used to advantage in theatrical productions.

The first system that I used for producing part of a theatre soundtrack was a Fairlight CMI (Computer Musical Instrument). It had a data resolution of 8 bits, came in three large road-boxes and included an experienced operator in the hire price. In the early 1980s, composer Ilona Seckacz wanted to use the device to manipulate recordings of a choir and wind, sea and thunder sound effects to form a musical soundtrack base for a production of *Twelfth Night* at the RSC in Stratford-upon-Avon. The ease with which we could access the sounds and replay them from a conventional music keyboard was a pointer to systems in use today. At that time, however, the technology was so expensive that it was far out of reach for most theatre companies.

As with most new technology, the prices came down and the boxes got smaller, and now many theatres have a sampler somewhere in their equipment specification. Currently I use samplers from the Akai range – either the S3200XL or the S6000. MIDI control of the unit is via an Apple Macintosh or Windows-based PC, using either a standard MIDI sequencer or one of the specialist show control programs now generally available.

In order to see how these devices can be used in theatre productions, we will need to look at how sounds are stored and recalled.

Samplers were originally created to allow a musician to record and replay a sample, i.e. a short digital recording of a musical instrument, from a synthesiser keyboard. If one note, say middle C, were recorded and then manipulated so that it could be played back at a pitch determined by the keyboard, it would be possible to recreate the sound of a musical instrument without actually having to have the instrument in one's possession. Changing the pitch of a single sample over four octaves did not produce particularly realistic sounds, so a further development produced samplers that were capable of storing one sample for each note on the keyboard, and later, for even more sophistication, more than one sample per note, the actual sample being played determined by the strength at which the note was played. For example, it would be possible to record a note on a piano being played pianissimo, piano, forte and mezzo forte, and then to allocate these four samples to the same note on the sampler. A simple program within the sample determines how hard a particular key has been hit and instructs the sampler to replay the correct sound.

This is fine for instruments that have a finite note duration such as percussion instruments, but for instruments that are capable of sustained note length, such as brass, woodwind or strings, a method had to be found to allow for variable note duration as well as variable dynamic. The method most commonly used allows the user to select a part of the sampled sound for looping. A sustained note played on a violin will have a beginning, or attack, a period where the note is held, or sustained, and an end, where the bow is lifted from the string. To sustain a note for an indefinite period, the violinist must continually move the bow back and forth on the string, usually applying a degree of vibrato with the finger holding down the string being bowed. In a sampler, the operator has the facility to select a section of the held note for looping, or repeating, until a note-off instruction is received from the device controlling the sampler. The operator may then choose to let the end of the sample play, or to let the sound decay according to another set of parameters.

The operator is also given the ability to change the dynamic of a sample by altering values relating to the envelope superimposed on a sample. The term 'envelope' refers to the way in which a particular instrument produces a sound. It is usually described in terms of four components: attack, decay, sustain and release (or ADSR). A single note on a piano, struck hard, has a fast attack, a fast decay, a sustain that depends on whether the sustain pedal is held down, and a release (or off-time) that depends on whether the damper is released; so the envelope characteristics are variable. Having specified an envelope, further alterations of the sound may be carried out by relating the pitch of the sound to its envelope. A sound that builds slowly from silence, may also gradually increase or decrease in pitch as it does so; similarly, a slow die-away may be accompanied by a slow rise or fall in pitch, depending on how the parameters are set within the sampler. A low-frequency oscillator may also be employed to control pitch in a cyclical manner, thus giving the effect of vibrato.

It is also possible to send a particular sound to a specific output of the sampler. Most samplers have multiple outputs so that groups of sounds can appear at specified inputs to a mixing desk. For example, stereo string sounds could appear at outputs one and two, whilst brass and woodwind could be routed to outputs three and four respectively; a lead guitar could output to channel five, bass to channel six, and stereo percussion to seven and eight. Most samplers will allow multiple sets of samples to be played together, restricted only by the number of separate sounds or voices that sampler can produce at any one time.

The latest generation of samplers will allow 256 'voices' or individual sounds to be routed to any of sixteen outputs at any one time, with up to 256 Mbytes of RAM available to hold these in the memory. This may seem more than enough, but in complex musical arrangements, two or more samplers may be required to fulfil the needs of the composer.

As well as storing samples in random access memory, modern samplers allow the playback of sounds directly from an internal or external hard-disk, thus removing the 'limited memory' problem and giving, in the case of the Akai 6000, playback of up to eight simultaneous hard-disk files alongside the notional 256 RAM-based samples, out of a choice of sixteen outputs.

There are many other ways in which the sampled sound may be manipulated and subsequently controlled from an external device such as a keyboard, or a music sequencer running alone or on a computer, and the final disposition of all the variables available to the operator can be recorded as a program and saved to disc for later recall.

In order to see how this technology is of use to the theatre sound designer, simply replace samples of musical instruments with sampled sound effects. Imagine a musical keyboard with a different sound for each key pressed: twelve different thunder claps spread across the first twelve keys, a continuous rain loop that plays for as long as the key is held down, crickets on another key, and dogs barking and growling on two others. Now imagine that you can spread a whole symphony of wind across the entire keyboard, with a different pitch or speed of wind for each key; and with the aid of a sampler that allows you to layer one program on top of another, you could have a second keyboard to play thunder, rain and animals, and yet a third to control the replay of musical sounds! This is exactly the way that many theatre sound designers prepare and replay their soundtracks, using computer programs rather than music keyboards. Some composer/designers generate the music for the show from samplers and produce the entire music and effects soundtrack this way, with complex music sequencer packages giving fine control over both music and effects playback.

There is an historical precedent for producing music and effects in this way using a piece of equipment known as the Mellotron. This was a keyboard instrument that used magnetic tape stored in its cabinet. Pressing a key was the equivalent of starting a tape player: a pinch roller and a constantly rotating capstan that ran the length of the machine were held together and the magnetic tape sandwiched in between was dragged past a replay head until the key was released. A spring-loaded pulley then dragged the tape back to the start, ready for the next key press. Typically, each tape held three sounds, and a mechanical linkage moved the replay head into a position that determined which of the three sounds were replayed. Initially developed for replacing large string, brass, woodwind or choirs for rock groups on tour, the devices met with much adverse reaction from the Musicians' Union and were not widely used, Their use in sound effects work for film and television was possibly slightly more prolonged.

MIDI

The degree of flexibility and control offered by samplers, synthesisers and a vast number of processing devices, is made possible by the use of a standard protocol for the transmission of data between them. This is known as the Musical Instrument Digital Interface, or MIDI, and as the name suggests, it was originally developed as a means to allow electronic musical instruments to interface with one another easily. Each note on the musical scale is allocated a unique number from 0 to 127 (or 1 to 128 if the instrument is Japanese in origin). The strength at which the note on a keyboard is hit is also given a value from 0 to 127. So middle C, hit as hard as possible, will have a note-on MIDI value of 60 and a MIDI velocity of 127. MIDI data can be transmitted over sixteen separate channels, with each channel able to carry data relating to the following parameter: note-on, note-off, key velocity, polyphonic key-pressure (sometimes called after-touch), control change, program change and pitch-bend. In addition, the MIDI standard allows for the transmission of time data (MIDI Time Code) and data relating specifically to a particular manufacturer (System Exclusive).

Other items that can come under MIDI control include signal processing devices such as reverberation and echo units, graphic equalisers, digital delays, audio patch bays and digital attenuators. In fact, most items of professional audio equipment with user-variable controls now offer remote variation of some, if not all, of those controls via a MIDI interface. The list now includes some theatre lighting boards and accessories as well. What started as a means of communication between synthesisers has now matured into a useful means of complete system control.

Hardware devices exist to allow channelling of MIDI information from a computer music sequencer through extra MIDI ports, allowing over 100 separate MIDI channels to be addressed at once (software and computer power permitting). Additional devices are available to allow MIDI control of non-MIDI replay machines such as CD players, tape machines, laser disc players and video recorders. More information on MIDI is given in the next section of the book, and additional documentation of both the MIDI and MIDI Show Control systems in included is the Appendix.

Putting Together a Soundtrack Using Samplers

Using a sampler for creating and reproducing sound effects requires a very different way of working from conventional methods. First, it is necessary to prepare and load the raw material into the sampler. Given that the sampler's memory is volatile, i.e. if the power is removed, the samples will not be retained in the memory, the material must be saved to a more permanent storage medium, either floppy-disks, or a mass storage device such as a Winchester-type hard-disk, either fixed or removable, or a magneto-optical hard-disk cartridge. The mass storage devices are preferable to floppies, simply because access time is much faster, and large amounts of data can be stored on one drive.

Some samplers have the ability to store samples in Flash-ROM, a type of memory that will retain the stored information when the power is removed, but can easily be overwritten if required.

Different samplers use different conventions for recording samples, but in general you will be able to choose the sampling rate at which you record, how much space you want the sample to occupy, expressed as minutes and seconds, and to set the recording level for the incoming signal. High-quality samples will take up a great deal of memory and disk space, so care is needed in deciding what to sample. As a rough guide, one minute of mono audio at the sampling rate of 44.1 kHz will occupy 5 Mbytes of disk space. Such a sample is too long to fit on a floppy disk, and must be stored on a hard-disk. For stereo samples, it is necessary to double the storage space requirements.

Most samplers provide useful tools to allow samples to occupy a smaller amount of space than would normally be the case. It is possible to define a loop within a sample so that it will repeat until a note-off command is received. In the case of a tolling bell, or a background of crickets, for example, it is only necessary to record a short section of the sound, and then to instruct the sampler to loop between a pair of defined points. Multiple loops are also available, so that a section of a sound may be looped for a certain length of time, then a further loop may be defined between a second pair of loop points, then a third, and a fourth, until the limit is reached. Thus, a short thunder rumble may be turned into a much longer one by defining multiple loop points within the original sample.

Time stretch and compression functions are included, as well as the ability to mix two samples together to form a third, or to join two samples end to end, with user-determined start and stop points. Selective editing of samples, allowing the user to remove sections from the middle of a sample and save the result, or to copy a section of a sample, is also available, as is the ability to carry out tonal correction and to scale the level of a sample up or down, although scaling up will also increase any unwanted noise as well as the wanted signal.

Once all samples have been prepared, identified and stored, the next part of the procedure can start. This involves preparing a program which will contain a number of keygroups. A keygroup can consist of a single note or a group of notes on a notional keyboard to which an individual sample, or group of samples, can be assigned. This may sound complicated, but it is quite easy in practice.

For example, a keygroup is created and assigned to the note middle C, or MIDI note 60. It is then possible to assign a sample to this note, say a pistol shot. Anytime the note middle C is played on a keyboard connected to the sample via MIDI, the sampler will play the sound of a pistol shot. More than one sample can be assigned to a note, either to play at the same time or at different key velocities, for example a quiet thunder rumble might be assigned to MIDI note 24 to be played at a key velocity of 0–30. A second, louder clap can be assigned to the same note, to be played at a key velocity of 31–62. A third and still louder clap for key velocities between 63 and 94, and a final cataclysmic clap at velocities from 95–127. If the key is struck gently, then the first clap will play, if slightly harder, then the second, if harder still, then the third, and at the hardest, the fourth clap. If a keygroup is created and assigned to more than one note, it is possible to vary the pitch of the sample depending on which note is pressed, thus creating instant pitch variations of the original sound.

Each MIDI note can have a sample or group of samples assigned to it, giving a total of 127 different effects per MIDI channel. More programs may then be constructed with different keygroups using different sound effects, up to the limit of the sampler. In the case of the Akai S6000, this is ninety-nine programs. Using the MIDI program change command, it is then possible to select a new program, or group of programs, and therefore a new set of effects, from either a keyboard or computer controller.

It is possible to modify the way in which a sample is played back from within a keygroup; pitch and loudness may be altered, a filter may be employed, and the envelope of the sound may be changed, so that a sample with an abrupt start may be tailored to fade in slowly.

It is also possible to apply pitch variations depending on a second envelope generator. Setting a long, slow attack and a long, slow release, and then applying this envelope to the pitch of the sample can result in a slow increase in pitch as the note-on command is given, followed by a slow decrease when the note is released.

One example utilising looping, envelope alteration and pitch variation via envelope, was the use of a multi-sample for the sound of an airship in Shaw's play *Heartbreak House*. The airship sound consisted of a short sample of an aircraft engine, slowed down and mixed with a sample of two cellos playing a low drone. The pitch of the cellos was matched to the pitch of the aircraft engine, and then looped within the sampler. All elements were kept as separate samples, but assigned to the same keygroup so that relative levels could be altered as required. During the course of the action, the airship has to start and stop its engines, so a decrease in pitch and level was required for stopping the engines, and an increase in pitch and level for the start-up. A loop was established for the drone, so that only a short sample needed to be held in memory, and an envelope with a slow attack and long release was programmed so that the drone would slowly increase in volume at the note-on message, and then decrease in level when the note-off command was received.

A second envelope controlling the pitch of the drone was also programmed, also with a long attack and decay. As the envelope ramped up, so the pitch of the drone increased, until, as the note was held, it reached a steady volume and a steady pitch. When the note was released, the pitch slowly fell, as did the volume. Similar methods may be use to simulate the effect of police sirens approaching and passing, or any form of machinery starting up or slowing down.

A keygroup may also contain information about how the sample should be replayed: whether the loop points set at the recording stage should be ignored, or whether the loop should continue until the note-off command is given, or continue during the decay time set for the sample envelope. Although this facility was intended for musical purposes, it can be extremely useful in effects work.

For example: In *Othello*, an alarm bell is rung after a fight between Cassio and Montano. Othello enters, and some lines later says the line, 'Silence that dreadful bell . . .' If the bell is on tape, the operator has to make sure that the fade-out between chimes is clean so that the natural die-away of the bell is preserved. This invariably sounds false, as the final die-away will always be much longer than the gap between chimes, but if the effect is of a fixed length there is always the possibility that something may occur to lengthen the action, in which case Othello's line may well be said in silence.

The sampler provides an easy solution. A sample is recorded of a bell tolling three times, with a natural start and end. A loop of the middle bell chime is programmed, and the sampler is instructed to play the sample, looping the middle chime until the note-off command is received. At that point, the remaining part of the sample, i.e. the natural decay of the last chime, is played. Thus the effect has a natural beginning, a middle section that is as long as is required, and a natural, untruncated end.

Most samplers have more than one output. The most basic stereo sampler has two outputs, and the more advanced samplers have eight or, in the case of an Akai S6000, sixteen. Each sample can be assigned to an individual output, giving immense flexibility for replay purposes. The sampler can be thought of as providing sixteen mono sources, eight stereo sources, or one sixteen-track source, or any combination in between. These combinations can change from cue to cue, and the sampler can also be used as a music source, if required.

Collections of samples assigned to their various keygroups are contained in a program, and the MIDI channel on which each program receives its MIDI information is determined by the user. For example, the programmer may wish to arrange all weather sound effects under one program, or to split them up into a series of programs, one for thunder, one for rain and one for wind, with each program assigned to a different MIDI channel. Splitting programs in this way makes accessing and editing the information much easier and keeps like samples grouped together.

There is another advantage to this way of working, as many samplers have inbuilt effects such as reverberation, delay, and pitch and phase change, that can be applied to programs rather than samples. Each program can have a specific effect applied to it, which will affect all samples held in that program. Many variations on these processes are possible, with programs and samples overlapping for complex layering of sound. Attempting to control this from an actual musical instrument keyboard would require the skill and dexterity of a concert pianist, and, in the case of multiple MIDI channels, would require as many keyboards as MIDI channels used, which is why the MIDI control programs are so vital to the use of samplers in theatre sound.

Computers and MIDI

Triggering of samples, control of other hardware, and altering system parameters via MIDI used to be a complex matter involving several different controllers, devices for merging the MIDI data and a tangle of cables and interface boxes. With the continuing development of MIDI-related computer software, it has become possible for most functions to be controlled from within one computer program. The normal method of transmitting MIDI data for use in musical applications is via a keyboard controller or a computer program known as a sequencer. It is possible to utilise these devices for theatre applications, but the interface between operator and controller can often be intimidating and unnecessarily complex. A number of manufacturers have produced programs for originating and manipulating MIDI data specifically for theatre applications, and these are available on a variety of computing platforms. I shall examine several such programs in the following section, and although these are by no means the only programs available, they should give the user an idea of how different types of programs can be used in theatre effects work.

In the early days of using MIDI for theatre, a number of sound designers opted to use software programs mainly intended for creating computer and sampler based music, often known simply as 'sequencers'. Of these, a program called Vision, and its more complex partner Studio Vision, found favour with a number of designers, particularly in the UK, for the extremely versatile and complex processes which could be achieved through its use. The fact that sequences could be triggered at random by assigning them to 'hot-keys' on the computer keyboard gave a degree of flexibility to the program that was much sought after – although the use of key combinations after the initial set of keys had been used up sometimes led to confusion. The need to assign sequences to a special module, called a Player, in order to run more than one at a time could also give rise to problems. Other music sequencer programs were also used in theatres, but the increasing sophistication of programs specially written for theatre has seen this use decline somewhat in recent years.

Many complex shows were created using music sequencers, however, and the addition of hard-disk based recording and playback in synchronisation with the MIDI data made them an extremely powerful tool for sound designers. The ability of the more sophisticated programs like Vision to incorporate MIDI System Exclusive commands and MIDI Machine Control commands made them versatile, if not particularly intuitive, show-controllers. At the time of writing, there is some doubt over the future of Vision, but other sequencer programs offer many of the same facilities and may continue to be used to great effect.

The Commodore Amiga-based Richmond Sound Design Stage-Manager program used in many theme parks and theatres as a show control program, has been replaced by ShowMan from the same company, running under the Windows NT operating system. This is a highly advanced show control program that is able to control multiple devices, using standard MIDI commands, MIDI Machine Control (MMC) commands, MIDI Show Control (MSC) commands,

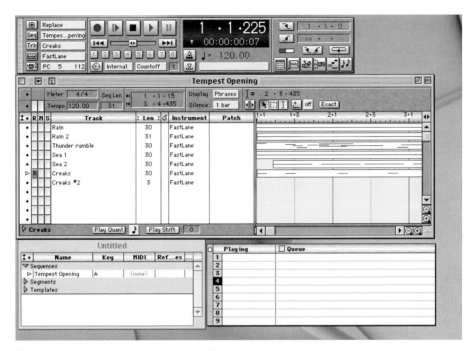

Figure 52 *A typical sequence in 'Vision'.*

and MIDI System Exclusive (SysEx) commands. Multiple cue lists, up to thirty-two if required, and a central control panel make this one of the most versatile show control programs available, and the company has a policy of continuous development in response to the wishes of its users.

Each cue in a list can be either a single event or a complex sequence, and there is no limit to the number of sequences that can be running at the same time, subject to equipment limitations. Using MSC commands, it is possible for cues in one list to trigger events in other lists, or in the same list, making looping extremely simple, and allowing the user to build a library of cues or sequences in one list that are easily called up by a single command from another list. ShowMan also features plug-ins for controlling many other devices via MIDI, RS 232/442 and Ethernet networks, as well as the ability to control an on-board CD-ROM player for playback of audio CDs.

Cue timing is either via the internal system clock, MIDI Time Code (MTC), or a real-time clock, allowing the user to program events to happen at certain times of day.

Matt McKenzie's MIDI Control Program (MCP, sometimes known as G-Type) is written for the Intel-based range of computers, running either under the MS-DOS operating system or Windows 98, and has a screen display based on modules that can be added or removed as required. As all information relevant to a cue or sequence of cues is displayed on screen at the same time, there is no problem about screen updates. The program incorporates a number of special

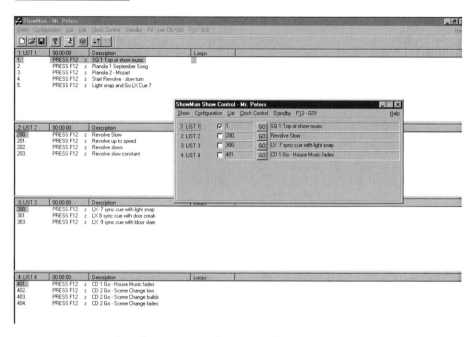

Figure 53 *Screenshot from RSD's ShowMan show control program.*

commands that allow the control of a number of non-MIDI devices, such as cartridge machines, tape recorders and CD players, and in the case of the Denon and Tascam pro CD players, frame-accurate location of cue points can be achieved.

Movement around the modules is effected via the computer keyboard or mouse, with event triggering being via purpose-built remote, or keyboard commands. Help screens are available for each part of the program. A version is available that will allow control of certain aspects of some CADAC mixing desks, including channel muting, VCA assignment and labelling and desk memory recall. System Exclusive commands may be included in cues, and Standard MIDI Files (SMF), where all MIDI information pertaining to a complete musical performance can be stored in a standard file, can also be imported and played back as part of a cue. Currently, MCP allows the user to have up to eight sequences running simultaneously.

This program is unique in that it is possible to load the same program and cue list on to two linked PCs and have the second machine track the actions of the first. In the event of a computer failure, the operator is automatically at the right place on the second machine.

Richard Bleasdale's SAM (Sound and MIDI) program is another show control program, this time running on the Apple Macintosh range of computers. It offers similar facilities to ShowMan and MCP and also offers plug-ins to allow direct control of a range of other devices that accept MIDI, MMC and MSC

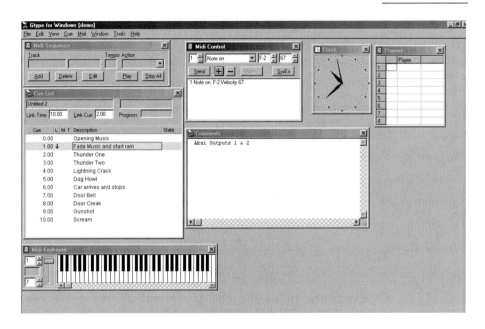

Figure 54 *Matt McKenzie's G-Type for Windows.*

commands. Like the other programs, the software is continually updated to reflect the ever-expanding range of equipment available to the technical theatre practitioner.

Stage Research's SFX program (see page 63) is finding favour with an increasing number of designers in the UK and USA, as it runs under Windows and is able to use multiple computer-hosted sound-cards to play back audio stored as .WAV files on the computer's hard-disk, as well as sound from CD-ROM. MIDI implementation is also included, as are MSC commands and the ability to synchronise with MIDI Time Code. The program can be configured to be as simple or as complex as the designer requires, at its simplest taking the form of a series of on-screen 'Go' buttons to fire specific cues; at its most complex it is a complete cue-list based show control system.

As previously stated, there are a number of other programs running on Apple Macintosh or Windows-based system that have their merits, but those mentioned above are used regularly on West-End and Broadway shows and have long pedigrees as theatre sound control software.

To use a sampler successfully, the designer must have a thorough working knowledge of MIDI, as well as being conversant with the workings of the sampler and control program being used. Instruction manuals for these devices are often aimed at the non-technical user, and can omit much useful information. If the designer is unfamiliar with the equipment, then a period of acclimatisation should be allowed for in the pre-production period.

For further information, see the MIDI Manufacturers Association (MMA) information sheet 'What is MIDI?' in Appendix C.

Editing

Inevitably, you will have to edit your recordings. Editing effects is fairly straightforward, and the chances are that you will be far more likely to be editing digital audio, using either computer-based editing software such as Digidesign's ProTools, BIAS's Peak, MacroMedia's SoundEdit, SoundForge, and so on, or in a sampler or MiniDisc recorder. It's also possible that you may be using reel-to-reel analogue tape and a razor blade so a brief description for this technique is also included.

If you're working with a computer-based system, what you will normally see is a screen display of the wave-form, and you will be able to use all the cut and paste trickery that your particular program offers. These programs are the audio equivalent of a word-processor; they allow you to do far more than simple edits. You can copy and repeat sections of the audio, reverse them, change the level, add effects and change the tonal quality, perform pitch-change and time stretch functions and do many other weird and wonderful things that previously required a battery of separate pieces of equipment. It's not within the scope of this book to examine all the possible permutations of editing hardware/software that are available, so the examples will be based on the ProTools program used in recording studios throughout the world.

Editing any sound effects that you may be using is often a simple matter of trimming the front and end of the sound, and cutting out any extraneous and unwanted noise that has found its way into your recording. An example would be a recording of a street atmosphere with a car horn sounding part way through. As the track is to be used as a basis for a loop, the car horn needs to be removed so that it does not repeat irritatingly at regular intervals. In ProTools, it is simply a matter of highlighting the offending area of the wave-form and hitting the 'delete' key on the keyboard. Once the sound has been removed, you can butt the two remaining wave-forms up against one another, or, if required, perform a cross-fade so that there is no sudden change in level and the two sounds merge. Unless you specify otherwise, ProTools is a non-destructive editor; in other words, the audio you remove will not be destroyed but will be skipped by the computer when you play your track back. If you change your mind, you can get it back and try again.

If you were to try this using a splicing block and razor blade, the technique would be as follows. With the tape machine in edit mode, i.e. with the tape in contact with the replay head but the reel motors off, move the tape past the replay head slowly, rotating the take-up spool until the beginning of the sound is heard from the monitoring loudspeakers. Then reverse the direction of the tape by moving the feed spool until the sound disappears. Of course, you'll be listening backwards, but you should still be able to determine when the sound starts and stops. Continue this process, rocking the spools slowly backwards and forwards until you have found the exact point at which the sound starts. Then, using a wax pencil (the white or yellow Chinagraph pencils are best for this), mark a thin vertical line on the backing of the tape at the centre of the replay head. Now move the tape on past the replay head until you find the end of the sound that you want to remove, and repeat the process.

Remove the tape from the machine and lay it in the splicing block, taking care that it is held firmly in the grooves. Position the first wax pencil mark so that it is level with the top of the cutting guide by carefully sliding the tape along the block. Now use the single-sided razor blade to make a clean cut in the tape. Find the second mark and repeat the process. Discard the piece of tape that you have extracted, but resist the temptation to destroy it, because if you've made a mistake you're going to have to put it back in. Butt the two ends of the tape together and cut a small piece of special splicing tape from the reel and apply it to the centre of the join, rubbing the splice lightly with a fingernail to ensure that all air bubbles have been removed. Peel the joined tape out of the block, rethread the tape in the machine and play through the splice to check that it's good. If it's not, you'll need to start again. Repeat this process until you have removed all unwanted parts of the audio, and then, if the tape is to be used in a production, it's probably wise to make a copy on fresh, unedited tape.

Although I enjoy editing with a block and blade, it's a time-consuming and messy business; computer-based editing is a much more desirable method.

Speech Editing

Editing speech is not as easy as it might appear. The usual reason for wanting to edit speech recordings is to remove mistakes, long pauses or material that's not relevant. The tricky part is to make sure that the resulting speech still has a natural sounding rhythm. Speakers will normally take a breath at the beginning of each sentence, for example, and it's important that these are retained. Similarly, cutting out all 'um's and 'er's can often make a speech sound too perfect, especially if the recording is of a real person rather than an actor.

Soft consonants such as 'h', 's', 'w', and 'y' can also cause problems in editing, as it is all too easy to miss the very start and end of the sound and intelligibility will suffer. Figure 55 shows the waveform produced by speaking the words 'window' and 'tart' and illustrates how care needs to be taken to ensure that the edit points are exact.

It may be that you are required to edit out an extraneous sound that occurs in a pause in speech recording, but to maintain the length of the pause. To avoid a noticeable gap in the recording, it will be necessary to edit in some 'clean' background sound from another part of the recording, and it is always sensible to record a minute or so of 'room-tone' – the naturally occurring sounds in the room in which the recording is being made – during any speech recording session so that it can be used to cover any such edits.

The best way to perfect speech editing is to practise with a variety of different

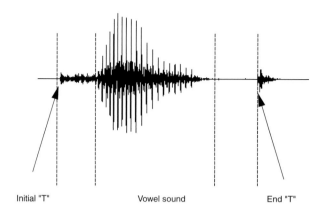

Initial "T"   Vowel sound   End "T"

Figure 55a *Waveform for the word 'tart'.*

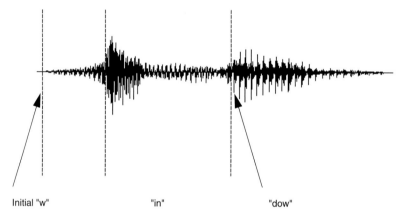

Initial "w"   "in"   "dow"

Figure 55b *Waveform for the word 'window'.*

speakers and to try and maintain the distinctive speech patterns for each. It's frequently possible to hear really bad speech editing on radio news programmes, where edits have to be performed extremely quickly to meet deadlines and finesse suffers because of time constraints.

Music Editing

Music editing in the classical recording world is normally the preserve of the producer, who may work with a specialist editor to assemble the best possible performance out of a number of takes. The advances in digital editing are such that it is possible to replace single notes in a performance, but usually the producer is more concerned with capturing complete performances and may only resort to this type of editing if an extraneous noise intrudes on what is otherwise a perfect take. It may also be the case that a take is perfect except for one or two

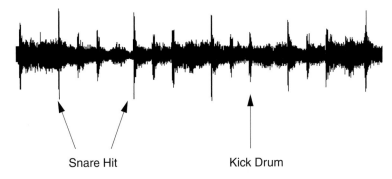

Snare Hit   Kick Drum

Figure 56 *Rock music edit points.*

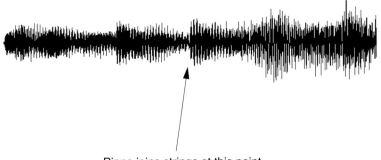

Piano joins strings at this point

Figure 57 *Classical music edit point.*

mistakes, and in order to rectify these without recording the entire piece again, the sections are rerecorded and edited in to the master take. The producer will sit in the control room with the recording engineer and a copy of the score, having discussed the performance with the performers, and will take careful note of how each take progresses. He or she will mark the score when mistakes occur and will liaise with the engineer to make sure that recording process captures the performance faithfully.

In theatre work, this level of editing may well be needed if you are recording music specially for a production and do not have the time to do retakes. However, it is more likely that you will be required to carry out simpler tasks, such as shortening or lengthening a piece of music, or jointing two pieces together. Over the years I have 'rewritten' a great deal of pre-recorded music in order to make it fit in with the production. With most popular music, this is a relatively easy task; simple song structures, simple time signatures and a strong drum rhythm make identifying edit points very simple. Removing a verse or a chorus from a pop song is usually extremely easy, as is adding an extra section. Figure 56 is a stereo track taken from a rock album, and the repetitive nature of the drums is easy to see: the snare drum hit comes on the second and fourth beat of each bar and provides an excellent editing point reference.

Figure 57 shows a more complex music format: visually and aurally identifying likely edit points is much more difficult, and it can take a great deal of time and patience to edit a piece of complex classical or jazz music so that an audience does not notice the join. Tempo and key changes can cause problems when editing more complex music, and at least a basic understanding of musical form is necessary if more advanced editing is to be undertaken.

Digital editing using a Digital Audio Workstation allows a great deal more freedom than tape-based editing or editing on a MiniDisc, where simple cut and join techniques are the only ones available. A computer-based system allows pieces of music to overlap during the editing process, and the construction of the cross-fade, i.e. how one piece of music fades out and how the other fades in, can be specified by the user. As most of these systems are non-destructive, the user can experiment with edits without fear of ruining the original music.

Integrating Sound Effects into a Production

Having gathered or prepared all the sound effects and music required for a production, the next stage is to make sure that they become an integral part of the show, and not just a series of sounds dropped in at the last moment. Some shows will be appear to be simple: music at the top and end of each act, a couple of spot effects of dogs barking, a telephone ringing in another room, a toilet flushing and a baby crying. No problems there, except of course that the toilet flush and the off-stage telephone are at different sides of the stage, the dog barks need to come from a position at the rear of the set as though outside the window, the baby crying is supposed to be in an upstairs room (the set has three solid walls, a perspex window and a ceiling piece), all the sound effects come as a sequence, one on top of the other, in response to various lines from the actors, and as the cacophony of dog, baby, telephone and toilet flush rises to a crescendo, the final curtain music starts on stage and gradually builds to the proscenium loudspeakers, climaxing with a final triumphal chord as the house curtain descends.

Immediately, we have six separate locations for sound, counting the proscenium system as a left/right pair, a need for five different sounds to be cued in precisely on time and then to run continuously, and separate level build times for the sound effects and the music. So a show that, on paper, seems to have four sound effects and some music, has turned into a nightmare that requires three hands to operate it. This is by no means an exaggeration; many straight plays have operational requirements that greatly exceed the ones described above, and part of being a sound designer is to know how to achieve these requirements in a way that seems effortless.

At the other end of the scale, some shows will require a mixture of realistic sound effects, mood-creating impressionistic soundscapes, music underscore, long sound effect background tracks, curtain-up and scene-change music and live microphone cues. And, just like the few effects described in the first example, these will all need to be played in at the right time, at the appropriate level and from the right location. Too loud or too busy and the mood created by the actors will be destroyed; too quiet and the audience will wonder why they can't hear the sound of the cherry orchard being chopped down when everyone on stage keeps referring to it; too late and the actor who has to rush off stage to answer the phone will have to improvise his way around the fact that it hasn't rung when it should; from the wrong location and the audience will wonder why the car has driven up outside in what is constantly referred to as the river.

The process of getting these things right requires a combination of the skills of the designer and the skills of the operator, and unless the show is completely automated, those two skills are vital to the production. I have to say that I have, at times, automated shows to the extent that the operator has no involvement other than pressing a button at the correct moment, and the sound equipment currently available makes this a viable possibility. Usually this has been for purely economic reasons; the producer cannot or will not afford the services of a skilled operator, or any operator at all, and the job is given to an assistant stage-manager who is also responsible for props and for understudying one of the minor roles. In many cases, however, the operator becomes as important a part of the production as any of the actors and needs to have a similar set of skills.

The designer's skill lies in being able to understand what is required from a production and then using both technical knowledge and artistic interpretation to create a sound world that fits the show. This is possibly the biggest challenge facing a sound designer, and I believe that it is as valid for simple productions as it is for the most complex. The problem is that sound is completely subjective; no two people will necessarily agree on what constitutes the right sound, or the right level, or the right piece of music for a particular show, or section of a show, and very often the sound designer has to achieve a compromise that satisfies all concerned in the production, including the audience. After a while, there is a danger that caution will prevail and that the sound designer will always go for safe options, for tricks and techniques that he or she knows will work, and sometimes this is a perfectly valid option, but the real magic happens when risks are taken and they pay off. This is true for all aspects of theatre, not just sound, and there is a great temptation to push that bit further with each new show. But unless there is a discipline in place that tells you that you don't push further without explaining to those involved why you want to do it, and that stops you from going too far too often, the result tends to be the opposite of what you intended.

Sometimes, the push comes from a director, sometimes from an actor, some-times from a composer – they all have a right to comment on things that you are doing that affect them, and in many cases their suggestions may be something that hasn't occurred to you. It's not a one-way process, either, although giving a leading actor notes on his or her interpretation is not always a sensible idea. Theatre is all about collaboration and, with some exceptions, suggestions made by members of the creative team can crack a particularly difficult problem simply because a view is given by someone who is not directly involved.

In a production of *Romeo And Juliet* for the Royal Shakespeare Company, the director, Michael Attenborough, wanted an almost continuous background track of crickets. This request started me thinking about the different patterns of noise made by different insects at different times of day, and I devised a constantly changing background track of crickets and other insect sounds that varied depending on the time of day, the location and the action, so that during the fight scenes, when there was a great deal of shouting and running around, the insect track stopped almost completely, to be replaced with the barking of dogs from all around the stage. After Tybalt is stabbed and dies, the sound of flies buzzing around the corpse faded in slowly to an almost imperceptible level and the different cricket chirps started up again as the play progressed. In Juliet's house, during the daytime, a single cricket chirped in the foreground whilst a muted chorus of crickets and insects could be heard outside the window. Michael encouraged me to be bold with these sounds, in the same way that he encouraged the lighting designer to be bold with the strength and colours of the lighting, and the entire production had an absolute sense of a hot, dusty town in Italy in high summer.

In *Macbeth*, a show that I have done ten times now, there is the sound of an owl that frightens Lady Macbeth whilst she is waiting for Macbeth to kill Duncan, and for the first time in a recent production I used two owl sounds – the first, a screech, caused the reaction 'Hark!', the second, a much more gentle call a few seconds later, gave the actress a reason to say the next words, 'Peace, it was the owl that shrieked ...' I introduced the second sound during a rehearsal without consulting either the actress or the director, but at a point where I knew that it would not cause a problem. The actress immediately got the idea and waited for the second sound before continuing and the cue stayed in. It was a small point, but one that I had never thought of before, and I think it helped the scene.

In the same production, I also used a variation on an idea that can be extremely useful for creating tension, or for adding atmosphere to a scene where dialogue is important, but spoken quietly – very low – frequency sound. In the case of *Macbeth*, it was a slowly changing, pitched drone, but at such a low frequency that it was felt rather than heard by the audience. It goes without saying that special low-frequency loudspeakers were available to me or the effect would simply not have worked, but once again it added a definite feeling of unease to certain scenes in the show, without being apparent as a sound effect.

In Racine's *Phaedre*, a character has to describe how a Sea God rises up out of the ocean and destroys another character. The director wanted to give both an aural and visual suggestion of the chain of events and used huge video projections of a specially made film on the tall windows of the palace and on to the white backcloth. The actor delivering the speech (which is three minutes long) used a very quiet, shocked tone of voice, but against this the director wanted a background sound that suggested the thunderous sounds that had accompanied the tragedy. Once again, the answer was to use a soundtrack with a great deal of low-frequency energy and I created a series of sounds that were based on waves crashing and monsters roaring, but that were played back at some two octaves below their normal pitch and had all the high-frequency content removed. Again, the force of the sounds was felt rather than heard by the audience, and the actor had no trouble in maintaining his quiet speech; indeed, the first time we ran the sequence he was barely aware that there was a soundtrack running at all.

In a production of *Measure For Measure*, the director was not happy with the way the show opened and was searching for an alternative. I suggested the sound of approaching footsteps and a series of doors slamming in a long echoey corridor, gradually building in level until the final door-slam cued the stage lights to snap up and the action began. I refrained from mentioning that I'd borrowed the idea from the opening of a television comedy series popular in the 1960s called *Get Smart*, however.

I have different methods of dealing with the many different directors, designers and composers that I work with, and experience has taught me how much I should push my ideas. I have worked with so-called 'old-school' directors who are working to tight schedules and have every cue mapped out in advance, and with other directors who have no ideas at all about a soundtrack for their show and want an enormous amount of creative input. In each case, the way in which everyone works will vary tremendously, and if I restricted myself to working with one specific type of director or production, then life would be very boring. Sometimes I surprise them, sometimes they surprise me, and quite often I surprise myself, which is possibly the most rewarding aspect of doing the job, but each show must be taken on its merits and the working method must change to reflect that. Flexibility and an open mind are the tools that will be the most use to any sound designer working in theatre.

Appendix A

Technical Information

The finer points of sound system design require a basic understanding of certain areas of maths and physics – this is the part of sound engineering that presents an often-insurmountable barrier to many would-be sound designers. With the detailed documentation provided with most modern sound equipment, it is tempting to ignore the maths and physics and simply put together a system using the building blocks of sound sources, mixing desk and treatment devices, amplifiers and loudspeakers, without having any technical knowledge at all, and indeed there are many designers who do precisely this. They rely on production sound engineers and rental companies to iron out the details.

This approach can sometimes work, but, like any other form of engineering, ignorance of the basics can lead to poor results, distortion and ultimately, system failure. It's very easy to construct a bridge across a stream using a convenient plank and make it relatively safe for one person to cross on foot, but only a fool would apply the same considerations to building a road or rail bridge across a deep river. So, if we're going to design systems that are functional, elegant, efficient and safe, we need to study the engineering involved.

I'm not about to turn this book into a maths or physics text-book, but I will cover some of the basic formulae that are usually required in putting together a sound system.

Ohm's Law

Ohm's Law states that in an electrical circuit, there is a relationship between the current (I) flowing through a device in that circuit , the voltage (V) across the device and the resistance (R) of the device. The formula for this law is simple and allows us to determine the value of any one of the three variables given the other two, thus:

$V = IR$ Voltage equals Current multiplied by Resistance
$I = V/R$ Current equals Voltage divided by Resistance
$R = V/I$ Resistance equals Voltage divided by Current.

Ohm's law also lets us calculate the power dissipated in a circuit (W) using the following formula:

$$W = I^2R = V^2/R = V \times I$$

This is all pretty straightforward when we're dealing with direct current (D.C.) in a simple circuit using a battery and a light-bulb, for example:

Given a 12 volt car battery and a headlamp bulb that produces 48 watts of power, the current flowing in the circuit and the resistance of the circuit can easily be calculated using the above formula:

$W = V \times I = 48 = 12 \times 4$. The current flowing is 4 amps.

Now, as resistance equals voltage divided by current, the next equation looks like this:

$R = V/I = R = 12/4$ The resistance of the circuit is 3 ohms.

Actually, this is not strictly accurate as the resistance will change somewhat as the temperature of the bulb filament increases, but it's sufficient for the current discussion.

In circuits that involve alternating current (A.C.), things get rather more complicated.

We need to state a voltage value for an cyclic voltage generator. This produces both positive and negative waveforms, like a microphone, which will dissipate the same power in a circuit as would a non-cyclic voltage generator such as a battery. The calculation to arrive at this in terms of a sine wave is to divide the peak voltage by the square root of 2, which simplifies down to multiplying the peak voltage by .707. The voltage arrived at is called the root mean square voltage, or r.m.s. Therefore, a sine wave that has a peak voltage of 10 volts over one complete cycle will give us a voltage of 7.07 volts r.m.s. to use in our calculation.

In addition, there are other components in audio systems that have a resistive effect on an alternating current. Capacitors and inductors both exhibit a frequency-dependent resistance known as reactance and the combined effect of these components along with resistance, gives us a new term, impedance, which is also measured in ohms.

Impedance matters in audio systems because it's important to ensure that one piece of equipment will pass its signal on to another piece in the chain with the maximum efficiency. Impedance mismatches can lead to increase in system noise and loss of signal level. Making sure that input and output impedances are correctly matched is an important part of designing a sound system.

Most modem microphones have an impedance value of a few hundred ohms and will be happy with a mixing desk that has an input impedance value which is the same or greater. Typically, most mixing desks have an input impedance of 3,000 ohms or greater.

Mixing desk output impedance's are usually 600 ohms, and the same rule applies, i.e. that they will deliver their maximum power when they are connected to the next piece of equipment with an input impedance that is the same or greater.

Most modern power amplifiers provide a very low source impedance and can be connected to loudspeakers with an impedance of 4, 8 or 16 ohms. The manufacturer should always indicate the amount of power that the amplifier will deliver for a stated input voltage with different loudspeaker impedances. The lower the impedance of the loudspeaker, the greater the power delivered by the amplifier.

The DeciBel

The deciBel, in its various manifestations is used throughout the audio industry and is the cause of more confusion than almost any other term. So why do we need it? Well, as we've discussed at the beginning of this book, the ear/brain can cope with a range of sound levels from the smallest whisper to the loudest rock band a ratio of around 5 million to one, and if we need to carry out calculations based on this range, we'd be dealing with huge and unwieldy numbers. The deciBel is a logarithmic expression that allows us to make calculations in audio systems much more simply. It also provides, in its various guises, references for making sure that equipment is matched in level as well as impedance.

What is a DeciBel?

Originally, the logarithmic expression of a ratio between two powers was called the Bel, after Alexander Graham Bell, but this resulted in numbers that were rather too large for convenience, so the deciBel, or one-tenth of a Bel was favoured instead. Note that, although I tend to use the older spelling, 'deciBel', 'decibel' is also acceptable. However, when abbreviating the term, 'dB' is preferable.

Let's look at the arithmetical progression involved and then see how the deciBel can help us in our calculations:

Taking 10 as our base number, if we multiply by a factor of 10, we get a progression that looks like this:

10
10 0
1,000
10,000
100,000
1,000,000

We can also express these numbers in exponential form as:

10, 10^2, 10^3, 10^4, 10^5, 10^6,

which is quicker to write, but still involves some pretty hefty calculations when multiplying or dividing. Logarithms let us express these large numbers in a simpler way and allow us to use addition and subtraction in place of multiplication and division. The definition of the deciBel is 10 times the logarithm to the base 10 of the ratio between two signal powers

or, dB = 10log(P1/P2) where P1 and P2 are the two powers.

For example: what is the power ratio between two amplifiers, one of 100 watts and one of 200 watts?

Using the formula, we get 10log(200/100) = 3dB

It's important to note that the deciBel relates to power and if we want to look at at voltages, we need to consider the relationship between voltage and power stated by Ohm's Law where Power (W) = V^2/R so the formula becomes:

dB = 10 log $(V1/V2)^2$ or 20 log(V1/V2)

Again, taking an example, what is the voltage gain we will achieve by doubling a signal voltage from 3 volts to 6 volts?

The formula gives us 20 log (6/3) = 6dB

We need to note that there is a difference between sound power and sound pressure: for our purposes, sound pressure relates to the amplitude of an acoustic signal and is therefore calculated using the 20 log (V1/V2) calculation.

Put simply, this means that doubling the voltage will give a voltage increse of 6dB and doubling the power will give a power increase of 3dB. This is true of any power and and any voltage: increasing the power of an amplifier from 10 to 20 watts will give the same result as increasing the power from 500 to 1000 watts – a change of 3dB. Increasing the voltage from 1 volt to 2 volts is the same as increasing the voltage from 10 volts to 20 volts – a change of 6dB.

dBu, dBm, dBV, dBA

More confusion comes when reading manufacturers' specifications and seeing the deciBel used in a different way, i.e. as an absolute expression of level, either electrical or acoustical power or voltage, rather than as a ratio between two powers or voltages. We can use the deciBel for this purpose, but we must state the reference as part of the expression. This is done by adding a qualifying suffix to the letters dB.

0dBu applies to a reference voltage level used in sound engineering to denote a voltage of .775 Volts rms irrespective of impedance. Signal levels above this are given a + prefix, and below it a – prefix. Most faders on mixing desks are marked with a 0dB point: this means that, with all other settings having been made correctly, the signal is passing through the desk at the reference level, with no gain, addition or reduction taking place.

The term 0dBm refers to a power level where 0dBm is equal to 1 milliwatt in a 600Ω resistive

150 dB	Jet engine at 1 metre
140 dB	Rock and Roll PA stack at 1 metre
130 dB	Threshold of Pain
120 dB	Pneumatic Drill
110 dB	Symphony Orchestra Forte Passage
100 dB	Train passing - close up.
90 dB	Heavy traffic
80 dB	Printing press
70 dB	City Street
60 dB	Noisy Bar or Restaurant
50dB	Open-plan office environment
40 dB	Normal conversation level
30 dB	Quiet office environment
20 dB	Quiet domestic environment
10 dB	Recording Studio
0 dB	Threshold of hearing in young adult

Figure 58 A rough guide to sound pressure levels, taking 0dB SPL as the threshold of hearing and 130dB SPL as the threshold of pain.

circuit. In older studio and broadcast equiment, 600Ω source and termination impedances were common and 0dBm could be regarded as a voltage of .775 V r.m.s.

Some manufacturers uses a reference voltage of 1 V r.m.s. irrespective of impedance, and in this case the reference level is termed 0dBV. Unfortunately, some engineers in the United States use dBv rather than dBu and this can lead to even more confusion.

When we want to express sound pressure level using the deciBel, we should add the qualifying suffix dB SPL. As the ear tends to react differently to certain frequencies depending on the sound pressure level, most devices for measuring the level of sound pressure have what's called a 'weighting network' included. This makes allowances for the anomalies in our ears. The most common of these is called an 'A-weighting' network. Measurements made using such devices should be written as 'XdB SPL A-weighted', but most manufacturers abbreviate this to 'XdBA'.

The Inverse Square Law and Acoustic Absorption

It's fairly obvious that the further away we get from a sound source, the quieter we perceive that sound to be. The law that relates to this is known as the inverse square law, because the intensity of the sound is inversely proportional to the square of the distance from the source. Sound radiates from a free-field vibrating point source as a sphere and the sound pressure level close to the source is concentrated over a small area of that sphere. The further away from the source one gets, the larger the area that the sound affects, but since the initial level is still the same, the sound becomes less intense. The maths involved in this calculation is complex, but the result is extremely simple: for each doubling of the distance from a source, the intensity of a sound will reduce by 6dB. This only holds true in free-field conditions, but it is useful rule of thumb in calculating level drop-off over distance: other factors must always be taken into account, such as the absorption of sound waves by the materials used in the construction and furnishing of the theatre and the set, and indeed the presence of an audience. Different materials absorb different amounts of acoustic energy and in some auditoria, special absorbers are installed to reduce the level of specific frequencies that may be artificially boosted by the shape of the building. Too much absorption in an auditorium can give rise to a space which is acoustically 'dead' and much time is spent fine tuning acoustics in new concert halls and theatres to arrive at a desirable amount of absorption. Absorption, reflection and the effects of the inverse square law all need to be considered when calculating the likely power requirements of a loudspeaker system in an auditorium of reasonable size.

Summary

I haven't gone into this subject in any great depth, because this book is intended to be an introduction to theatre sound and not a maths textbook, but it is important that at some stage in your education you develop a thorough understanding of the maths and physics involved in sound system design. The books listed in Appendix E are all highly recommended.

Appendix B

Documenting a Sound Design

For many reasons, producing a set of documents that show how your sound design goes together is a worthwhile proposition. There are several stages to this process, starting from the very first days of rehearsal, through to the final plans for archiving purposes once the show has opened. How you proceed with this depends on whether you are producing a design for a well-stocked repertory or festival theatre, or for a production in a fringe theatre, or for a major Broadway or West-End musical, or somewhere in between. Remember that others may need to read and be able to understand your paperwork, and that in future years you may also need to refer back to it yourself, so producing a comprehensive archive of every stage in your sound design can save you and others a great deal of time in the future.

Contractual Information

The designer, or the designer's agent, should have obtained a contract which is agreed and signed by the designer and the producer. The contract is a legally binding document and must be read carefully by the designer to ensure that he or she is able to perform the duties required as specified. If there are any exceptions or alterations that need to be made to the contract, these should be agreed by both parties and either written into a new contract, or appended to the original contract, and signed by both parties. In the unfortunate event of a dispute, the contract will be used as the definition of the duties of the designer and the employer so it's important to make sure that it is in order. Dates of productions can sometimes change radically, and it may be necessary under these circumstances for the designer either to leave the production or to arrange cover for times when he or she is not available. In these circumstances, the designer and the director may have to reach an acceptable compromise, but once again, this should be documented and signed by both parties.

Initial Design

The play-text should be your original reference document: many designers will place the script in a ring-binder so that they can insert notes, additional information or alterations, as well as cue sheets, initial speaker plots, music scores and equipment lists.

Once a basic form for the show begins to take shape, the designer can make a more definitive list of equipment that might be needed and this may be sent to a number of rental companies if the equipment is to be hired in. This is often referred to as the initial bid document and will be the basis of estimating the likely rental costs of the equipment for the run of the production.

At this stage, it should also be apparent, if the show is not a musical, whether the music is to be selected from commercially available sources or produced by the sound designer or a separate composer. If the former, then music sources should be researched, documented and offered to the director for comment. As soon as a decision is reached, the relevant licensing authorities should be contacted, listing the music under consideration and asking for preliminary clearance for use. If the music is to be specially composed, an idea of the number of musicians needed should be obtained, and a preliminary booking should be made for recording studio time, if required. All correspondence should state that these are preliminary bookings only, unless a firm date and time can be set at this point. A Musicians' Union approved fixer should be approached with details of the musical requirements and the possible dates of the recording session.

An initial budget can now be drawn up and circulated to the relevant parties for approval, i.e. finance department, production manager and to the producers if the show is a commercial venture.

As soon as a firm system design has been agreed, a revised equipment list should be sent to the approved rental company with a request for a revised rental cost. This list should include, as far as possible, all equipment, connecting cables, rigging equipment, electrical connection requirements, and any other items that may conceivably be required. Many rental companies will only supply exactly what the designer lists, while some others will make informed decisions on any extras that they think may be needed. If these items are not specified by the designer, they should be supplied on a goodwill basis and not charged to the show unless agreed by the designer.

If a production sound engineer is to be engaged, he or she should be provided with a copy of a plan and elevation drawing of the theatre and the stage settings, as well as a system drawing: this may take the form of a block diagram or schematic using recognisable symbols to represent the system design. It may also include a graphical representation of desk layout and equipment racks which should also be presented to the rental company providing the equipment so that they can build the system to the designer's exact requirements.

If the show is a musical, it may be necessary to produce a drawing of the orchestra pit with a suggested layout for the musicians, following discussions with the musical director. Microphone locations, stand types and seating can then be drawn on to the plan as required.

If the production is large, and involves patch-bays, then a patching plot should also be provided both to the production sound engineer and to the rental company. Any changes in the system should result in drawing revisions that are clearly marked and dated (e.g. Drawing 001, Revision 2 4/10/2001).

All drawings should include the name of the show, the producing company, the name of the venue and of the members of the creative team. Drawing scale should also be marked on the plan: in Europe and Canada, the standard scale is 1:25, whilst in the USA, the standard scale is 1:24.

Drawings should include a key which displays an example of each symbol used against its relevant device, with description and model number, if appropriate, along with any other special considerations;

e.g. Microphone: Neuman U87/Cardioid/10dB pad, LF cut.
   Loudspeaker: Meyer UPM1-P/local power via PowerCon connector required.

The system schematic should also show any special requirements for mixing desk and auxiliary equipment, although this may not be required on simpler shows.

In North America, The Canadian Standards Association Z99 'Graphic Symbols for Electrical and Electronics Diagrams Including Sound Equipment' has been acknowledged by the Sound Design Commission as the appropriate reference for graphic symbolism to be used in theatrical sound system drawings, although many designers choose to use their own set of symbols.

Once the set design is completed, the sound designer should, in consultation with the set and lighting designers, produce a detailed rigging plot for the loudspeaker system, showing horizontal and vertical placement and any special rigging requirements. Once finalised, this should be passed to the production sound engineer with copies to the production lighting engineer, master carpenter and flyman, if the nature of the system demands special rigging.

Sound and Music Sources

During the course of the rehearsal process, notes should be made of all relevant music sources, with details of composer, record company, performer, album and track titles and duration and use of music; i.e. whether pre-show, curtain up/drop and entre-act, or music used as part of the action (sometimes called interpolated music). Once the choice of music has been finalised, written details should be sent to the relevant licensing authorities. Ideally, this should happen before the production opens to the public, but this is not always possible, so preparations should be made for alternative pieces if permission is refused by a copyright holder. As previously mentioned, the process for clearing music for use in theatre performances is long and complicated, so as much time as possible should be allowed.

Sound effects sources should be documented, and, if location recordings are to be made, written permission should be obtained from property owners or administrators, along with any agreement over the payment of fees.

If music is to be specially recorded, detailed track-sheets should be kept of the recording session, detailing the recording system, sampling rate, if digital recording is used, track titles, track lengths, take numbers and an indication of 'best take'. If the recording is a multi-track, track disposition should also be noted. The musician's contractor or fixer should deal with the booking and payment of musicians and will provide details of any extra payments, instrumental doubling, porterage, etc., that may arise. A note of session start and stop times should be kept and agreed with the studio engineers at the end of the session.

Sampler Loading

If a sampler is to be used, the designer should maintain a list of samples, their relevant keygroups and sampler outputs, along with other information such as pitch change, envelope or looping parameters. A copy of the sampler's complete program parameters can usually be saved to a 3.5" floppy disc. The complete sample contents should be backed up to an external storage medium and updated as necessary. Magneto-Optical and removable cartridge drives are useful for this purpose.

Cue Sheets

A show's cue sheets should include the following information:
- Production title and venue
- Cue sheet number
- Cue number or name
- Type of execution, e.g. Go, Build, Fade, Stop, Preset
- Source, i.e. Sampler, CD, Mic.
- Source fader level at start and finish of action
- Master fader level
- Auxiliary send levels
- Channel routing including Pan Pot if necessary
- Duration of execution, e.g. snap, 5 seconds, etc.
- Any other notes, e.g. cue-line, visual cue, etc.

When the show is finished, all materials should be returned to the designer or the producers for archiving purposes. If the producers are to hold the archive, the sound designer should take a duplicate of all materials including all sound sources.

Appendix C

What is MIDI?

With thanks to the MIDI Manufacturers' Association:

MIDI stands for Musical Instrument Digital Interface and was developed by a number of manufacturers in the United States, Europe and the Far East to allow an easy exchange of information between electronic musical instruments of different manufacture. Before MIDI, there were a bewildering number of different protocols for transferring even the most basic information such as note pitch and duration and it is a tribute to the thoroughness with which the MIDI Manufacturers' Association (MMA) prepared the MIDI protocol that it has survived intact to the present. Various extensions to the original protocol, such as MIDI Time Code amd MIDI Show Control have been developed and offer almost limitless possibilities in controlling sound, lighting and many other aspects of theatre technology. There are three parts to MIDI: the communications protocol, or language; the hardware – connectors and interface, and a method of distributing MIDI via disk or telephony – the Standard MIDI File, or SMF.

Protocol

The MIDI protocol is an entire music description language in binary form. Every part of a musical performance can be broken down into a series of digital codes in binary form. Each note in a musical scale is assigned a specific number from 1 to 127 and in order to 'play' that note on a synthesiser or any other MIDI-controlled sound source, a 'note-on' message relating to that particular note must be transmitted from the controller, whether it be a computer program, a remote keyboard or another piece of MIDI-based equipment. To determine how loud the note is played, a 'velocity' message is sent, and finally, a 'note-off' message will turn the note off. So a complete MIDI message to play middle C on a synthesiser at maximum volume would consist of a binary string comprising the following information: 'NOTE ON – MIDI NOTE NUMBER 60 – VELOCITY 127 – NOTE OFF'. The information is transmitted serially, with the various parts of the message being sent one after the other to the receiving equipment. These chunks of information can be transmitted in real time, or stored in a computer program, known as a sequencer, for playback at a later date. The full MIDI protocol can cope with almost all the variables in a musical performance and includes variable controls for left/right panning of sounds, level, sustain, pitch and many others. Each one of these control variables is assigned its own unique controller number, with some of the most used being Controller 7 (which sets the overall volume of a sound), Controller 10 (which sets left/right panning), Controller 64 (which is the equivalent of the sustain pedal on a piano) and Controller 67 (which is the equivalent of the soft pedal on a piano). Controller 123 is reserved for a special 'ALL NOTES OFF' message which will cause any sound currently being produced to stop playing – a sort of 'emergency stop' function. Each controller has settings from 0 to 127, with 0 being an 'off' setting and 127 being a maximum setting. Exceptions are the controllers dealing with pitch and panning, where 64 is the central or normal position and numbers above or below 64 will either increase or decrease the pitch of a note, or cause the sound to come from left or right.

The complete MIDI protocol description is too long to be included here, but can be obtained from the MIDI Manufacturers Association at the address given in Appendix D.

Standard MIDI Files

Despite MIDI being a standard protocol, different sequencer manufacturers choose to store their information in their own formats. To enable a sequence prepared on one computer program to be played back on another, it's possible to save MIDI sequences in a form that is universally readable, that of the Standard MIDI File, or SMF. The SMF contains all the note on/off information and all other variables, but is also time-stamped so that the sequences will play back at the correct speed. Standard MIDI Files can be saved to disk for physical transportation between computers or synthesisers, but they can also be sent over the Internet, stored on CD-ROMs and embedded in computer games, or with computer-based movies or animations. As all that is being stored or transmitted is a relatively simple digital message, SMFs are very small and can be sent over the Internet extremely quickly and easily and then played back on the computer.

Hardware

The only approved connector for MIDI is the 5-pin DIN connector; the wiring is shown below. However, this connector is not particularly robust and the MMA may look at specifying an alternative connector when a later revision of the MIDI specification is released. The maximum cable length permitted is 15 metres, but in practice, providing a good quality twin screened cable is used, lengths up to 100 metres have been used with no problems. A number of companies make devices called MIDI Line Drivers that boost the MIDI signal for transmission over long distances, but these are not always reliable. It's worth trying without one before renting or buying a line driver. It's also common in theatre to make special MIDI converter cables which have a 5-pin DIN plug at one end and an XLR 3 male or female at the other. The MIDI signal can then be sent down balanced microphone lines and re-converted at the other end for connection to the remote piece of equipment.

As much of the work undertaken using MIDI in theatre sound involves computers, the interface between the computer and the MIDI device needs to be as robust as possible. Windows-based personal computers usually derive their MIDI signal either from a sound card or from a cable plugged into the serial port. Not all sound cards and adaptor cables comply with the electrical specification laid down by the MMA, and it's always worth buying a MIDI interface from a reputable source. The MIDI adapters costing a few pounds or dollars from your local music store are unlikely to be as reliable as a purpose-built MIDI interface from a reputable manufacturer.

Users of older Apple Macintosh computers have the advantage that MIDI sequencers and MIDI interfaces have been in production for far longer than for the Wintel-based PCs and a large number of reliable interfaces are available from a number of different manufacturers. The adoption by Apple of the Universal Serial Bus (USB) instead of a standard serial port has posed a problem recently, but more and more manufacturers are bringing out USB-based MIDI interfaces for both Macintosh and Wintel-based PCs.

As always, it is vital to test any control interface thoroughly well in advance of technical rehearsals, so that any potential problems can be identified and eliminated.

MIDI Show Control

The following is an edited version of the complete MIDI Show Control Specification and is included to give the reader an idea of the range of commands available to the user. For the full implentation of the standard, please write to:

MIDI Manufacturers' Association
PO Box 3173, La Habra, CA 90632-3173 USA
Tel: +1-310/947-8689 Fax: +1-310/947-4569

Introduction

The purpose of MIDI Show Control is to allow MIDI systems to communicate with and to control dedicated intelligent control equipment in theatrical, live performance, multimedia, audio-visual and similar environments.

Applications may range from a simple interface through which a single lighting controller can be instructed to GO, STOP or RESUME, to complex communications with large, timed and synchronised systems utilising many controllers of all types of performance technology.

The set of commands is modelled on the command structure of currently existing computer memory lighting, sound and show control systems. The intent is that translation between the MIDI Show Control specification and dedicated controller commands will be relatively straightforward, being based on the same operating principles. On the other hand, it has been assumed that translation will involve more than table look-up, and considerable variation will be found in data specifications and other communications details. In essence, MIDI Show Control is intended to communicate easily with devices which are designed to execute the same set or similar sets of operations.

Universal System Exclusive Format

MIDI Show Control uses a single Universal Real Time System Exclusive ID number (sub-ID #1 = 02H) for all transmissions between Controller and Controlled Device.

A guiding philosophy behind live performance control is that failures of individual Controlled Devices should not impair communications with other Controlled Devices. This principle may be implemented in either 'open-loop' or 'closed-loop' variations.

In open-loop control, no command responses from Controlled Device to Controller are specified or required. Open-loop control represents the most economical usage of communications bandwidth, and is fundamental to MIDI usage. MIDI Show Control includes open-loop practice for consistency with other Channel and System messages.

Closed-loop control, on the other hand, expects specified responses from Controlled Devices. Closed-loop practice requires more intelligent devices and uses more communications bandwidth, but provides more exact coordination between Controller and Controlled Devices. (The closed-loop implementation of MSC is currently under review.)

In this document, all transmitted characters are represented in hex unless otherwise noted. The initials 'msc' will be used to denote the new MIDI Show Control sub-ID #1 (= 02H).

The format of a Show Control message is as follows:

F0 7F <device_ID> <msc> <command_format> <command> <data> F7

Notes
1. No more than one command can be transmitted in a Sysex.
2. The total number of bytes in a Show Control message should not exceed 128.
3. Sysex's must always be closed with an F7H as soon as all currently prepared information has been transmitted.

Device Identification

<device_ID> is always a DESTINATION device address.

Commands are most often addressed to one device at a time. For example, to command two lighting consoles to GO, transmit:

    F0 7F <device_ID=1> <msc> <command_format=lighting> <GO> F7
    F0 7F <device_ID=2> <msc> <command_format=lighting> <GO> F7

<device_ID> values:

00-6F	Individual ID's
70-7E	Group ID's 1-15 (optional)
7F	'All-call' ID for system wide broadcasts

Every device must be able to respond to both an individual and the 'all-call' (7F) ID.

The group addressing mode is optional. A device may respond to one or more individual ID and one or more group ID. Both <device_ID> and <command_format> of a message must match the <device_ID> and <command_format> of a controlled device before the message is recognised.

If two separate controlled devices responding to the same <command_format> are set to respond to the same <device_ID> then only one message need be sent for both to respond.

The 'all-call' <device_ID> (7FH) is used for system wide 'broadcasts' of identical commands to devices of the same <command_format> (or to all devices when used with <command_format=all-types>).

Before fully interpreting the <device_ID> byte, parsing routines will need to look at <msc> and <command_format>, both of which follow <device_ID>, in order to first determine that the Sysex contains Show Control commands in the appropriate format.

A typical system will consist of at least one Controller attached to one or more Controlled Devices. It is possible for the same machine to be both a Controlled Device and a Controller at the same time. In this case, the machine may act as a translator, interpreter or converter of Show Control commands. According to its programmed instructions, the receipt of one type of command may result in the transmission of similar or different commands.

It is also a possibility that multiple Controller outputs could be merged and distributed to one or more Controlled Devices.

Optionally, Controlled Devices may be able to transmit (from a MIDI Out connector), MIDI Show Control commands of the type required by themselves to produce a desired result. In this condition, the Controlled Device will be transmitting a valid MIDI Show Control command but may not necessarily be doing so as a Controller.

This is useful when the Controller has the ability (through MIDI in) to capture valid MIDI Show Control messages in order to conveniently create and edit the database of messages needed for the performances being controlled. In this case, the Controlled Device will be transmitting to the Controller, but only for the purposes of capturing messages to store and re-transmit during performance.

Another application allowed by the transmission of Show Control commands by Controlled devices is the slaving of multiple Devices of similar type. For example, if a dedicated lighting console transmits a Show Control command to 'GO' when its GO button is pressed, then any other dedicated lighting console that obeys MIDI Show Control commands will also GO if it receives MIDI from the first console. In this way, many Controlled Devices may be controlled by another

Controlled Device acting as the Controller. Interconnection would follow the same pattern as the normal Controller to Controlled Device arrangement.

<Command_Formats>

<Command_formats> fall into the categories of General, Specific and All-types. General <command_formats> have a least significant nibble equal to 0, except for lighting which is 01H. Specific <command_formats> are related to the General <command_format> with the most significant nibble of the same value, but represent a more restricted range of functions within the format.

<Command_format> 'All-types' (7FH) is used for system wide 'broadcasts' of identical commands to devices of the same <device_ID> (or to all devices when used with <device_ID=All-call>). For example, use of the All-types <command_format> along with the All-call <device_ID> allows a complete system to be RESET with a single message.

Controlled Devices will normally respond to only one <command_format> besides All-types. Occasionally, more complex control systems will respond to more than one <command_format> since they will be in control of more than one technical performance element. Controllers, of course,

Hex	command_format
00	reserved for extensions
01	Lighting (General Category)
02	Moving Lights
03	Colour Changers
04	Strobes
05	Lasers
06	Chasers
10	Sound (General Category)
11	Music
12	CD Players
13	EPROM Playback
14	Audio Tape Machines
15	Intercoms
16	Amplifiers
17	Audio Effects Devices
18	Equalisers
20	Machinery (General Category)
21	Rigging
22	Flys
23	Lifts
24	Turntables
25	Trusses
26	Robots
27	Animation
28	Floats
29	Breakaways
2A	Barges
30	Video (General Category)
31	Video Tape Machines

Hex	command_format
32	Video Cassette Machines
33	Video Disc Players
34	Video Switchers
35	Video Effects
36	Video Character Generators
37	Video Still Stores
38	Video Monitors
40	Projection (General Category)
41	Film Projectors
42	Slide Projectors
43	Video Projectors
44	Dissolvers
45	Shutter Controls
50	Process Control (General Category)
51	Hydraulic Oil
52	H_2O
53	CO_2
54	Compressed Air
55	Natural Gas
56	Fog
57	Smoke
58	Cracked Haze
60	Pyro (General Category)
61	Fireworks
62	Explosions
63	Flame
64	Smoke pots
7F	All-types

should normally be able to create and send commands in all <command_formats>, otherwise their usefulness will be limited.

Although it can be seen that a wide variety of potentially dangerous and life-threatening performance processes may be under MIDI Show Control, the intent of this specification is to allow the user considerably more exacting and precise control over the type of <command_format> and command which will normally be provided·in a non-electronic cueing situation. The major advantages to the use of MIDI Show Control in these conditions are:

1. Less likelihood of errors in cueing. Digital communications can be demonstrated to be extremely reliable in repetitive duty conditions – much more so than tired or inexperienced stagehands.
2. More precise timing. Likewise, digital communications and computer control can be consistently accurate in automatic timing sequences and exactly as accurate as their human operators when under manual control.

N.B. In no way is this specification intended to replace any aspect of normal performance safety which is either required or makes good sense when dangerous equipment is in use. Manual controls such as emergency stops, deadman switches, confirmation enable controls or similar safety devices shall be used for maximum safety.

Automatic safety devices such as limit switches, proximity sensors, gas detectors, infrared cameras and pressure and motion detectors shall be used for maximum safety. MIDI show control is not intended to tell dangerous equipment when it is safe to go: it is only intended to signal what is desired if all conditions are acceptable and ideal for safe performance. Only properly designed safety systems and trained safety personnel can establish if conditions are acceptable and ideal at any time.

Two-phase commit methodology is exceptionally error-free and can be utilised to add safety features to show control systems; however this must still be implemented according to the parameters of this specification and only in addition to the above safety caveats.

General Commands

The following commands are basic to the current implementation of Memory Lighting systems and probably apply to all dedicated theatrical Show Control Systems in a general sense. Although it is not required that Controlled Devices incorporate all of these commands, it is highly recommended:

Hex	command	Number of data recommended bytes	Minimum Sets
00	Reserved for Extensions		
01	GO	variable	123
02	STOP	variable	123
03	RESUME	variable	123
04	TIMED_GO	variable	23
05	LOAD	variable	23
06	SET	4 or 9	23
07	FIRE	1	23
08	ALL_OFF	0	23
09	RESTORE	0	23
0A	RESET	0	23
0B	GO_OFF	variable	23

Sound Commands

The following commands, in addition to the above, are basic to the current implementation of Computer Controlled Sound Memory Programming Systems and are widely used by Show Control Systems in more comprehensive applications. It is recommended that Controllers support the transmission of these commands:

Hex	command	Number of data recommended bytes	Minimum Sets
10	GO/JAM_CLOCK	variable	3
11	STANDBY_+	variable	23
12	STANDBY_-	variable	23
13	SEQUENCE_+	variable	23
14	SEQUENCE_-	variable	23
15	START_CLOCK	variable	3
16	STOP_CLOCK	variable	3
17	ZERO_CLOCK	variable	3
18	SET_CLOCK	variable	3
19	MTC_CHASE_ON	variable	3
1A	MTC_CHASE_OFF	variable	3
1B	OPEN_CUE_LIST	variable	23
1C	CLOSE_CUE_LIST	variable	23
1D	OPEN_CUE_PATH	variable	23
1E	CLOSE_CUE_PATH	variable	23

Bibliography

This is not intended as an exhaustive bibliography. Some works are out of print but are worth looking up in a library. Some are vastly too technical for the beginner, but will repay reading at a later stage, and some are very expensive, but should be considered as an investment for the future. Of the books specific to theatre sound, those by John Bracewell, Burris-Meyer, David Collison and Kaye & LeBrecht are essential reading, as is anything by John Watkinson – one of the most informative and entertaining technical writers it has ever been my pleasure to read.

Title: *The Complete MIDI 1.0 Detailed Specification* (v 95.1)
Publisher: MIDI Manufacturer's Association, La Habra, CA phone +1-310/947-8689

Author: Alkin
Title: *Sound Recording Reproduction,* (3rd edition)
Publisher: Focal Press
ISBN: 0-240-51467-x

Author: Alten
Title: *Audio in Media, The Recording Studio*
Publisher: Wadsworth Publishing Company, 1996
Comment: A textbook for any student of sound recording

Editor: Ballou
Title: *Handbook for Sound Engineers: The New Audio Cyclopedia*
Publisher: Howard W. Sams & Co. div of McMillan, Inc., 1987
ISBN: 0-672-21983-2

Author: Bartlett
Title: *Introduction to Professional Recording Techniques*
Publisher: Howard W. Sams & Co., 1987

Author: Bartlett
Title: *Stereo Microphone Techniques*
Publisher: Focal Press, 1991
Comment: A look at microphone techniques for stereo

Editor: Benson
Title: *Audio Engineering Handbook*
Publisher: McGraw-Hill Book Co., 1988

Editor: Borwick
Title: *APRS Sound Recording Practice,* (4th edition)
Publisher: Oxford University Press, 1996
ISBN: 0-19-311927-7

Author: Borwick
Title: *Microphones, Technology and Technique*
Publisher: Focal Press, 1990

Author: Bracewell
Title: *Sound Design in the Theatre*
Publisher: Prentice Hall, 1993

Authors: Burris-Meyer, Mallory (and Goodfriend)
Title: *Sound in the Theatre*
Publisher: Theatre Art, New York, 1959

Author: Collison
Title: *Stage Sound* (poss. 2nd edition)
Publisher: Drama Publishers, 1976

Authors: Davies & Jones
Title: *The Yamaha Sound Reinforcement Handbook* (2nd edition)
Publisher: Hal Leonard Corp., 1989
ISBN: 0-88188-900-8

Author: Davis & Davis
Title: *Sound System Engineering* (2nd edition)
Publisher: Howard W. Sams & Co., 1989

ISBN: 0-672-21857-7

Author: Eargle
Title: *Sound Recording, 2nd Edition*
Publisher: Van Nostrand Reinhold, 1980
ISBN: 0-442-22557-1

Author: Green
Title: *Stage Noises and Effects*
Publisher: Jenkins, London, 1958

Authors: Kaye & LeBrecht
Title: *Sound and Music for the Theatre*
Publisher: Backstage Books, 1992

Author: Mapp
Title: *The Audio System Designer Technical Reference*
Publisher: Klark-Teknik Plc.

Author: Nesbit
Title: *The Studio Sound* (5th edition)
Publisher: Focal Press
ISBN: 0-240-51292-8

Author: Rumsey & McCormick
Title: *Sound and Recording* (3rd edition)
Publisher: Focal Press
ISBN: 0-240-51487-4

Author: Runstein & Huber
Title: *Modern Recording Techniques* (2nd edition)
Publisher: Howard W. Sams & Co., 1986
ISBN: 0-672-22451-8

Author: Sanford
Title: *Performance Criteria for Theatrical Sound Effects Systems*
Publisher: Journal of the AES, May, Sept. 1973

Author: Walne
Title: *Sound for the Theatre*
Publisher: A&C Black, London
ISBN: 0-7136-3135-X

Author: Watkinson
Title: *An Introduction to Digital Audio*
Publisher: Focal Press
ISBN: 0-240-51378-9

Appendix F

Useful Addresses

Audio Engineering Society (AES)
Audio Engineering Society, Inc.,
International Headquarters,
60 East 42nd Street,
Room 2520, New York,
New York, 10165-2520,
USA
Tel: +1 212 661 8528,
Fax: +1 212 682 0477
Email: HQ@aes.org,
Internet: http://www.aes.org

**Association of British Theatre Technicians
  (ABTT)**
47 Bermondsey Street
London, SE1 3XT
UK
Tel. +44 (0) 20 7403 3778
Fax. +44 (0) 20 7378 6170
Email: office@abtt.org.uk
Internet: http://www.abtt.org.uk

Institute of Acoustics
77A St Peter's Street
St Albans
Hertfordshire, AL1 3BN
UK
Tel. +44 (0) 172 784 8195
Fax. +44 (0) 172 785 0553
Email: ioa@ioa.org.uk
Internet: http://www.ioa.org.uk

MIDI Manufacturer's Association
P.O. Box 3173
La Habra CA 90632-3173
USA
Email: mma@midi.org
Internet: http://www.midi.org

**Organization of International Scenographers
  And Theatre Technicians**
General Secretariat of OISTAT
P.O. Box 15172
1001 MD Amsterdam
The Netherlands

Tel. +31 74 2505095
Fax. +31 26 4457235
Email: secretariat@oistat.nl
Internet: http://www.oistat.nl

Joint Frequencies Management Group (Radio
  Frequency allocation and licensing)
JFMG Ltd
72 Upper Ground
London SE1 9LT
UK
Tel. +44 (0)20 7261 3797
Fax.+44 (0)20 7737 8499
Email: info@jfmg.co.uk
Internet: http://www.jfmg.co.uk

Performing Rights Society
Copyright House
29/33 Berners Street
London W1T 3AB
UK
Tel. +44 (0) 20 7580-5544
Fax. +44 (0) 20 7306 4455
Email: info@prs.co.uk
Internet: http://www.prs.co.uk

Mechanical Copyright Protection Society
29-33 Berners Street
London W1T 3AB
UK
Tel. +44 (0) 20 7580 5544
Fax. +44 (0) 20 7306 4455
Email: info@mcps.co.uk
Internet: http://www.mcps.co.uk

Phonographic Performances Ltd.
Granton House,
14 - 22 Granton Street
London W1V 1LB
UK
Tel. +44 (0) 20 7584 1030
Fax. +44 (0) 20 7534 1363
Email: GLD.info@ppluk.com
Internet: http://www.ppluk.com

British Musicians' Union
60-64 Clapham Road
London SW9 0JJ
UK
Tel. +44 (0) 20 7582 5566
Fax. +44 (0) 20 7582 9805
Email: info@musiciansunion.org.uk
Internet: www.musiciansunion.org.uk

BECTU - Technicians' trade union in the UK
  Broadcasting, Entertainment,
  Cinematographers and Theatre Union
111 Wardour Street
London W1V 4AY
UK
Tel. +44 (0) 20 7437 8506
Fax. +44 (0) 20 7437 8268
Email: smacdonald@bectu.org.uk
Internet: http://www.bectu.org.uk

IATSE - Technicians' union in the USA
International Alliance of Theatrical Stage
  Employees Local 1
320 West 46th Street,
New York, NY 10036-8399
USA
Tel. (212) 333-2500 · Outside NYC +1 (800)
745-0045
Fax. +1 (212) 586-2437
Email: snowball@interport.net
Internet: http://www.iatse-local1.org

**National Sound Archive at The British
  Library** - archive material and natural
  sounds.
The British Library National Sound Archive
96 Euston Road
London NW1 2DB
UK
Tel. +44 (0) 20 7412 7440
Fax. +44 (0) 20 7412 7441
Email: nsa@bl.uk
Internet: http://www.portico.bl.uk

BBC Worldwide - sound effects and archive
  material: very expensive.
BBC Resources
Unit 7, Ariel Way
London W12 7SL
U.K.
Tel. +44 (0) 20 7765 1155
Email: sales@bbcworldwide.co.uk
Internet: http://www.bbcworldwide.com

Sound Ideas Sound Effects - massive library
  covering most areas.
Sound Ideas
105 West Beaver Creek Road
Suite 4, Richmond Hill, Ontario
Canada L4B 1C6
Tel. +1 (905) 886-5000
Fax. +1 (905) 886-6800
Email: info@sound-ideas.com
Internet: http://www.sound-ideas.com

Sound Ideas US Distributor
Gefen, Inc
6265 Variel Avenue
Woodland Hills,
California,
USA
Tel. +1 818 884 6294 or + 1800 545 6900
Email: gsinfo@gefen.com
Internet: http://www.Gefen.com

Sound Ideas UK Distributor:
De Wolfe Limited
Shropshire House, 2nd Floor East
11/20 Capper Street
London WC1E 6JA,
UK
Tel. +44 (0) 20 7631 3600
Fax. +44 (0) 20 7631 3700
Email: info@dewolfemusic.co.uk
Internet: http://www.dewolfemusic.co.uk/

Hollywood Edge Sound Effects - another huge
library.
The Hollywood Edge
7080 Hollywood Blvd.
Suite 519,
Hollywood,
CA 90028.
USA
Tel. +1800 2923795
Email. info@hollywoodedge.com
Internet. http://www.hollywoodedge.com

Hollywood Edge US Distributor:
Gefen, Inc.
6265 Variel Avenue,
Woodland Hills,
California,
USA
Tel. +1 818 884 6294 or + 1800 545 6900
Email: gsinfo@gefen.com
Internet: http://www.Gefen.com

Hollywood Edge UK Distributor:
J W Media Music Ltd.
4 Whitfield Street
London W1T 2RD
UK
Tel. +44 (0) 20 7681 8900
Fax. +44 (0) 20 7681 8911
Email: salesinfo@jwmediamusic.co.uk
Internet: http://www.jwmediamusic.com

Digiffects Sound Effects - mainly European-
sourced effects –
Digiffects
Email: bengt.skoog@ljudproduktion.se
Internet: http://www.ljudproduktion.se

Digiffects US Distributor:
Gefen, Inc.
6265 Variel Avenue Woodland Hills,
California, USA
Tel. +1 818 884 6294 or + 1800 545 6900
Email: gsinfo@gefen.com
Internet: http://www.Gefen.com

Digiffects UK Distributor:
Music House International Ltd
5 Newburgh Street
London, W1V 1LH
UK
Tel. +44 (0) 20 7434 9678
Fax. +44 (0) 20 7434 1470

DeWolfe Sound Effects - Their own effects
library and also distributors of various
effects libraries in the UK
Shropshire House, 2nd Floor East
11/20 Capper Street
London, WC1E 6JA
UK
Tel. +44 (0) 20 7631 3600
Fax. +44 (0) 20 7631 3700
Email: info@dewolfemusic.co.uk
Internet: http://www.dewolfemusic.co.uk/

JW Media Music Ltd - distributors of various
effects libraries in the UK
JW Media Music Ltd
4 Whitfield Street
London W1T 2RD
Tel. +44 (0) 20 7681 8900
Fax. +44 (0) 20 7681 8911
UK
Email: salesinfo@jwmediamusic.co.uk
Internet: www.jwmediamusic.com

Gefen Systems - distributors of most sound
effects libraries in the US
Gefen, Inc.
6265 Variel Avenue Woodland Hills,
California, USA
Tel. +1 818 884 6294 or + 1800 545 6900
Email: gsinfo@gefen.com
Internet: http://www.Gefen.com

Masque Sound Studios - huge library of sound
effects- fast and efficient service for theatre in
the USA.
630 Ninth Avenue, Suite 410,
NYC, NY 10036, USA
Tel: +1 212 245 4623
Fax: +1 212 262 4013
Internet: http://www.masque-sound.com/
studio.htm

Aura Sound Design Ltd - custom provision of
sound effects in the UK
23 Charlotte Road
London EC2A 3PB
UK
Tel. +44 (0) 20 7739 6057
Fax. +44 (0) 20 7729 1820
Email: info@aurasound.co.uk
Internet: http://www.aurasound.co.uk

Bits And Pieces - Simon Kahn's Sound Effects
series
Email: simon@bitsandpieces.co.uk
Internet: http://www.bits.dircon.co.uk

Bits and Pieces UK Distributor:
Canford Audio PLC
Crowther Road
Washington, Tyne On Wear
NE38 0BW, United Kingdom
Tel. +44 (0) 191 418 1000
Fax. +44 (0) 191 418 1001
Email: info@canford.co.uk
Internet: http://www.canford.co.uk

Sounddogs - Internet sound effects services
selling effects on a one-off basis via the
Internet: expensive, but good for last-
minute panics.
Email: sounddogs@sounddogs.com
Internet: http://www.sounddogs.com

Lighting And Sound International
38 St Leonards Road
Eastbourne
East Sussex BN21 3UT
UK

Tel. +44 (0) 1323 642639
Fax. +44 (0) 1323 646905
Email: info@plasa.org
Internet: http://www.plasa.org

The Stage - UK weekly newspaper
47 Bermondsey Street
London SE1 3XT
UK
Tel. +44 (0) 20 7403 1818
Email: info@thestage.co.uk
Internet: http://www.thestage.co.uk

Backstage - US weekly newspaper
Back Stage East: 770 Broadway,
New York, NY 10003
USA
Tel. +1 800-634-6810
Internet: www.backstage.com

Live! - monthly magazine
Nexus House, Swanely,
Kent BR8 8HU
UK
Tel. +44 (0) 1322 660070
Fax. +44 (0) 1322 616319
Email: 113251.662@compuserve.com

ProSound News - monthly magazine

Pro Sound News Europe
Miller Freeman Entertainment Group
8 Montague Close, London Bridge,
London SE1 9UR
UK
Tel. +44 (0) 20 7940 8500
Fax. +44 (0) 20 7407 7102
Email: info@unfm.com

Studio Sound - monthly magazine
Studio Sound, United Business Media Ltd
Tower House, Lathkill Street,
Market Harborough, Leicestershire, LE16 9EF
UK
Tel: +44 (0) 1858 435361
Fax: +44 (0) 1858 434958
Email: natalie.marley@towerpublishing.co.uk
Internet: http://www.prostudio.com/
   studiosound

**United States Institute of Theatre Technology
   (USITT)**
6443 Ridings Road
Syracuse, NY 13206-1111
USA
Tel. +1 800-938-7488 or +1 315-463-6463
Fax. +1315-463-6525
Internet http://www.usitt.org

Index